CONCENTRATE Q&A
EVIDENCE

CONCENTRATE
Q&A
EVIDENCE

Maureen Spencer
MA (Oxon), MA (Open), LLM, PhD
John Spencer
MA (Oxon), LLM, MMath, Barrister

SECOND EDITION

OXFORD
UNIVERSITY PRESS

Great Clarendon Street, Oxford, OX2 6DP,
United Kingdom

Oxford University Press is a department of the University of Oxford.
It furthers the University's objective of excellence in research, scholarship,
and education by publishing worldwide. Oxford is a registered trade mark of
Oxford University Press in the UK and in certain other countries

Published in the United States of America by Oxford University Press
198 Madison Avenue, New York, NY 10016, United States of America

British Library Cataloguing in Publication Data
Data available

Library of Congress Control Number: 2018949481

ISBN 978–0–19–881990–5

Printed in Great Britain by
Ashford Colour Press Ltd, Gosport, Hampshire

Contents

Editor's acknowledgements

The brand-new Concentrate Q&A series from Oxford University Press has been developed alongside hundreds of students and lecturers from a range of universities across the UK.

I'd like to take this opportunity to thank all those law students who've filled in questionnaires, completed in-depth reviews of sample materials, attended focus groups and provided us with the insight and feedback we needed to shape a series relevant for today's law students.

Also to the lecturers the length and breadth of the UK who have given so generously of their time by being heavily involved in our lengthy review process; their inside information gained from experience as teachers and examiners has been vital in the shaping of this new series.

You told us that you wanted a Q&A book that:

- gives you tips to help you understand exactly what the question is asking
- offers focused guidance on how to structure your answer and develop your arguments
- uses clear and simple diagrams to help you see how to structure your answers at a glance
- highlights key debates and extra points for you to add to your answers to get the highest marks
- flags common mistakes to avoid when answering questions
- offers detailed advice on coursework assignments as well as exams
- provides focused reading suggestions to help you develop in-depth knowledge for when you are looking for the highest marks
- is accompanied by a great range of online support

We listened and we have delivered.

We are confident that because they provide exactly what you told us you need, the Concentrate Q&As offer you better support and a greater chance for succeeding than any competing series.

We wish you all the best throughout your law course and in your exams and hope that these guides give you the confidence to tackle any question that you encounter, and give you the skills you need to excel during your studies and beyond.

Good luck
Carol Barber, Senior Publishing Editor

This is what you said:

'The content is exceptional; the best Q&A books that I've read'

Wendy Chinenye Akaigwe, law student, London Metropolitan University

'Since I started using the OUP Q&A guides my grades have dramatically improved'

Glen Sylvester, law student, Bournemouth University

'A sure-fire way to get a 1st class result'

Naomi M, law student, Coventry University

'100% would recommend. Makes you feel like you will pass with flying colours'

Elysia Marie Vaughan, law student, University of Hertfordshire

'Excellent. Very detailed which makes a change from the brief answers in other Q&A books … fantastic'

Frances Easton, law student, University of Birmingham

This is what your lecturers said:

'Much more substantial and less superficial than competitor Q&As. Some guides are rather too simplistic but the OUP guides are much better than the norm'

Dr Tony Harvey, Principal law lecturer, Liverpool John Moores University

'Cleverly and carefully put together. Every bit as good as one would expect from OUP, you really have cornered the market in the revision guides sector. I am also a huge fan of the OUP Concentrate series and I think that these books sit neatly alongside this'

Alice Blythe, law lecturer, University of Bolton

'I think Q&A guides are crucial and advise my students to buy early on'

Loretta Trickett, law lecturer, Nottingham Trent University

'Students often lack experience in writing full answers but seeing suggested answers like this provides them with confidence and structure. I will be recommending this book to my students not just for revision purposes but for the duration of the unit'

Nick Longworth, law lecturer, Manchester Metropolitan University

Preface

'So what's the answer?' said Laura, a rather literal-minded girl who wrote down everything Robyn said in tutorials. 'Is it a train or a tram?'

   'Both or either,' said Robyn. 'It doesn't really matter. Go on Marion.'

   'Hang about,' said Vic. 'You can't have it both ways.'

Nice Work by David Lodge (Secker and Warburg, London, 1988)

Like David Lodge's fictional English Literature tutor, Evidence lecturers are fonder of setting questions than giving answers. This study aid is intended to help students prepare for assessments in a systematic and analytical way. It encourages them to research and plan their work using the wide range of electronic and paper sources now available. It gives guidance on a variety of assessments including seen exams and research-based coursework. Students are prepared thereby to approach the tasks with intellectual curiosity and forensic diligence. They must be aware that all writing involves frequent re-writing and revisions.

   The authors express gratitude to the ever-patient staff at the OUP for their invaluable support and guidance. This edition reflects the law as it was in March 2018.

Maureen Spencer
John Spencer

Guide to the Book

Every book in the Concentrate Q&A series contains the following features:

Are you ready to face the exam? This box at the start of each chapter identifies the key topics and cases that you need to have learned, revised, and understood before tackling the questions in each chapter.

Not sure where to begin? Clear diagram answer plans at the start of each question help you see how to structure your answer at a glance, and take you through each point step-by-step.

Demonstrating your knowledge of the crucial debates is a sure-fire way to impress examiners. These at-a-glance boxes help remind you of the key debates relevant to each topic, which you should discuss in your answers to get the highest marks.

What makes a great answer great? Our authors show you the thought process behind their own answers, and how you can do the same in your exam. Key sentences are highlighted and advice is given on how to structure your answer well and develop your arguments.

Each question represents a typical essay or problem question so that you know exactly what to expect in your exam.

Don't settle for a good answer—make it great! This feature gives you extra points to include in the exam if you want to gain more marks and make your answer stand out.

Don't fall into any traps! This feature points out common mistakes that students make, and which you need to avoid when answering each question.

Really push yourself and impress your examiner by going beyond what is expected. Focused further reading suggestions allow you to develop in-depth knowledge of the subject for when you are looking for the highest marks.

Guide to the Online Resources

Every book in the Concentrate Q&A series is supported by additional online materials to aid your study and revision: www.oup.com/uk/qanda/

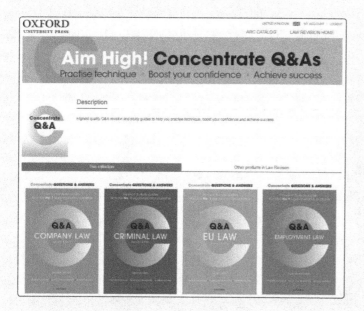

- Extra essay and problem questions.
- Bonus questions to help you practise and refine your technique. Questions are annotated, highlighting key terms and legal issues to help you plan your own answers. An indication of what your answers should cover is also provided.

- Online versions of the diagram answer plans.
- Video guidance on how to put an answer plan together.
- Flashcard glossaries of key terms.
- Audio advice on revision and exam technique from Nigel Foster.

Table of Cases

Table of Statutes

International treaties and conventions

Table of Statutory Instruments

Exam skills for success in evidence

1

Evidence is often regarded as one of the more complex subjects studied in undergraduate law courses. It is a mixture of arcane old rules and opaque new statutes and sometimes seems to offend common sense. Technical precepts are intermingled with judicial discretion and matters of high constitutional principle. The subject covers such wide-ranging areas as the defendant's right to silence, the treatment of the presumed victim in the trial process, and whether or not intercept evidence should be used in court.

Until the early years of this century, less so since 2003, there has been much legislative activity in the field of evidence, some dealing with questions which are or were politically controversial. The courts struggled to digest complex new law while upholding the human rights of the various parties to litigation, both criminal and civil. The **Human Rights Act 1998** and the application of **Art. 6** has had a powerful impact on defendants' rights in areas such as the admissibility of improperly obtained evidence and the allocation of the burden of proof. On the other hand, there has been a parallel advance in making prosecutors protectors of victims. Indeed, the Government in 2002 proclaimed its aim to put victims 'at the heart' of the criminal justice system (Home Office, *Justice for All* (Cm 5563, 2002), para. 0.2). One outcome was the wide-ranging **Criminal Justice Act 2003**, notably the provisions on character and hearsay evidence. As well as absorbing his or her course material, the alert student will follow the contemporary debates over these developments both in the general media and in legal journals. In this way students will appreciate the intellectual richness of the subject.

Preparing for the examination

Question and Answer books are not a substitute for learning the law from your lectures, seminar discussions, and recommended readings. They are a supplementary resource in that they enable students to practise answering questions as revision for examinations and coursework. These are not model answers to be slavishly imitated (of course, this could constitute plagiarism), but rather examples to help the student understand the topic and see how it might be approached. You can test yourself throughout the course by comparing your answers to questions with those suggested in this book.

Unseen examinations

The questions in this book are for the most part designed to help you prepare for unseen examinations, usually lasting two or three hours, consisting usually of assessments where you do not know the actual questions in advance. The last chapter in the book however gives guidance on coursework questions although of course the answers in all the chapters will help prepare you also for these. Examinations and coursework assessments may have a mixture of problem and essay questions but you will usually in the coursework be expected to produce a more sustained and well-referenced analytical submission.

Put crudely, the examinee's objective in any examination is to accumulate in the time allowed as many marks as possible. To be manageable, this task needs to be broken down into three stages: planning, execution, and review.

Planning for the examination

It goes without saying that you must organise yourself well in advance to prepare for the examination. Ideally you will have completed all the formative work throughout the year, sought and acted upon feedback from your tutor, and tested yourself by answering previous examination questions or MCT tests (you will find a range of these in the companion *Concentrate* volume). You will have learnt that an important skill in answering Evidence questions involves addressing yourself directly to the practical or abstract theoretical question set in both problem and essay questions.

Problem questions

Briefly, in answering problem questions, the student must first identify the areas of law in which the problem falls. Almost invariably, there will be more than one issue and it is important that you identify them at the start. Having done so, you should be able to outline the legal principles which are relevant to the issues in the problem, citing the relevant cases and statutes. The next stage is to apply these authorities to the facts. This involves discussion of the facts in the light of the relevant principles, analysis of the facts to select which are significant, and, where appropriate, a comparison of the problem's facts with those of the authorities, in such a way as to support your argument. Finally, come to a practical conclusion, which need not be a definitive answer, may suggest more than one alternative, and should where necessary indicate what additional factual material would be required to give a definitive response. Although the sources and authorities for your answer will largely be case law and statute, you will also gain credit for, where appropriate, referring to academic debate on the particular topic. This is particularly relevant where the case law reveals conflicting authorities.

You will find the IRAC method (*Identify* legal issues, state *Relevant* law, *Apply* the law to the facts, come to a *Conclusion*) which is employed in this book a good guide to structuring your answers. In problem questions it is vital to focus on the actual issues you are asked and avoid irrelevant diversions which will not impress the examiner. To give one example, if the question is about the admissibility of confessions and there is no suggestion in the facts of oppression having been exercised do not waste time on **s. 76(2)(a) of the Police and Criminal Evidence Act 1984** but go straight to **s. 76(2)(b)** and **s. 78**. Be driven by the specific factual scenario in the question.

Essay questions

A different approach is required when answering essay questions. Essay questions will usually be centred on an area of controversy or ambiguity in the law. Your preparation here will be largely reading widely not just your set textbooks, weighty though they are, but also articles from the leading journals. Thus the approach required to answering questions will vary with the type of question. It is important in essay questions to show understanding of the academic debates particularly over the controversial areas of the law such as the erosion of the right to silence. Good students will have spent time during the year researching such publications as the *International Journal of Evidence and Proof, Criminal Law Review, Law Quarterly Review*, and *Public Law*. Even if you have not done so throughout, it is well worth spending a few hours of revision time before the examination in the library, including of course its online version, looking through recent issues and making a note of evidence topics which have drawn academic comment. In many cases this is where the examiner will have looked when drafting the exam paper. Background reading will help you to see what the question-setter is looking for in answer to essay questions. Ensure you have answered the question which, given that Evidence is usually a second- or third-year option, requires a deep analysis of a legal practice or principle. Avoid a narrative account since to do well requires a high level of abstract thinking and a capacity to make connections between concepts. To give one example, if you are asked to comment on the operation of the exclusionary discretion under **s. 78 of the Police and Criminal Evidence Act 1984** you will gain a good grade if you demonstrate you have a theoretical framework around which to structure your answer. This might include preserving the legitimacy of the criminal justice system as the House of Lords analysed it in the landmark case of *R v Looseley* **[2001] UKHL 53**.

The examiners are not expecting identikit answers. Rather they are looking for indications of a well-structured, well-evidenced analysis which succinctly responds to the question they have set. A small tip is to make sure your first paragraph is impressive. This will make the examiner sit up and relish reading the thoughtful argument you are presenting to her. All lecturers are delighted when they find signs at the beginning of an answer of an intellectually curious student who is sure of her ground and scholarly in her exposition.

Examination day arrives

When you are given the examination paper, read it, read the rubric (the instructions at the top of the paper) carefully. Then take five minutes to read the paper itself right through before you start answering a question. You will usually be required to answer a set number of questions (say, four out of ten). You must answer the number of questions required and manage your time on each accord-ing to their weighting in marks. A surprising number of candidates fail because they answer fewer questions than required. Check whether there are compulsory questions.

Having chosen the required number of questions, sketch out in telegraphic note form your answer to each. In problem questions in law examinations this is very often a matter of spotting the issues, as several different areas of the subject are mixed together. The table at the end of this chapter will help you spot the variety of legal issues in mixed questions. If at this point you can recall the names of the cases which are authority for particular propositions in the area concerned, all the better. If you can't, pass on to the next of your chosen questions. By the end of this pro-cess, which should not take more than perhaps 15 minutes, you will have sketched out in rough form your answer to each of your chosen questions. Many of your fellow examinees will already be scribbling frantically. Don't panic. Before you go to the stage of execution, make a simple cal-culation. Take the length of the examination in minutes (180 minutes for the classic three-hour examination). Subtract the time you have spent on the planning stage (perhaps 15 minutes) and allow five minutes review time for the end of the examination. Then divide the remainder equally between the questions you have chosen.

Writing and review

Now you can start writing your first answer. Bear in mind that there is often no obvious right answer to a practical question. The authorities may conflict, or you may need to point out that more information is needed than the question provides. What is important is not so much arriving at a conclusion as demonstrating clearly in your reasoning that you appreciate the complexities and sometimes ambiguities of the law. Break your answer into paragraphs, underline the names of cases, and avoid writing between the lines or in the margins.

It is very important to remember that the examiner is interested in what you do know, not what you don't know. So if you are uncertain about a particular point, it is generally better to put down what you think is the answer, provided it is relevant to answering the question. If you are right, you will gain marks; if you are wrong, you will usually not have marks taken away. Don't be tempted to exceed your time limit. You are more likely to pick up marks at the beginning of your answer than at the end. Once your self-imposed time limit is up, stop writing and go on to the next question.

About half way through the examination your concentration may start to sag. It is at this point that you will appreciate having made your sketch answer to your third question at the beginning of the examination period. Your fellow examinees who rushed to get pen to paper at the start of the examination will be flagging too, but they won't have tried to think through the issues in the question when they were fresh. Your aim will be to get as many marks for your last answer as for your first.

You should analyse the question to establish whether you are asked to discuss, explain, or criticise a particular area of Evidence law or comment on the state of the law more generally.

Textbooks and sources

The suggested answers in this book frequently make reference to the leading textbooks on Evidence. These are listed in the next section. They have different features and virtues. Some give more attention to the socio-legal aspects of the law, some are more in the nature of practitioners' manuals, others are more philosophical. Your tutors will guide you on the most appropriate ones for your course. They all will convey to you the healthy debates and controversies in the world of Evidence scholarship.

Some answers in this book contain quotations from the textbooks and journal articles. Obviously in an examination you will not remember them verbatim. However, it will improve your grades if you familiarise yourself in advance with at least some of the arguments of these leading scholars. One example is the criticisms Dennis has of the operation of **s. 34 of the Criminal Justice and Public Order Act 1994** (see Dennis 2013, pp. 196–209). In any case you should be guided throughout the year by accounts made by leading scholars in the field of the fascinating subject of Evidence law.

Textbooks

There are a number of excellent textbooks on Evidence. Some of these are cited in the answers in this volume. These references have not been included in the 'Taking Things Further' lists in each chapter but are set out here:

- Choo, A.L.-T., *Evidence*, 5th edn (Oxford: OUP, 2018).
- Dennis, I., *The Law of Evidence*, 4th edn (London: Sweet & Maxwell, 2013).
- Doak, J. and McGourlay, C., *Evidence in Context*, 5th edn (Abingdon: Routledge, 2018).
- Durston, G., *Evidence: Text and Materials*, 2nd edn (Oxford: OUP, 2011).

- Emson, R., *Evidence*, 5th edn (Basingstoke: Palgrave Macmillan Law Masters, 2010).
- Glover, R., *Murphy on Evidence*, 15th edn (Oxford: OUP, 2017).
- Keane, A. and McKeown, P., *The Modern Law of Evidence*, 12th edn (Oxford: OUP, 2018).
- Munday, R., *Evidence. Core Text Series*, 9th edn (Oxford: OUP, 2017).
- Roberts, P. and Zuckerman, A., *Criminal Evidence*, 2nd edn (Oxford: OUP, 2010).
- Tapper, C., *Cross and Tapper on Evidence*, 10th edn (London: LexisNexis, 2010).
- Zuckerman, A.A.S., *The Principles of Criminal Evidence* (Oxford: Clarendon Press, 1989).
  Now out of date but contains a most perceptive theoretical analysis.

Guide to areas of Evidence law covered in questions

Area of evidence	Comment on application in problem questions
1. Relevance	The pre-condition of all admissibility. It may be appropriate to show your powers of logical analysis and fact management by explaining why a particular piece of evidence is relevant to the trial, the test being whether it increases or decreases the probability of a fact in issue.
2. Burden and standard of proof	This is implicit or explicit in every trial-based question and you are generally expected to comment. You might be given an extract from a statute, possibly an imaginary one, which refers to the need to 'prove' and be required to construe the wording in the light of the changes brought about by the **Human Rights Act 1998** to the allocation of legal and evidential burdens.
3. Confessions/silence of defendant	Bear in mind that confessions can be made to non-state agents, may be ambiguous, and could even, under the common law, involve silence if the parties are on 'even terms'. However, only apply the **CJPOA, ss. 34, 36, and 37** if the silence is in the face of questioning by constables charged with the duty of investigating offences or charging offenders.
4. References to spouses, co-defendants who are reluctant to testify, defendants who are undecided about testifying, or witnesses who are very young or mentally incapacitated	These are indications that competence and compellability may be in issue.
5. Character evidence	Usually only included in questions concerning crime, but be aware also of similar fact in civil cases. Note the different rules on the admissibility of character evidence for defendants and non-defendant witnesses in criminal trials.

(continued)

Area of evidence	Comment on application in problem questions
6. Improperly obtained evidence	Usually only raised in criminal evidence questions with suggestion of impropriety or illegality including entrapment. **Section 78 of the Police and Criminal Evidence Act 1984** may apply to exclude prosecution evidence or there may be a stay of prosecution.
7. Supporting evidence	The formal rules here have now been either abolished or simplified but you should still be prepared to comment on the desirability of supporting evidence, particularly in relation to identification evidence, lies told by the defendant, admissible hearsay, and inferences from silence of the accused.
8. Examination and cross-examination	There are many procedural rules here. The special rules relating to vulnerable witnesses, such as alleged victims in sex cases, are perhaps the most significant. Make sure you know the details of Special Measures Directions.
9. Out-of-court statements	When there is a reference to an out-of-court oral or written statement, including one made by a witness who is testifying, consider whether the hearsay rule applies. But bear in mind that the important question is not only the *form* the statement is in but also the *purpose* for which it is being tendered in evidence. Note that civil and criminal rules are different.
10. Communications with lawyer	This raises legal professional privilege. In civil cases, communications with a third party may also be privileged if there is pending litigation. In criminal cases, bear this in mind in considering **ss. 34–38 of the Criminal Justice and Public Order Act 1994.**
11. Public interest immunity	This may come up in questions on civil or criminal evidence, more usually the former. In criminal evidence a frequently raised issue is disclosure of the identity of police informers.
12. Opinion evidence	This usually refers to expert evidence and is easily recognised. The grey areas include the admissibility of expert evidence in relation to psychology

Burden and standard of proof: presumptions

2

In order to perform well you need to have revised:

- the difference between the evidential and the legal burden in criminal and civil trials
- justifications for reversing the burden of proof on some or all of the elements of an offence
- the importance of **art. 6** and the impact of the **Human Rights Act 1998**
- the standard of proof in criminal and civil trials
- the significance of presumptions in Evidence

KEY DEBATES

Debate: should there be a third standard of proof in civil cases which have a criminal element?

There has been considerable debate over what some term an 'overhasty' rejection of a higher standard of proof in such cases but recent authority seems to have settled the argument. There is only one standard, balance of probabilities. It is arguable that this is appropriate and the added protection is not needed since the trier of fact, the judge, is less likely to be persuaded by irrelevant considerations or poor argument than a jury in a criminal trial.

Debate: would it be better to decriminalise some minor regulatory offences rather than place the legal burden on the accused?

Arguments in favour of this approach are that such offences carry little stigma and that the criminal law is best reserved for offences that are truly criminal where the legal burden of proof should be

○

on the prosecution. The present position of allocating the burden on a case-by-case basis creates uncertainty. On the other hand, it could be argued that even minor offences such as breaches of health and safety legislation are socially harmful and society's disapproval should be shown. Note also that the ECtHR could decide that even an administrative offence was criminal and **Art. 6(2)** would apply.

Debate: is the distinction between procedural and substantive rights in relation to the burden of proof undermining justice?

Article 6 protects only procedural not substantive rights. It follows that strict liability offences could increase in number without engaging **Art. 6** and securing the full scrutiny of the courts. Some commentators argue that this upholds parliamentary supremacy while others recommend addressing the problem of blurring the presumption of innocence in relation to *mens rea* by making it a constitutional principle of the substantive law that there should be no criminal liability without fault.

QUESTION | 1

In order to merit its reputation as a fundamental constitutional guarantee, the presumption [of innocence] must be reasonably extensive and not too easily defeated.

(Roberts and Zuckerman, *Criminal Evidence* (Oxford: OUP, 2010), p. 223.)

How far does the current law in this area meet the requirements set out by Roberts and Zuckerman?

CAUTION!

- Avoid giving an answer based on a narrative account of the case law. Try to derive an analysis of the constitutional principle of the presumption of innocence and explain the difference between a procedural and a substantive right.

- You need to analyse what is meant by 'constitutional', a word which usually has connotations of upholding a principle rather than pragmatically adjusting to circumstances.

- There is a huge amount of academic literature on this area, make sure you are familiar with at least some recent academic commentaries.

DIAGRAM ANSWER PLAN

Introduction: analysis of why the presumption of innocence should be regarded as a constitutional right and how far it is safeguarded in current law; outline of structure of essay

Argument to show burden of proof historically not always on prosecution, see *Woolmington* and exceptions to the principle of presumption of innocence

Problem of regulatory offences: *Hunt* and *Edwards*. Possibility of decriminalisation

Argument to show courts after *Lambert* should preserve presumption of innocence: *Lambert* and post-*Lambert*; however some 'assault' on Lord Steyn in a 'case by case' approach

Clash of principles in relationship between Parliament and the courts: the will of Parliament; procedural and **substantive law**

Conclusion: possible conflict between pragmatism and principle

SUGGESTED ANSWER

The presumption of innocence is recognised in many jurisdictions as one of the most important constitutional foundations. The presumption recognises the vulnerability of the defendant faced with state prosecution and concomitant 'inequality of arms'.[1] The prosecution, in other words, should have the weightier task. It therefore has the burden of proof, must carry out the task of amassing and presenting the evidence, and in order to succeed has to do this to an exacting standard. In other words, the prosecution bears the risk of losing. Reference to the presumption is found in all major international human rights treaties but until the enactment of the **Human Rights Act 1998**, its acknowledgement by English law was found in judicial observations. The most notable articulation is Viscount Sankey's 'golden thread' speech in *Woolmington v DPP* **[1935] AC 462**.[2]

This question centres on what is meant by a 'fundamental constitutional guarantee' and if so whether it has been applied consistently in practice.

Burden of Proof Not Always on Prosecution

Roberts and Zuckerman suggest that there may be, in special circumstances, some departures from the presumption of innocence and that

[1] Try to explain the meaning of the presumption of innocence and link it to fair trial rights and the equality of arms.

[2] There is probably no need to quote the exact words of Viscount Sankey's remarks on the 'golden thread'.

[3] You may explain that the insanity exception, based on nineteenth-century case law, is somewhat of a historical anomaly.

[4] Research by Ashworth and Blake (1996) revealed that 40 per cent of offences triable in the Crown Court appeared to violate the presumption of innocence by placing a legal burden of proof on the defendant or imposing a form of strict liability. Doubtless the number has increased subsequently.

[5] The interpretation of **s. 101 of the Magistrates' Courts Act 1980** and the significance of provisos etc. raise the question of implied statutory exceptions.

[6] Although these cases have been to some extent overtaken by the **Human Rights Act 1998**, they are still important and the major Evidence textbooks devote considerable space to them.

[7] You will have had to prepare carefully a framework for understanding the large amount of case law on the allocation of the burden of proof. You will find a very useful typology is offered in the article by Dennis, 'Reverse Onuses and the Presumption of Innocence' [2005] Crim LR 901. A good revision exercise is to add recent cases to the table at the end of the article.

[8] You will see, later in the answer, that according to Glover, there was later an 'assault on Lord Steyn' by the Court of Appeal. A well-planned essay will therefore include a reference to Lord Steyn's speech.

is historically the case. The **Woolmington** principle has never been an absolute one.[3] **Woolmington** itself cited exceptions, notably the common law defence of insanity and statutory reversals of the burden. The constitutional principle of parliamentary sovereignty meant that Parliament could expressly shift the burden of an element of the offence to the defendant.[4] Particular controversy arose over the clearer acknowledgement, post-**Woolmington**, of a third exception to the 'golden thread', namely implied statutory exceptions. Historically, s. 101 of the Magistrates' Courts Act 1980 was the starting point.[5]

Regulatory Offences

One objective was to make it easier for the authorities to prosecute certain regulatory offences, such as driving without a licence. The approach of the courts, however, was to extend the possibility of shifting the burden to the defendant in a wider range of circumstances. **R v Edwards** [1975] QB 27 and **R v Hunt** [1987] AC 352 illustrate this.[6] General guidelines were set out in **Hunt**. First, the courts should recognise that Parliament can never lightly be taken to have intended to shift the burden of proof onto the defendant. Secondly, a factor of great importance was the ease or difficulty that parties met in discharging the probative burden. Finally, the gravity of the offence should be borne in mind. A number of critics, while applauding the actual decision, pointed out its troubling implications. By abdicating on the matter of principle the House arguably opened the door to inroads on the presumption of innocence. In cases of ambiguity in the statute, instead of relying unequivocally on the presumption of innocence, their Lordships were prepared only to see the necessity of avoiding the imposition of 'onerous burdens' on the defendant.

Setting limits to reverse burdens: the Human Rights Act

If **Hunt** and **Edwards** marked a retreat from constitutional principle then the **Human Rights Act 1998** signalled a return and the courts have set clearer limits to the shifting of the burden in interpreting statutes. The Act requires the courts to take account of the Strasbourg jurisprudence in interpreting legislation. The outcome was, initially at least, a return to the **Woolmington** principled approach. This has been examined by the House of Lords in several landmark cases.[7]

R v Lambert and Post-Lambert

In **R v Lambert** [2002] 2 AC 545 by a majority of four to one the House decided that in the context of reverse burdens of proof, 'prove' in a statute could be interpreted as imposing an 'evidential burden'. Lord Steyn, giving the majority judgment, stated that 'legislative interference with the presumption of innocence requires justification and must not be freer than necessary'.[8] The principle of proportionality must be observed. In **R v Johnstone** [2003] 1 WLR 1736 the House of Lords gave fuller guidance on reverse burden provisions. They were permitted so long as they were confined within reasonable limits that took account of the importance of what was at stake and maintained the rights of the defence. Subsequent case law has demonstrated that the courts place importance on the nature of the offence and are more ready to allow a shift of the burden in the case of regulatory offences. Reverse legal burdens were probably justified if the overall burden remained on the prosecution but Parliament had for significant reasons concluded that it was fair and reasonable to make an exception in respect of a particular aspect of the offence (*Attorney General's Reference (No. 1 of 2004)* [2004] 2 Cr App R 424). In that case the reasoning supporting a reverse onus included the public interest in deterring landlords from evicting tenants unlawfully. However, in *DPP v Wright* [2010] QB 224 it was disproportionate to place a legal burden on an accused who sought to rely on an exemption under **s. 1 of the Hunting Act 2004.** Parliament's intentions may be disregarded if the fairness of the trial is threatened as in *Attorney General's Reference (No. 4 of 2002)* [2004] UKHL 43.[9] In the case involving the application of **s. 5(2) of the Terrorism Act 2000**, placing a burden on the accused unjustifiably infringed the presumption of innocence.

Unresolved Questions

Lambert itself left a number of unanswered questions. First, Lord Hutton argued in a powerful dissenting speech that the effect of upholding the defendant's rights was to endanger society. Defendants would more easily be able to raise defences under the statute. Secondly, the law was left in a state of some uncertainty. However, some commentators argue that too robust an attachment to applying the presumption of innocence can make for a poor constitutional outcome. For example, Roberts and Zuckerman (2010, pp. 286–7) comment that by using **Art. 6(2)**, as they did in *Lambert*, to apply to affirmative defences as if they were elements of the offence, the courts are opening the door to Parliament extending the ambit of strict liability offences.[10] Roberts is critical of the reasoning in *Lambert*. He commented (2002, p. 36) that the courts were in effect using the evidential principle of the presumption of innocence to undermine the substantive law in relation to strict liability offences. There is a clash of the two constitutional principles, parliamentary sovereignty and the presumption of innocence. Note that in *R v Foye* [2013] EWCA Crim 475 the Court of Appeal applied the statutory rule that the burden of establishing diminished responsibility lies on the defendant, on the balance of probabilities. It observed it was 'entirely reasonable that a matter so personal to the defendant should be for him to prove, albeit only on the balance of probabilities' (para. 33). The judgment continued by stressing a pragmatic point: 'It would be a practical impossibility in many cases for the

[9] There was no doubt that Parliament in the **Terrorism Act 2000** intended to shift the legal burden but 'it was not the intention of Parliament in the 1998 Act' (para. 51) and the House imposed only an evidential burden on the accused. This marked a challenge to parliamentary supremacy.

[10] However note that the Court of Appeal in *Foye* did highlight the difference between elements of the offence and statutory defences. In the case of the latter, reverse burdens were less objectionable.

Crown to disprove (beyond reasonable doubt) an assertion that he was insane or suffering from diminished responsibility' (para. 35).

Glover (2017, p. 116) refers to 'an assault on Lord Steyn' and the resulting shift towards a case-by-case development of the law. Thus in *Williams (Orette)* **[2013] 1 WLR 1200** a legal burden on the defence was a 'necessary, reasonable and proportionate derogation of the presumption of innocence'.[11]

[11] The case involved the application of s. 5(1) of the Firearms Act 1968.

Parliament and the Courts

These observations illustrate the difficulty of deciding the parameters of a 'fundamental constitutional guarantee' and that the courts have not taken an absolutist stance. They have been prepared, however, on occasion to depart from the intention of Parliament, which does suggest that the presumption of innocence may override the popular will. The constitutional significance of the presumption of innocence was at the heart of Lord Bingham's rejection of the Court of Appeal's reasoning and refusal to accept the ten guiding principles in *Attorney General's Reference (No. 4 of 2002)*, a case conjoined with *Sheldrake v DPP* **[2004]**. As Tausz and Ashworth (2005, p. 218) comment, there 'Lord Bingham expressly rejected one of the less satisfactory principles, the assumption that Parliament would not have made an exception (to the presumption of innocence) without good reason.'

This principled approach was followed by the Court of Appeal in *R v Keogh* **[2007] 1 WLR 1500**. There the reverse-onus defences in **ss. 2(3) and 3(4) of the Official Secrets Act 1989** were interpreted to apply only to the evidential burden.

Thus, in English law, as in the Strasbourg jurisprudence, the presumption of innocence is not quite an absolute.[12] In *Lambert*, however, the court moved closer to the *Woolmington* principle by requiring close examination of all statutory reverse-onus provisions. As the analysis has shown, the current position has left some uncertainty and theoretical incoherence. One way forward suggested by Roberts and Zuckerman (2010, p. 289) is a 'planned programme of de-criminalisation' of the regulatory offences which are most often at issue in this area of statutory interpretation.

[12] *Lambert*, however, provides the theoretical framework. Glover (2017, p. 116) points out in relation to subsequent case law that 'as a general observation it should be said that they all appear to have taken into consideration the factors identified in *Lambert*'.

Conclusion

The legal landscape in relation to the presumption of innocence thus demonstrates that the position advocated by Roberts and Zuckerman is difficult to achieve. The courts and Parliament, particularly by the mechanism of separating the evidential and legal burdens on occasion, acknowledge that public policy considerations impact on constitutional rights to a fair trial.

The above account has illustrated, that it is also accepted that there may be compromises to the constitutional guarantee referred to in the question. The burden of elements of the offence or a defence may be shifted to the defendant in some cases as imposed by Parliament or the judges. In *Lambert* the House of Lords, stretching the linguistic interpretation somewhat, signalled a return to the principled approach of *Woolmington* away from the pragmatism of *Hunt*. The principles of the presumption of innocence should, the majority held, not be easily defeated. Instrumental arguments for the opposite stance did not prevail, a stance that showed more respect for the presumption of innocence as subsequent case law showed than Strasbourg showed in *Salabiaku v France* **(1988) 13 EHRR 379.**[13] However, principle and pragmatism currently go hand in hand, creating what Roberts and Zuckerman have called (2010, p. 281) a 'blizzard of single instances'.

[13] See Ashworth (2001, p. 865). He points out the importance of judgments concerning the presumption of innocence in Commonwealth courts in prompting British judges to 'give greater sharpness to the right'.

LOOKING FOR EXTRA MARKS?

- Since a number of the judgments are majority ones, it would improve your answer to have grasped details of the reasoning of the minority in such cases.
- Expand your analysis of various reform proposals, for example decriminalisation of regulatory offences.

QUESTION | 2

Answer all parts, each part is worth equal marks:

(a) Harry was refused entrance to a nightclub by a bouncer called George. A scuffle broke out and George suffered a broken nose. Harry is prosecuted for assault and claims that George struck the first blow. In her summing-up the judge states: 'Ladies and gentlemen of the jury, you have heard the defendant claim that he acted in self-defence. It is for the defendant to prove that he did act in self-defence. You may only convict the defendant if you are satisfied that he intentionally committed the offence.'

Comment on the judge's summing-up.

(b) Are we to infer that *M'Naghten* (and *Woolmington*) have been overruled, to the extent that the accused no longer has to prove insanity (on the balance of probabilities) but only to raise enough evidence to pass the judge?

(P. Roberts, 'Criminal Procedure, Drug Dealing and the Presumption of Innocence: The Human Rights Act (Almost) Bites' (2002) 6(2) International Journal of Evidence and Proof 17 at 37.)

Critically comment on this observation.

(c) Janet is facing two charges under the (imaginary) Tenant Protection Act 2015. Section 1(1) reads 'it is an offence to include car parking space in the tenancy except where the landlord has a licence from the local authority'. Section 1(2) reads: 'it is an offence for a landlord to enter a tenanted room after 10.00 p.m. without having secured permission from the tenant and with-out a reasonable excuse'. The prosecution allege that Janet let a parking space to her tenant Zara without a licence. They also allege that Janet entered the flat of her tenant Abdul while he was away and without his permission at 2.00 a.m. Janet claims she entered because she had received an anonymous phone call about a smoke alarm going off.

Advise Janet on the burden and standard of proof on both these charges.

CAUTION!

- These three questions require you to be familiar with very specific situations. A general answer describing the law would be inadequate.
- You must be careful to use the correct terminology and in particular to understand the difference between the legal and the evidential burdens.
- There is a significant amount of academic literature in this area and your answers must show appreciation of this.
- Plan your answers carefully and give each part of the question equal treatment.

DIAGRAM ANSWER PLAN

Identify the issues	The legal issues are: (a) the evidential rules on a claim of self-defence; (b) a historical development of the law on insanity; (c) construing a statutory provision to place a burden on the defendant.
Relevant law	(a) Evidential burden for common law defences; (b) *Woolmington*; (c) *Woolmington*; Magistrates' Courts Act 1980.
Apply the law	(a) The legal burden of proof on self-defence is on the prosecution, the standard is beyond reasonable doubt; (b) no intellectual justification for insanity exception, current reform proposals; (c) likely reversal of burden of proof.
Conclude	Advise Janet.

(a) Burden of Proof

The judge in her summing-up directed the jury's attention to Harry's use of self-defence based on the common law. It is a well-established principle that the prosecution does not have to anticipate every claim the defendant makes.[1] If the defendant wishes to plead self-defence then he must adduce sufficient evidence to convince the judge that this can be a live issue at the trial. In other words, the defendant has what is popularly known as the evidential burden. As Roberts (2002, p. 34) points out, the 'evidential burden is not a burden of proof at all, but only a burden of adducing evidence'.[2] In order for the defence to be put, the judge must be convinced that there was a reasonable possibility of the existence of that defence (*Jayasena v R* [1970] AC 618). She therefore does not have to refer to the evidential burden in her summing-up because admissibility on this issue is not a matter for the jury. The judge is incorrect in failing to direct the jury that the legal burden remains with the prosecution on this issue (*R v Lobell* [1957] 1 QB 547). A failure to do this could lead to an appeal (*R v Moon* [1969] 1 WLR 1705). In *R v O'Brien* [2004] EWCA Crim 2900 the Court of Appeal held that a failure by the judge to direct the jury that it was the task of the prosecution to prove the defendant was not acting in self-defence was 'an important misdirection in relation to a very significant aspect of the law of self-defence'.

Standard of proof

In the question set there is scant reference to the standard of proof in the summing-up. There is considerable case law on the words judges should use in directing juries on the standard of proof. Where the prosecution bears the legal burden the standard of proof required for conviction is beyond reasonable doubt. The Crown Court Compendium (successor to the Judicial Studies Board) recommend the wording:

The prosecution must prove that D is guilty. D does not have to prove anything to you. He does not have to prove that he is innocent. The prosecution will only succeed in proving that D is guilty if you have been made sure of his guilt. If, after considering all the evidence, you are sure that D is guilty your verdict must be 'Guilty'. If you are not sure that he is guilty or sure that he is innocent your verdict must be 'Not Guilty'.

However Glover comments (2017, p. 128) that 'it is submitted that the traditional formula "beyond reasonable doubt" is to be preferred'.[3] He refers to *R v Majid* [2009] EWCA Crim 2563 where the judge tried to distinguish 'being sure' from 'being certain', a distinction which Moses LJ said should be avoided. Keane and McKeowan (2018, p. 111) suggest that the inclusion of the phrase 'or sure he is innocent'

[1] The answer should here give a general explanation of the burden of 'passing the judge'.

[2] It is generally acknowledged that the term evidential burden of proof may be misleading and it is as well to be careful in the use of terminology.

[3] Note also that in *Smith (Scott)* [2012] EWCA Crim 702 the jury went so far as to ask for help in understanding the meaning of 'sure'.

in the guidance on wording by the Crown Court Compendium is 'troubling' and could lead the jury to return a unanimous guilty verdict if they are not sure the defendant is innocent.

The judge would be expected to include in her summing-up a direction along those lines. The Court of Appeal has over the years pronounced on unacceptable judicial directions in this area. In *R v Yap Chuan Ching* (1976) 63 Cr App R 7 Lawton LJ observed that 'if judges stopped trying to define that which is almost impossible to define there would be fewer appeals'. In this case, however, the Appeal Court stated that judges should avoid defining 'reasonable doubt'.

Thus the judge's summing-up in this instance is wrong on placing the burden of proving self-defence on the defendant. She is correct on the placing of the burden of proof on the prosecution in relation to the elements of the offence but her summing-up is incomplete on the question of the standard of proof.

(b) Critique of *Lambert*

In *Woolmington* Lord Sankey identified two exceptions to the placing of the legal burden of proof on the prosecution, namely statutory exceptions and that created in *M'Naghten's Case* (1843).

The quotation in this question acknowledges the importance of this exception to the 'golden thread' while at the same time acknowledging its status may be under threat from current judicial attitudes. To take the first point, it is salutary to realise that, as Roberts and Zuckerman point out, the insanity exception is 'of limited practical significance' (2010, p. 266).[4] They point out that a finding of 'not guilty by reason of insanity' meant 'mandatory detention in a secure hospital', and although other sentencing options are now available, 'a plea of insanity remains an unattractive option for most accused, and the defence is seldom raised'.

Roberts in the article quoted goes further by outlining the shaky intellectual basis for the insanity exception. The House of Lords in *Lambert*, argues Roberts, is close to saying that the only burdens on the defence should be evidential ones. He criticises the judgment because the analysis fails to acknowledge the conclusive nature of the specific statutory section, namely that it creates an offence of strict liability and therefore the discussion on burden of proof in relation to guilty knowledge is theoretically incoherent.

In the article Roberts goes on to speculate about the possible implications of *Lambert* for other seemingly entrenched doctrines, including the burden of proof on an insanity defence. He comments that the Canadian courts have re-examined this question in the light of fair trial right considerations, although this is not specifically included in the House of Lords' *Lambert* ruling.[5]

[4] See the Law Commission Paper, cited in the following section, for further discussion on the statistics of insanity defences.

[5] Examiners will give credit for references to other common law jurisdictions where relevant.

In short, Roberts is arguing that while putting an evidential burden rather than a legal burden on the defence might be welcome from a human rights standpoint, the general uncertainty and intellectual confusion the judgment has prompted is troubling.

Reform of law

With regard to the principled question in relation to insanity, namely should the burden of proof be on the defendant, it is certainly arguable that the *M'Naghten* decision itself is a historical anomaly and is arguably difficult to justify in the light of **Art. 6** provisions. The European Court of Human Rights has held that the rule does not violate the presumption of innocence: *H v UK* **(1990) App. No. 15023/89 ECHR**. Jones (1995, p. 475), however, cites arguments that the burden on the defence should be evidential only. Jones acknowledges that the courts are just as concerned with social protection as they are with issues of individual fairness or responsibility and that 'there is a constant tension between these two competing values, which goes some way to explaining (but not justifying) the complexities and paradoxes which pervade this area of law'.

The Law Commission has produced a Discussion Paper in which it proposed that the general law relating to mental illness should be rationalised and a new term 'mental disorder' should replace 'insanity'.[6] The burden of proving the defence would remain on the accused on the balance of probabilities. See http://www.lawcom.gov.uk/wp-content/uploads/2015/06/insanity_discussion.pdf.

The Paper argues that the law lags behind psychiatric understanding, and this partly explains why, in practice, the defence is underused and medical professionals do not apply the correct legal test.[7]

(c) Letting Parking Space

The two elements of the first offence are letting a parking space to a tenant without a licence. The courts will be likely to consider this scenario as being covered by **s. 101 of the Magistrates' Courts Act 1980**. Janet should be advised that it is immaterial in relation to this provision whether the trial takes place in the magistrates' court or the Crown Court.[8] The Crown will have to prove the *actus reus* of letting the parking space and, presumptively, the *mens rea*. Janet should be advised, however, that the court is likely to decide that she has the burden of proving the existence of a licence. The use of the word 'except' clearly signals that the existence of the licence would be an 'excuse', 'proviso', or 'exception' which would provide a defence to criminal liability.

Invasion of room

The court will examine whether 'without reasonable excuse' constitutes an exception which must be proved by the defendant. Following the **Human Rights Act 1998**, the courts will apply a series of tests to

[6] Your revision plan should always include consulting the Law Commission website for recent reports.

[7] This is an area where a knowledge of psychology could well improve your answer.

[8] Attention to procedural matters, such as whether the trial is summary or on indictment, is important.

decide if a reversal of the burden of proof in a statute is a proportionate response. In **Sheldrake v DPP [2005] 1 AC 264** which concerned the **Road Traffic Act 1988** the House of Lords examined the status of the burden of proof.[9] At issue was whether, where the defendant was on trial for being in charge of a car while intoxicated, the defence under **s. 5(2)** placed the burden on him or on the prosecution. The defence was held to be available on proof that there was no likelihood of the defendant driving his car. In **Sheldrake** the House placed the burden on the defendant. The prosecution will argue therefore in Janet's case that she should have the burden since the existence of the phone call was within her knowledge and there was a strong public interest in protecting the privacy of tenants. The offence appears to be a regulatory one, not one where there would be limited moral opprobrium. Even if there is moral blameworthiness, the prosecution may additionally rely on **R v Johnstone [2003] 1 WLR 1736** and **R v Davies [2002] EWCA Crim 2949**. In those cases the perpetrator engaged in a regulated activity but there was some element of moral blameworthiness, such as breaching the **Trade Marks Act 1994**. Here Janet has had a benefit as landlord since she gets to inspect her property by breaching the time regulation. On the other hand, it is possible Janet may rely on **R v Charles [2010] Crim LR 303** which turned on the interpretation of **s. 1(10) of the Crime and Disorder Act 1998**. The Court of Appeal held that the prosecution must prove a breach of the order to the criminal standard.[10] The court could take a pragmatic approach and hold that placing the legal burden on Janet would undermine the fairness of the trial while placing the evidential burden only on Janet would preserve the **Woolmington** principle.

Conclusion

Janet will have to prove the existence of the licence and the legal burden is likely to be on her to prove she had reasonable excuse to enter the premises to the standard of the balance of probabilities.

[9] The point here is to give examples of what might be called regulatory offences such that there is no opprobrium for a conviction.

[10] This is one example of civil sanctions which have a criminal element.

LOOKING FOR EXTRA MARKS?

- For part (a) demonstrate you are aware of the discussion of the use of 'sure' in the summing-up.
- For part (b) refer to the analysis of Loughran (2007) who has suggested that a concept of 'manifest madness' may provide a theoretical frame for interpreting the evidentiary and procedural aspect of the defence. She suggests that the defence is in effect limited to cases where the madness is encoded in the defendant's acts and its nature is intelligible to lay observers.
- For part (c) develop your analysis that there may be several elements to one statutory offence and the burden may be allocated differently on each.

The owners of Legacy Athletics Arena (LAA) are suing Arnold, a former employee.

They claim that he took away a sports bag of equipment when he left their employment. Arnold defends the claim of fraudulent conversion and relies on a clause in his contract which exempted him from liability for retaining LAA sports equipment provided he had introduced 20 new members to the LAA in the 12 months before his employment ended.

In a separate action the chief officer of police has applied for a civil banning order against Harold under the (imaginary) Athletics Arenas Protection Act 2014 under which spectators may be banned from attending athletics meetings if there is reasonable cause to suspect that a banning order will help prevent disorder or violence. Arnold has just been convicted of sending threatening offensive tweets to members of a team visiting the LAA for a competition.

Advise the parties on burden and standard of proof in the above two civil proceedings.

CAUTION!

- The question centres on the correct standard of proof in civil proceedings when there is an allegation of a quasi-criminal nature.

- Address the burden in the exemption clause and its proviso.

- One issue concerns the application for a banning order which will be made in a civil court, but the question arises as to whether this is akin to a number of exceptions to the principle of the standard of proof being the balance of probabilities.

DIAGRAM ANSWER PLAN

Identify the issues	▦ The legal issues are: burden and standard of proof on the fraudulent conversion claim; status of exemption clause; burden and standard of proof on the banning order.
Relevant law	▦ Case law on burden and standard of proof in quasi-criminal claims; court's construction of exemption clauses; precedent for anti-social behaviour orders.
Apply the law	▦ Asserter has the burden, standard balance of probabilities; criminal standard applied in anti-social banning orders.
Conclude	▦ The parties are advised that the burden and standard of proof will shift as the litigation proceeds and where some matters may be conceded. The standard of proof for the banning order is likely to be beyond reasonable doubt.

SUGGESTED ANSWER

Burden of Proof on Fraudulent Conversion Claim

The general principle in civil litigation is that the burden of proof lies on the asserter of a claim. The incidence of the legal burden of proof will decide the outcome of the case if the tribunal is not able to come to a decision which to prefer.[1] In *Rhesa Shipping Co. SA v Edmunds* **[1985] 1 WLR 948** the House of Lords, overturning the Court of Appeal, held that the judge had not been obliged to choose between two versions merely because the defendants had chosen to put forward their explanation of events.

It is thus for the LAA to prove the removal of the sports bag.[2] The incidence of the burden is here a matter of substantive law for a claim or a defence and the House of Lords held that it is usually clear from the pleadings: *Joseph Constantine Steamship Line v Imperial Smelting Corp.* **[1942] AC 154.** The LAA therefore have the legal burden of proof on this issue. They also have the evidential burden in the sense that they must put in some evidence to convince the court there is an arguable case.[3] Arnold may simply deny liability but he runs the risk tactically of losing. He appears, however, to be putting up a specific defence, namely that the sports bag was due to him for

[1] Although in a problem question, unlike an essay question, there is not the same need for a general explanation of the law; it is appropriate here to set out the general principle since it is a matter of current debate.

[2] Note that the claimant will have to establish all the relevant facts which are not accepted by the other side.

[3] Although the distinction between the evidential burden and the legal burden is not as crucial in civil cases as in criminal cases, it is necessary to refer to it for the sake of completeness.

[4]You are now going to introduce
the more complex question of the
standard of proof in civil trials.

introducing new members to the LAA. He has the legal and evidential
burden of mounting this defence and the standard of proof is on the
balance of probabilities.[4] There is a possible further consideration in
that the LAA are alleging that Arnold held the bag fraudulently.

[5]It is occasionally, as here, useful to
cite professional guidance on these
issues.

The Bar's professional standards code provides that counsel may
not draft an allegation of fraud without specific instructions and unless he or she has reasonably credible material which, as it stands,
establishes a prima facie case of fraud.[5]

Standard of Proof

There have been some examples in civil cases where courts have held
that certain matters must be proved to the criminal standard of proof.
Re a Solicitor [1992] QB 69 is one such example. The issue was the
standard of proof in a case before a solicitors' disciplinary tribunal,
where allegations of professional misconduct were made. The Divisional

[6]Since you are examining
precedents on the standard of proof
in this question, it is good practice
to refer to the court which decided
the case.

Court held that since what was alleged was tantamount to a criminal
offence the criminal standard should apply.[6] However, this has not been
generally followed. In *Hornal v Neuberger Products Ltd* [1957] 1
QB 247, a case involving an allegation of fraudulent misrepresentation,
the Court of Appeal rejected the view that there was a higher standard
necessary than balance of probability but rather puzzlingly commented
per Denning LJ at p. 258 'the more serious the allegation the higher the
degree of probability that is required' and per Morris LJ at p. 266 'the
very elements of gravity become a part of the whole range of circumstances which have to be weighed in the scale when deciding as to the
balance of probabilities'. In *Re H and Others (Minors) (Sexual Abuse:
Standard of Proof)* [1996] AC 563 the House of Lords in a majority
decision rejected the concept of a third standard in civil cases of this sort.

[7]Again here you are signalling that
this is a binding precedent. In that
case Lord Hoffmann stated (at para.
13) 'I think that the time has come
to say, once and for all, that there is
only one civil standard of proof that
is proof that the fact in issue more
probably occurred than not'.

The issue seems to have been conclusively settled by subsequent
House of Lords decisions, see *Re B (Children)* [2008] UKHL 35.[7] On
the facts as they are given here it is likely that the position stated in
Re B should be applied and that the standard of proof required will be
on the balance of probabilities but that cogent evidence of Arnold's
alleged fraud will be required.

Exemption Clause

As regards the exclusion clause, it is for Arnold to prove the bag falls
within the exemption clause, although this is a matter of construction for the court: *Munro Brice and Co. v War Risks Association*

[8]It is easy to overlook the proviso
in an exemption clause so read the
question very carefully.

[1918] 2 KB 78. However, it is arguable that if a claimant relies upon
a proviso to an exemption clause, the burden of proving that the facts
fall within the proviso may be on the claimant, as *The Glendarroch*
[1894] P 226 illustrates.[8] Arnold may argue by analogy with this reasoning that the LAA will have to prove that he did not secure 20 new
members.

Athletics Banning Order

The application for a banning order will take place in a civil court but the question is whether the (imaginary) Athletics Arenas Protection Act 2012 is analogous to those statutes where the courts have held that a standard of proof which is in effect identical to the criminal standard applies.[9] Thus, for example, in *R (McCann) v Crown Court at Manchester* [2003] 1 AC 787 the House of Lords held that applications for anti-social behaviour orders under **s. 1(1)(a) of the Crime and Disorder Act 1998** should only be made where the preliminary conditions had been proved beyond reasonable doubt. See also *Gough v Chief Constable of the Derbyshire Constabulary* [2002] QB 1213 in relation to football banning orders under **s. 14B of the Football Spectators Act 1989**. It is likely that the banning order will only be made against Arnold if it can be proved beyond reasonable doubt that he is likely to cause violence. The earlier conviction will be relevant evidence.[10] The conviction had only 'just' taken place so the **Rehabilitation of Offenders Act 1974** will not apply.

[9] You are not given the extract of the relevant section of the statute so it is acceptable to speculate.

[10] See also *Re B* (2008) (para. 69), '. . . there are some proceedings, though civil in form, whose nature is such that it is appropriate to apply the criminal standard of proof'.

 LOOKING FOR EXTRA MARKS?

- This is a problem question and you are not asked to comment on the strength or weakness of the law. It would gain you no marks therefore to discuss possible reform proposals here.
- Extend your account of how a civil case may be decided on burden of proof using the example of *Rhesa Shipping Co. SA v Edmunds* [1985].
- Make it clear that you understand the general rule that civil standard of proof is balance of probabilities.
- Examine cases where a quasi-criminal accusation is made in a civil case; despite some deviation from balance of probabilities, the House of Lords has decided there is no third standard.

 QUESTION | **4**

Jane and Harry were legally married in 2000 in Birmingham. In 2002 Harry left to join a revolutionary group in Bolivia, but told Jane he would return in a year. In fact Jane did not hear from him again and in 2004 received a letter from the group leader saying Harry had been missing for six months following an expedition against counter-revolutionaries. Jane heard no more and in 2014 married Oliver, a man older than her, in Paris. In 2015 Jane gave birth to twins Barry and John and in 2016 to Margaret. In 2017 Jane and Oliver were both killed instantly in a car crash. Shortly before he was killed, Oliver told his sister, Sarah, that Margaret could not be his child because he had not had intercourse with Jane for a year before her birth. At the funeral, Alan, an old college friend of Jane and Harry's, who has been out of touch for years, told John that he saw Harry in a cafe in La

Paz in 2004 but said Harry disappeared before he could speak to him. Jane's will said that if she died after Oliver her estate should be divided between her children and a charity for distressed Bolivian revolutionaries. Oliver's will left all his property to his 'legitimate children'. When Sarah, after the car crash, looked through old photographs in the attic she came across one showing Oliver and an unknown woman. On the back was noted 'Wedding day, 29 March 2010'.

Advise whether Margaret can claim under Oliver's will and whether all the children can succeed under Jane's will.

CAUTION!

- This is conceptually quite a tricky area and you need to keep in mind the difference between presumptions in civil cases and criminal cases.

- Make sure you appreciate the traditional classification of irrebuttable presumptions of law, rebuttable presumptions of law, and presumptions of fact. It is mainly the second with which you need to be concerned in this question.

- Alongside this you need to distinguish persuasive presumptions, that is those where the effect of the presumption is to put the legal burden of disproof on the party who wishes to challenge it, and evidential presumptions where the evidential burden only is placed on the party against whom it operates.

- In this question the examiner is looking for a clear application of the law on presumptions to the facts, rather than discussion on the rationale of presumptions more appropriate to an essay question.

It is helpful to draw up a chronology.

- 2000 Jane and Harry marry—presumption of validity of marriage.

- 2014 Jane and Oliver marry—does presumption of Harry's death operate?

- What is the effect of the 2004 sighting of Harry? Is validity of marriage challenged by 2010 'wedding photograph' of Oliver and unknown woman?

- 2015 John and Barry born.

- 2016 Margaret born—presumption of legitimacy but does what Oliver told Sarah rebut presumption of Margaret's legitimacy? Does the 'wedding photograph' affect all children's legitimacy?

- 2017 Jane and Oliver killed—presumption of order of death and effect on inheritance.

DIAGRAM ANSWER PLAN

Identify the issues	▨ The legal issues are: presumptions of legitimacy of marriage, death, and legitimacy; evidence needed to challenge the presumptions; significance of location of marriage.
Relevant law	▨ Common law; statutes include: Law of Property Act; Family Law Reform Act 1969; Matrimonial Causes Act 1973; Presumption of Death Act 2013
Apply the law	▨ Oliver's eligibility to marry; Jane's position depends on evidence and is a question of fact; legal burden of proof on John and Barry to disprove Margaret's claim.
Conclude	▨ Possibility of DNA testing.

SUGGESTED ANSWER

Order of Death

[1] Note the effect of **s. 1 of the Intestates' Estate Act 1952** where one spouse dies intestate.

The order of death of Jane and Oliver is determined by their seniority **(Law of Property Act 1925, s. 184).**[1] As Jane is the younger of the two, Oliver will be presumed to have died first, thus in accordance with the terms of her will her estate is divided between John, Barry, and Margaret and the Bolivian charity.

Inheritance and Validity of Marriage

[2] It is important in a factual scenario as complex as this to highlight the individual pieces of evidence.

Oliver's estate raises more complicated issues. John, Barry, and Margaret can inherit only if they are legitimate. The validity of the marriage between Jane and Oliver could affect the legitimacy of all three. The validity of the marriage is threatened by two pieces of evidence.[2] One is the evidence of Alan that Harry may have been alive after he was presumed to have died. The other is the photograph which suggests that Oliver was not free to marry Jane. The presumption of the validity of a marriage is a very strong one. There are two presumptions which may be operative here. On proof of the celebration of a marriage ceremony, that is one which is capable of producing a valid marriage, the law will presume the formal validity of the marriage, that is to say that the formalities have been complied with.

The primary facts thus are the evidence of the ceremony that is valid according to local law. In *Mahadervan v Mahadervan* **[1964] P 233** it was argued that the presumption did not apply in favour of a foreign marriage but Sir Jocelyn Simon P said (at p. 247):[3]

> To accept it would give expression to a legal chauvinism that has no place in any rational system of private international law. Our courts in my view apply exactly the same weight of presumption in favour of a foreign marriage as of an English one, and the nationality of any later marriage brought into question is quite immaterial.

It is not significant therefore that the marriage took place in Paris.[4]

This presumption is a persuasive one and there is a legal burden on the party seeking to rebut formal validity. The standard of proof to be met by that party is high. In *Mahadervan* Sir Jocelyn Simon P held that the presumption can only be rebutted by evidence which establishes beyond reasonable doubt that there was no marriage.[5]

Capacity to Marry

On proof of the celebration of a marriage ceremony, relying on the same primary facts, the 'essential validity' of the marriage will be assumed. This is that the parties had the necessary capacity of marrying and that their respective consents were genuine. There appears to be little doubt about the formal validity of the marriage of Jane and Oliver: the issue is its essential validity. In other words, were the parties free to marry?[6] Again, in civil proceedings, the presumption is a persuasive rather than an evidential presumption, but the standard of proof is lower than that in the case of the presumption of formal validity. In *Re Peete, Peete v Crompton* **[1952] 2 All ER 599** the issue arose as to the essential validity of a formally valid marriage in 1919. There was some evidence of the existence of an earlier marriage and the presumption of validity of the 1919 marriage failed. Even so, the photograph in itself is unlikely to be sufficient evidence to undermine the presumption that Oliver was free to marry Jane.[7]

The issue whether Jane was free to marry is more complicated. Evidently, she relied on the presumption that Harry was dead when she went through the ceremony with Oliver. The rules relating to presumption of death were a matter of common law set out in *Chard v Chard* **[1956] P 259**. Harry would be presumed dead when four circumstances apply: there is no acceptable evidence that he has been alive for at least seven continuous years; there are persons likely to have heard of him, had he been alive; who during that period have not so heard; and all due inquiries have failed to locate him. We aren't told whether Jane made inquiries about Harry after his disappearance, but, assuming she did, she was entitled by 2014 to presume his death.[8] The procedure is laid down by the **Presumption of Death Act 2013** repealing s. 19 of the

[3] It will obviously not be possible for you to commit to memory many quotations from cases but it is quite acceptable to paraphrase the point, particularly when it is as pertinent as here.

[4] This part of the answer comes to a clear assertion of the advice to the parties.

[5] Students often worry about how many cases to recall. Note that here just one leading case has given authority for two propositions integral to the question. It shows the importance of revising the case law carefully.

[6] Examiners will look for clear writing style as well as analytical skills and knowledge. As long as you do not do it to excess, it is acceptable to ask a rhetorical question.

[7] Again you have come back sharply to the facts as given.

[8] Questions cannot always give an extensive account of the facts so it is acceptable to state that you may need 'further and better particulars'.

Matrimonial Causes Act 1973. The 2013 Act introduced a new and simpler procedure which provides that anyone with sufficient interest may apply for a declaration that a missing person is dead. The court would make the declaration if satisfied that the missing person had died or had not been known to be alive for at least the previous seven years. A spouse or other close relative automatically has sufficient interest to make the application. The court can make the declaration even if it is not satisfied that the person is dead provided it is satisfied that he was last known to be alive at a date more than seven years previously. The missing person's name would be entered on the Register of Presumed Deaths maintained by the Registrar-General. Were he to reappear alive, application could be made to the High Court to revoke the declaration.[9]

[9] The repealed section contained a much more cumbersome procedure. The relevant **s. 19(3)** read: '. . . the fact that for a period of seven years or more the other party to the marriage has been continually absent from the petitioner and the petitioner has no reason to believe that the other party has been living within that time shall be evidence that the other party is dead until the contrary is proved'.

Challenge to Presumption

If she had married Oliver without petitioning for a decree under the Presumption of Death Act, the marriage would not necessarily have been an act of bigamy since she could still rely on the common law presumption. Those wishing to challenge the presumption will have the evidential burden. In *Prudential Assurance Co. v Edmonds* **(1877) 2 App Cas 487** a niece standing in a crowded street in Australia had briefly caught sight of a man she recognised as her uncle. The judge had first to decide whether or not she was mistaken. If she was, it made no difference to the presumption. If she was not, the onus was on the side claiming that he was dead to establish that he was. The House of Lords held that it was for the tribunal of fact to decide whether or not to accept the niece's evidence and that if the jury had been satisfied that she was mistaken the basic facts giving rise to the presumption were established. Here Alan is available for cross-examination and the preliminary issue is ultimately one of fact.

Margaret's Legitimacy

The next issue concerns Margaret. Does what Oliver told Sarah affect her legitimacy and claim under Oliver's will? There is a presumption that a child born to the wife in lawful wedlock and conceived while the husband was alive is legitimate. This persuasive presumption can be rebutted by evidence which shows that it is more probable than not that the person is illegitimate and it is not necessary to prove that fact beyond reasonable doubt: **Family Law Reform Act 1969, s. 26** and *S v S* **[1972] AC 24**. Oliver's remark to Sarah (admissible at trial under the **Civil Evidence Act 1995;** see **Chapter 5**) is evidence which might be capable of rebutting the presumption that Margaret is legitimate. The presumption is a persuasive one.[10] Thus the legal burden of disproof falls on John and Barry, assuming it is their representatives who

[10] Here you see the importance of setting out in your plan which presumptions are persuasive.

are challenging Margaret's claim. However, against the remark should be set the provisional presumption (or presumption of fact) that sexual intercourse between husband and wife is likely to follow where opportunities for it occur. This is a weaker presumption: ***Piggott v Piggott* (1938) 61 CLR 378** probably destroyed here by the remark itself. John and Barry have only the tactical burden of disproving it.

Conclusion: Possibility of DNA Testing

[11] It is sensible to refer realistically to possible current scientific aids.

Finally the issue might be resolved by DNA testing. [11]

LOOKING FOR EXTRA MARKS?

- Clearly acknowledge that the primary facts must first be proved; if they are, the specific presumption must be drawn from them, although it may be rebutted by other conflicting facts.
- Develop a clear outline structure. First, see if the presumptions apply and then see if they can be rebutted.
- Give closer attention to the facts given—for example, the marriage takes place in Paris—is this significant?

TAKING THINGS FURTHER

- Ashworth, A., 'Criminal Proceedings after the Human Rights Act: The First Year' [2001] Crim LR 855.
  Contrasts English judgments upholding the presumption of innocence favourably against Strasbourg decisions.
- Ashworth, A., 'Four Threats to the Presumption of Innocence' (2006) 10 E & P 241.
  Analyses contemporary threats as: confinement, erosion, evasion, and sidestepping and argues that the presumption should be recognised as fundamental.
- Ashworth, A. and Blake, M., 'The Presumption of Innocence in English Criminal Law' [1996] Crim LR 306.
  A review of the statutes where the criminal burden of proof is reversed. It would be a useful exercise for students to add to the list when they read of later statutes.
- Dennis, I., 'Reverse Onuses and the Presumption of Innocence' [2005] Crim LR 901.
  Gives a detailed typology of cases on the allocation of the burden of proof and argues that it is important to distinguish the procedural and substantive aspects of the presumption of innocence.
- Jones, T.H., 'Insanity, Automatism and the Burden of Proof on the Accused' (1995) 111 LQR 475.
  See references in text to answers.

- Loughran, A., '"Manifest Madness": Towards a New Understanding of the Insanity Defence' (2007) 70 MLR 379.

  A carefully researched analysis of the nature of mental illness which would give a powerful socio-medical thrust to your answers.

- Roberts, P., 'Drug Dealing and the Presumption of Innocence: The Human Rights Act (Almost) Bites' (2002) 6 E & P 17.

  See references in text to answers.

- Roberts P. and Zuckerman A., *Criminal Evidence* (Oxford: OUP, 2010).

  This book is a must for students who wish to appreciate the challenging theoretical evidential issues.

- Tausz, D. and Ashworth, A., 'Case Comment, *Sheldrake v DPP* [2004] UKHL 43' [2005] Crim LR 215.

  A rounded critique of the judgment and its implications.

Online Resources

www.oup.com/uk/qanda/

Go online for extra essay and problem questions, a glossary of key terms, online versions of all the answer plans and audio commentary on how selected ones were put together, and a range of podcasts which include advice on exam and coursework technique and advice for other assessment methods.

Witnesses: competence and compellability; Special Measures Directions

3

ARE YOU READY?

In order to perform well you will need to have revised:

- the statutory provisions and relevant case law on the general rules on competence and compellability of witnesses in criminal and civil trials
- the specific position relating to spouses and civil partners as witnesses in criminal trials
- the law relating to the non-testifying defendant
- the statutory provisions whereby non-defendant vulnerable witnesses may be granted Special Measures Directions in criminal trials
- the more limited provisions for the protection of vulnerable defendants in criminal trials

KEY DEBATES

Debate: should spousal privilege be maintained?

Spousal privilege is based on the social desirability of protecting the stability of the institution of marriage. Some argue that this is still an important goal which cements a healthy functioning society. However, others maintain that it is an outdated concept that no longer accords with current conditions and that, for example, elderly witnesses may deserve protecting as much as children. It is argued that the specified list of exemptions is not coherent.

Debate: is the current provision for intermediaries adequate?

The **Youth Justice and Criminal Evidence Act 1999** acknowledged that vulnerable witnesses may need intermediaries in court. Vulnerable defendants do not fall within the statutory scheme

⊙

◁

although the court, with its common law inherent jurisdiction to ensure a fair trial, may make provision. It is argued that the scheme is currently inadequate and that the PACE Codes in this area should be amended.

(Q) QUESTION | 1

Explain, giving reasons for your answer, whether you think that the current law on the compellability at trial of spouses and civil partners is both justifiable and consistent.

(!) CAUTION!

▨ The question requires you to be familiar with the case of *R v L* [2008] 2 Cr App R 18.

▨ Note that there are in effect two parts to the answer, namely is the current law consistent and is it justifiable. Ensure your answer is structured well in that it addresses these two points of the question, uses academic and legal references to give authority to your propositions, and adopts an analytical not a purely narrative stance.

(O) DIAGRAM ANSWER PLAN

Explain the reason for the exception for the general presumption of competence.

▼

Give arguments why spousal privilege is justifiable.

▼

Give arguments why spousal privilege is not justifiable.

▼

Discuss how the law is consistent.

▼

Discuss how the law is inconsistent.

▼

Conclusion including assessment of academic arguments.

Introduction: The General Rule and Exceptions

The general rule in relation to competence is straightforward. All witnesses are assumed to be competent by virtue of **s. 53(1) of the Youth Justice and Criminal Evidence Act 1999**. However, in relation to spouses and civil partners otherwise competent partners are not compellable. The statutory provisions on the compellability of these witnesses are a matter of debate on the two grounds the question identifies, namely whether they are justifiable and whether they are consistent. This answer will review the arguments in both of these areas. It should be stressed initially that this is an evolving area of the law and a brief historical overview reveals that the goal of consistency and the achievement of a justifiable legal framework is socially conditioned. There will rarely be a fixed acceptable answer. Thus what might appear consistent and justifiable to some has to be seen in the light of the prevailing social climate. A brief historical overview illustrates this.[1]

[1] In a coursework question you would be able to expand on the historical background but in the examination you are simply indicating that you appreciate that the law has evolved over time.

Common Law

The non-competence of spouses to testify for the prosecution was a common law rule, the justification being that such testimony would put strain on the marriage relationship. The law upheld the legal fiction of the single personality of the husband and wife. However, this was not upheld consistently since there was an exception in cases involving violence by one spouse against the other. In such cases the spouse was competent although not compellable. This background informs the current law set out in **s. 80 of the Police and Criminal Evidence Act 1984 (PACE).**[2] A wife is competent to testify for the prosecution but only compellable for 'specified offences' namely those involving physical or sexual violence to the spouse or civil partner or to a person under 16. This essay will first address the question of justifiability of the law and secondly consistency.[3]

[2] You should not give too much narrative information about the law in the introduction. Set out simply the central thrust of the law.

[3] It is important to give the examiner an outline of the structure of your essay early on.

Justifying Non-Compellability

The foundational justification for the law was stated by Lord Salmon in *R v Hoskyn* **[1979] AC 474**, a majority judgment.[4] He referred to 'the supreme importance attached by the common law to the special status of marriage' and also to what he claimed was 'the natural repugnance of the public at the prospect of the wife giving evidence against her husband'. Whether compelling a reluctant spouse to testify really did threaten the stability of a marriage was not subjected to empirical investigation and it might well be argued that if serious violence was alleged the marriage might be beyond repair. However, although the gender-based observation by Lord Salmon sounds

[4] It is unlikely you will be able to recall exact quotations in an examination but you may put to memory telling phrases that convey the flavour of the time. This quotation from Lord Salmon [1979] AC 474 at 495 gives a succinct picture of the law and how it reflects what are assumed to be prevailing attitudes.

somewhat quaint several decades later, other, albeit more nuanced, opinion argues also for a presumption of non-compellability with limited exceptions on the grounds that the law should be concerned with upholding marriage. The 11th Report of the Criminal Law Revision Committee (1972), in recommending that the wife should be competent for the prosecution in all cases, referred to the 'preservation of marital harmony' while deploring 'excessive concern' for it.[5] The reforms enacted in **PACE** accepted the need to treat spouses differently from other witnesses.

More broadly there are academic commentators who have put powerful arguments for the maintenance of the spousal privilege. Thus Brabyn claims that the present law helps preserve marriage and that it is in society's long-term interests to put this objective above securing the conviction of the guilty.[6] She adopts a pragmatic stance as well as a principled one in suggesting that the quality of the evidence obtained from a spouse who was compelled to give evidence is uncertain. In Brabyn's view the provisions in **PACE** are based on 'unprincipled distinctions' including the decision in the controversial case of *R v L* **[2008] 1 WLR 626** which she says was based on 'an abusive misuse of hearsay'.[7] The views of this academic, however, must be set against those of the many academics who do not accept that non-compellability is justified.

Justifying Compellability

The principled arguments in favour of general compellability range from an assessment of actual social conditions to more jurisprudential reasoning about access to evidence. Roberts and Zuckerman (2010, p. 313) point out that marriages are much more readily dissolved today so it is not as necessary to rely on the law of evidence to help cement an unhappy relationship as it was when couples faced difficulties in obtaining a divorce. Other objections to the law deriving from social conditions include the point that many couples cohabit and this can form the basis of a long-standing relationship as significant as marriage. In *R v Pearce* **[2002] 1 WLR 1553** the Court of Appeal refused to extend spousal privilege to cohabitees. By contrast the Grand Chamber has held in *Van der Heijden v Netherlands* **[2012] ECHR 588** that it would be a violation of **Art. 8** to compel a cohabitee of 18 years to give testimony against her partner, although in this instance the breach was necessary for the prevention of crime.

Jurisprudential arguments for opposing spousal privilege include those put forward by the American academic and neo-Benthamite, Laudan. He argues in favour of free proof and is critical of what he calls 'relationship privileges' (2005, p. 165). Spousal privilege according to Laudan is theoretically incoherent. He points out that if a husband tells his wife that he robbed a bank, she could not be compelled

[5] See the 1972 Report (Cmd 4991) at para. 147.

[6] It is wise to give voice in a law essay to opposing viewpoints. In other words, do not 'editorialise' by promoting just one opinion. You are being examined on your assessment of the evidence for a proposition and although you will be expected to make your own assessment, this must be in the context of setting out differences of academic opinion.

[7] This controversial case is central to the discussion in this essay. See also *R v Horsnell* **[2012] EWCA Crim 227**.

to testify against him but if he told his young daughter she could. He questions whether a parent–child relationship is less threatened by the revelation of confidences than a spousal one. His most robust objection to the non-compellability of the spouse is its obstruction to the truth-seeking process.

Consistency of the Law

The strongest argument that the law is consistent is that it has attempted to uphold the underlying substance of a marriage- or family-based relationship rather than cling to some outdated perception of legal form. The extension of the privilege to civil partners illustrates this very well (although the exclusion of cohabitees from the privilege, as outlined earlier, has to be set against this reform). **Section 80 PACE** was subsequently amended to place civil partners on the same footing as spouses. Finally the case of *R v Registrar-General for Births, Marriages and Deaths, ex p CPS* **[2002] QB 1222, CACD** illustrates the consistent importance the courts attach to the status of marriage. The Queen's Bench Division held that even where the objective of a marriage with a remand prisoner was to prevent a spouse being compelled to give evidence against him, there was no power to prevent it.

Inconsistency of the Law

As the account above indicated, the defence of spousal privilege articulated by Brabyn was prompted by the decision in *R v L* **(2008)**. A statement made in police interview was held to be admissible hearsay under **s. 114(1)(d) of the Criminal Justice Act 2003**. The spouse had not been warned at interview she was not compellable and at the trial she declined to testify. The upholding of a consistent approach to spousal privilege was held to be secondary to the exercise of judicial discretion to admit hearsay evidence in the interest of justice. Other inconsistencies in this area of law include, first, the fact that the spouse is generally compellable in civil cases although arguably here also the stability of a marriage may be threatened. Secondly, **s. 80A PACE** provides that 'the failure of the spouse or civil partner of a person charged in any proceedings to give evidence in the proceedings shall not be made the subject of any comment by the prosecution'. In *R v Davey* **[2006] EWCA Crim 565** comment was precluded even where it was based on a logical inference. This is inconsistent with the approach to the non-testifying defendant exemplified in **s. 35 of the Criminal Justice and Public Order Act 1994.** Thirdly if the accused is charged with more than one offence, the spouse may be compellable for some offences but not on others.[8] Fourthly, the wording of **s. 80(3)** may give rise to inconsistencies since as Munday puts it (2015, p. 114) 'it is not

[8] The Court of Appeal made comment on this in *R v A (B)* [2012] 1WLR 3378.

[9] The husband was charged with an offence under **s. 2(a) of the Criminal Damage Act 1971.** After a quarrel with his wife it was alleged that he pressed the portable gas igniter and left the house leaving the hobs and oven turned on. The indictment stated: '[The husband] without lawful excuse, made to [his wife] a threat to destroy or damage property, namely her flat . . ., intending that [the wife] would fear that the threat would be carried out'.

[10] The husband had, according to the pre-trial statement of the wife, threatened to burn down the house with her and the children in it.

straightforward' in relation to specified offences. One problem is the scope of the word 'involves'. Thus in *R v A (B)* [2012] 1 WLR 3378 arson was excluded from the list of specified offences under **s. 80(2A)(b) PACE**.[9] At the trial the wife declined to give evidence and the judge ruled that the offence with which the husband was charged was not a specified offence within the meaning of **s. 80(2A)(b) PACE** and therefore the wife was not a compellable witness. The Court of Appeal heard the prosecution's appeal that the issue should be decided by reference to the evidence adduced about the circumstances of the particular offence and not only on the terms of the indictment. The Court of Appeal adopted a purposive interpretation and held that the[10] judge's ruling was correct.

Hoyano in a riposte to Brabyn's defence of spousal privilege argued, 'Whilst few modern commentators would doubt the beneficial effect for society of marriage and analogous committed relationships, this commentator has never seen any empirical evidence to support the assertion that "fewer relationships may form" if spousal immunity were abolished' ([2013] **Crim LR 170**).

Conclusion

The above discussion has illustrated that the question of whether the law on spousal privilege should be amended is a value-laden one. In essence the essay has centred on the issue of whether subjective and perhaps anachronistic perceptions of ways of achieving social harmony should prevail over truth-seeking in a criminal trial. May the spousal privilege lead to wrongful acquittals? The experience of other countries such as Australia suggests that increased use of judicial discretion on compellability may be one way out of the theoretical incoherence and arbitrariness of the present position.[11] The weight of academic opinion in favour of abolition of the privilege is convincing on the grounds that it privileges the institution of marriage (or civil partnership) over the needs of the wider criminal justice system.

[11] Since this is a subject which impacts on common law jurisdictions globally, you could make references in the essay to approaches in, for example, Australia, which might form a model for reform.

LOOKING FOR EXTRA MARKS?

- Include more discussion in your answer on the jurisprudential debate which centres on the Benthamite argument for free proof. Should the only criterion for admissibility be truth-seeking?

- Improve your grade with a short historical account in the introduction of the evolution of this area of law suggesting that there are ongoing attempts to both rationalise the provisions and to bring them in line with social change.

QUESTION | 2

Daphne is charged with causing criminal damage to the valuable rose bushes in the front garden of a house at 6 Churchill Road. She had been hawking garden waste bags door to door along with her daughter Judith, aged 12. Mr and Mrs Baldwin, the occupants of number 6, refused to buy from Daphne and slammed the door in her face. As Daphne left she allegedly destroyed the rose bushes in anger. Hector, the Baldwins' 20-year-old son, who has a mental age of ten, was looking out of the window. James, aged 17, who also saw the incident from the top of a bus as it passed along Churchill Road, is worried about testifying. He was bullied by Daphne's nephew at school and is afraid he might be attacked if he testifies against her. Daphne plans to plead not guilty.
The prosecution wish to call Judith, James, and Hector as witnesses.

Advise on whether Judith, James, and Hector are competent and compellable witnesses and, if they do testify, how they may give evidence in court.

CAUTION!

- It is crucial you adopt a clear structure to this answer. It is best to take each potential witness in turn in relation to competence and compellability.

- Be aware that the question asks you to cover three aspects for each witness, namely are they competent, are they compellable, and if they do testify would there be any special arrangements at court for their appearance.

- Note that you are given brief background circumstance of each of the three potential witnesses so you are alerted to the fact that they may be 'vulnerable' and that you will be required to demonstrate your understanding of Special Measures Directions (SMDs). In the interests of efficient time management in an unseen examination it is probably best to cover all three witnesses together in the part of your answer on the complexities of SMDs.

DIAGRAM ANSWER PLAN

Identify the issues	■ The legal issues are: the competence and compellability of children and those with mental incapacity, the availability of SMDs.
Relevant law	■ Competency provisions in **YJCEA**, ss. 53, 55(2), and 56, SMDs in **YJCEA**, ss. 16–21, hearsay provisions in **CJA 2003**.
Apply the law	■ YJCEA and Judith's and James's competency in view of their age, Hector's mental capacity and possibility of SMDs. ■ Assessment for each witness and possibility also of submission of evidence by hearsay.
Conclude	■ Note on penalties for refusing to obey witness summons.

SUGGESTED ANSWER

Exceptions to Presumption of Competence

This question centres on the legal position of witnesses who may deviate from the norm of universal competence and compellability in criminal trials. This requires an application of the relevant provisions in the **Youth Justice and Criminal Evidence Act 1999 (YJCEA)** and its case law.[1] Under **s. 53(1) of the YJCEA** all witnesses are assumed to be competent, although there are a number of exceptions. The answer will examine the specific facts given for Judith, James, and Hector in relation to competence and compellability. It will then consider whether Special Measures Directions may apply to one or more of them. It will conclude with a brief consideration about the possibility of hearsay evidence being admitted.

Judith

Judith is presumed to be a competent witness (**YJCEA, s. 53**) and compellable for the prosecution or defence. As a child under 14 Judith must give evidence unsworn: **YJCEA, ss. 55(2)** and **56.** Under **s. 53(3)** the evidence of children under 14 is to be given unsworn and a child's evidence must be received unless it appears to the court that the child is incapable of understanding questions put to her and unable to give answers which can be understood.[2] It is submitted that a normal

<hr>

[1] It is good practice to outline the way you are going to structure your answer to the question in an introductory paragraph.

[2] The court must decide not whether she is competent on grounds of age but whether she is capable of giving intelligible evidence.

12-year-old would be capable. The importance of giving truthful evidence must be explained to her by the tribunal as part of the process of putting her at her ease.

The Pigot Committee on Video Evidence set up by the Home Office, reporting in 1989, condemned the existing position as being founded on an archaic belief that children could not be honest and coherent witnesses.[3] The present practice is that the child should give evidence and only be stopped from doing so if it becomes clear she could not give an intelligible account. The result is that there is now no minimum age below which a child cannot give evidence, although in practice judicial discretion may be exercised. The present state of the law arguably brings it into line with psychological research on the veracity of children.

The changes in the law relating to children's evidence were the result particularly of the difficulty of achieving successful prosecutions in the case of child victims of sexual abusers. In short, Judith is likely to be called as a witness.

Hector

As regards Hector, the court will take a pragmatic view. In *R v Barker* **[2010] EWCA Crim 4** the court held that a child aged four and a half could give evidence in a case of rape. Referring to **s. 53 of the YJCEA** the court stated (at para. 38): 'These statutory provisions are not limited to the evidence of children. They apply to individuals of unsound mind. They apply to the infirm. The question in each case is whether the individual witness, or, as in this case, the individual child, is competent to give evidence in the particular trial. The question is entirely witness or child specific. There are no presumptions or preconceptions. The witness need not understand the special importance that the truth should be told in court, and the witness need not understand every single question or give a readily understood answer to every question'. Thus under the rules set out in **ss. 53–57** persons suffering from a degree of mental difficulty are subject to the same tests as any other witness.[4]

The Court of Appeal has set out a number of questions that should be addressed in deciding whether a witness is competent, see *R v McPherson* **[2005] EWCA Crim 3625**. That case made it clear that questions of credibility and reliability are not relevant to competence but are matters of weight which might be considered at the end of the prosecution case by way of a submission of no case to answer. Expert evidence may be admitted as to the witness's mental state (see **s. 54(5))**. *R v Sed* **[2004] 1 WLR 3218** gave further guidance.[5] Thus Hector may find that the judge in considering competence will not require that he has total comprehension. However, it is important to make clear that in *Sed* the witness was the alleged victim of a serious crime and so her evidence would be more crucial than that of Hector to the trial.[6]

[3] Evidence courses differ insofar as they cover the socio-legal background to the law. You should take guidance from your tutor on whether to make some reference to this in answering a problem question since it may be that it is felt only relevant to an essay not a problem question.

[4] The competence of witnesses may be raised by the parties or by the court of its own motion (**s. 54(1)**). It is for the party calling the witness to satisfy the court on the balance of probabilities that the witness is competent (**s. 54(2)**).

[5] The witness was an 81-year-old rape victim who suffered from Alzheimer's disease. She was held to be competent (although her evidence was given by video recording). Auld LJ stated (at para. 46) that it was 'for the judge to determine the question of competence almost as a matter of feel'.

[6] It is good practice to draw out differences in facts between the case you are citing and the imaginary scenario in the question.

It is possible the defence may raise that Hector has insufficient appreciation of the solemnity of the occasion and of the particular responsibility to tell the truth which is involved in taking an oath (**s. 55(2)(b)**). If he is able to give intelligible testimony he is presumed to have such appreciation unless evidence to the contrary is adduced. In that event, then, he may be able to give evidence unsworn provided he passes the basic test of competence (**s. 56(1)** and **(2)**).

James

[7] It is as well to prepare carefully your appreciation of how statutes vary in defining childhood. Age is not specified under **s. 53(3)** of the YJCEA in relation to competence but it is specified in relation to the availability of SMDs. If you are given the age of a witness in a question be aware that it is going to be relevant to your answer.

James who is 17 years old is assumed to be a competent and compellable witness, under **s. 53 of the YJCEA**.[7]

Special Measures Directions (SMDs)

Hector

Hector might experience special difficulty in testifying. Under **ss. 16(1)(b)** and **16(2)** witnesses other than the accused who suffer from a physical or mental disorder, or have a disability or impairment of intelligence and social functioning that is likely to diminish the quality of their evidence, may give evidence by means such as live video link or pre-recording. Since Hector is likely to be considered as eligible for SMD under **s. 16(1)(b)**, the court in deciding whether to award them must consider Hector's views of whether special measures are needed (see **s. 19(3)(a)**).

[8] Where relevant, answers to Evidence questions should refer to Art. 6 rights.

If the prosecution is allowed to use SMD for Hector's testimony then Daphne will have difficulty in arguing that this is unfair.[8] In *R (on the application of D) v Camberwell Green Youth Court* **[2005] 1 WLR 393**, the House of Lords held that special measures provisions, here involving children, were compatible with **Art. 6(3)(a)**, which embodies the defendant's right 'to examine or have examined witnesses against him'.

[9] The House of Lords upheld the Divisional Court's ruling.

Although the specific provisions which were the subject of the action have since been amended, the case is still of interest in illustrating fair trial considerations.[9]

James and Judith

As persons under 18 years, James and Judith may also be eligible for Special Measures Directions. Under **s. 21(1)(a) of the YJCEA**, as amended by the **Coroners and Justice Act 2009**, the primary rule in requiring admission of a video interview as examination-in-chief and cross-examination through a live link at trial, applies presumptively to all non-defendant witnesses under 18, regardless of the nature of the offence.

[10] You could set out the factors the court will consider. These are set out in **s. 21(4C)** and include the age and maturity of the witness, the witness's social and cultural background, and the relationship between the witness and the accused.

However, under **s. 21(4)(c)** if the court determines that under the primary rule special measures would be unlikely to maximise the quality of the witness's evidence so far as is practicable optional measures such as a screen must be considered.[10] It is open to James and Judith to elect to give oral evidence-in-chief and/or testify in the courtroom rather than using the live link (**s. 21(4)(ba)**).

Although James, if not Judith, is arguably of an age where he might be expected to be able to give live testimony, the background factor of the alleged bullying would also be taken into account. If James or Judith elect to give evidence by live link they may be accompanied by an adult to provide support. The adult must be independent of the witness and his family, have no previous knowledge of or personal involvement in the case, and be trained in obligations imposed by national standards relating to witness support. Under **s. 27(5)(b)** if the prosecution wish to ask James or Judith supplementary questions in examination-in-chief they will require leave of the court if the matter had been dealt with in the video interview. The judge will decide if it is in the interests of justice to permit the additional questions.

Related Areas of Evidence

If Hector is held incompetent as a witness it is unlikely that his evidence will be admitted under the statutory exceptions to the hearsay rule. The hearsay provisions are now found in **ss. 114–136 of the Criminal Justice Act (CJA) 2003**. Under **s. 114 of the CJA 2003**, in deciding whether a hearsay statement is to be admitted the court must have regard, inter alia, to 'how reliable the maker of the statement appears to be' (**s. 114(2)(e)**). The Court of Appeal held in *R v Setz-Dempsey* **[1994] Crim LR 123** that the admission of documentary statements from a mentally ill witness was a material irregularity under s. 23(1)(a) of the CJA 1988 (the predecessor to the 2003 Act). The judge had erred in law in not exercising discretion under **s. 26** and should have considered the psychiatrist's evidence about the likely quality of any evidence given by the witness. In *R v Ferdinand* **[2014] EWCA Crim 1243**, the court stated that it may be appropriate for the possibility of SMDs to be considered.

Hearsay may, however, be a possibility for James, since he fears bullying if he testifies. Under **s. 116(2)(e)** one of the acceptable reasons for not calling the witness and allowing first-hand hearsay is that the witness does not give evidence through fear. Further information is needed to determine if James could claim this protection.

Conclusion

The decision on whether witnesses are competent and compellable is a matter of law for the judge. James, Judith, and Hector should be warned that if they are judged compellable and refuse to attend court, or attend and refuse to testify, they risk being held in contempt of court and may face imprisonment. The fact that Judith as a child could not be imprisoned for failure to comply is not a good reason for refusing to issue a witness summons to compel her attendance: *R v Greenwich Justices, ex p Carter* **[1973] Crim LR 444**.

LOOKING FOR EXTRA MARKS?

■ Although this is primarily a question about competence, compellability, and SMDs you could discuss further related areas such as the guidance on examination and cross-examination of vulnerable witnesses in para. 3E.4 Criminal Practice Directions.

■ You will gain extra marks by explaining that the court will have regard to the following factors in considering **s. 21(4)(c)**: (a) the child's age and maturity; (b) the child's ability to understand the consequences of giving evidence in a different way; (c) the relationship (if any) between the witness and the accused; (d) the child's social and cultural background and ethnic origins; and (e) the nature and alleged circumstances of the offence to which the proceedings relate.

■ It will improve your answer to show you are aware of how the intellectual and psychological approach to children's evidence has radically changed over time and the key role of the Pigot Committee.

QUESTION | 3

Jane, aged 30, and her assistant Stacey, aged 40, are charged with physically assaulting Freda who is 20 years old. The prosecution case is that they struck her with the handle of a knife because she mistreated a horse in the riding stables run by Jane. Freda is very frightened about appearing as a witness. Stacey has a mental age of 12 but has been declared fit to plead. She is nervous about appearing in court and unhappy about testifying. She pleads not guilty. Jane has pleaded guilty. In a separate civil action Jane is being sued for negligence since a pupil of the riding school, Grace, aged 13, has been injured in a fall from a horse which bolted.

(a) **Advise whether Stacey and Freda may be eligible for Special Measures Directions and what will be the consequence if Stacey elects not to testify.**

(b) **Advise also how Jane is likely to be treated as a witness in the trial where Stacey is prosecuted.**

(c) **Advise how Grace, if called as a witness, is likely to be treated in the civil case.**

Each part of the question is worth equal marks.

CAUTION!

■ Note that the question mixes civil and criminal evidence.

■ Careless reading of the question could be fatal and you should note that you are required to be familiar with the statutory provisions on competence and compellability of 'ex-defendants', that is those who have pleaded guilty or been convicted.

■ Do not attempt this question unless you have studied the limited special measures available for vulnerable defendants.

DIAGRAM ANSWER PLAN

Identify the issues	▪ The legal issues are: competence and compellability of ex-defendants in criminal trials; SMDs; competence and compellability of witnesses in civil trials.
Relevant law	▪ YJCEA, ss. 17, 33, and 53(5); CJPOA, s. 35; Children Act 1989, s. 96; Civil Evidence Act 1972.
Apply the law	▪ Jane, compellability of ex-co-defendants; ▪ Stacey, limited SMDs for defendants; failure to testify; ▪ Freda, SMDs; ▪ Grace, protection for child witnesses in civil cases.
Conclude	▪ Assess outcome for each witness.

SUGGESTED ANSWER

The question requires an examination of the provisions on competence and compellability of ex-defendants in the **Youth Justice and Criminal Evidence Act 1999 (YJCEA)**. It also includes giving advice to a defendant who is 'vulnerable' and who may benefit from the limited special measures available in **ss. 33A, 33B, 33BA, and 33BB of the YJCEA**. The advice to be given includes that for the criminal and the civil trial. The answer will take each potential witness in turn for the criminal and then the civil trial; it will apply the relevant law to the specific facts in the question.

Jane

By pleading guilty Jane is no longer a defendant. She is therefore competent and compellable as a witness for the prosecution or defence, according to **s. 53(5) of the YJCEA**. She can thus give evidence for Stacey or the prosecution. Of course if she is compellable it is not necessarily the case that she will be called as a witness but if she is called and refuses she may be in contempt of court.

Stacey

Some limited protection has been introduced for vulnerable defend-ants and is now to be found in **ss. 33A, 33B, 33BA**, and **33BB of the YJCEA**. It is arguable that Stacey falls into one eligible category in that she is over 18 years and suffers from a significant impairment of intelligence and social function in that she is unable to participate effectively in the proceedings as a witness giving oral evidence in court (**s. 33A(5)(a)** and **(b)**). In that case she may be allowed a live link (**s. 33(5)(c)**) or be examined through an intermediary (**s. 33BA**) if these measures are judged likely to enable her to participate effec-tively in the proceedings. Stacey must be warned that she has quite a high hurdle to mount if she is to be offered these limited SMDs. Critics of the provisions for defendants contrast their requirements with those of ordinary witnesses.[1] Hoyano (2010), for example, points out that according to the statutory provisions the mentally vulnerable defendant 'must be shown to be *unable* to participate effectively in the proceedings as a witness by reason of that incapacity, whereas for the ordinary witness it need only be shown that the quality of his or her evidence would be *diminished* by the incapacitating condition'.

Stacey is considering whether to testify. Presumably her decision will be influenced by whether she is granted a SMD or not. She should be warned that **s. 35 of the Criminal Justice and Public Order Act 1994 (CJPOA)** may apply if she chooses not to testify. Under this provision a defendant who chooses not to testify faces the possibility of adverse comment on his silence by the prosecution. *R v Cowan* **[1996] QB 373** sets out guidelines for how the judge should direct the jury to treat such failure to give evidence. He or she must remind them that the burden of proof lies on the prosecution, that the defendant is entitled to remain silent, that an inference from silence alone cannot prove guilt, that the jury must be satisfied that the prosecution have established a case to answer before drawing inferences from silence, and that if the jury conclude that the silence can only be attributed to the defendant's having no real answer, or one that would stand up to cross-examination, they may then draw an adverse inference. In par-ticular Stacey must be warned that her mental difficulty does not nec-essarily help her avoid an inference being drawn. In *R v Friend* **[1997] 1 WLR 1433** even though the defendant had a mental age of nine the Court of Appeal held that the judge had been correct to direct the jury that they could draw an adverse inference.[2] The conviction was, how-ever, quashed in *R v Friend (No. 2)* **[2004] EWCA Crim 2661** when new medical evidence was introduced. In the second appeal, reference was made to the undesirability of a competent defendant testifying if he suffers from intellectual or cognitive defects.

[1] Depending on the time allocated for this question you could expand on the academic criticisms made of the limited protections for vulnerable defendants, particularly the work of Hoyano cited in the section 'Taking Things Further'.

[2] These two cases have also aroused academic commentary, see for example Keane and McKeown (2018, p. 454). They turn on the interpretation of **s. 35(1)(b)** of the CJPOA where the possibility of prosecution comment under **s. 35(2)** on the failure of a defendant to testify does not apply if 'it appears to the court that the physical or mental condition of the accused makes it undesirable for him to give evidence'. Keane and McKeown point out that in the 1997 case 'it was said that the language of **s. 35(1)(b)** was such as to give a wide discretion to the trial judge, whose decision can only be impugned if *Wednesbury* unreasonable'.

Freda

We are told that a knife handle was involved in the attack on Freda. It is possible therefore that Freda is now a vulnerable witness under **ss. 17** and **18**. These sections cover witnesses where the quality of evidence is likely to be diminished by reason of the witness's fear or distress about testifying. Under **Sch. 1A** to the Act such witnesses presumptively include witnesses where the offence is one in the **Offences Against the Person Act 1861** where it is alleged that a firearm or knife caused the wound or harm in question.[3] Unless Freda has informed the court that she does not want to be eligible she will be entitled to SMDs listed in the statute. In *R v Lubemba* **[2014] EWCA Crim 2064** the court gave guidance on the questioning of vulnerable witnesses such as Freda.

Finally Stacey's defence counsel should be aware that **s. 32 of the YJCEA** provides that where in a trial on indictment evidence has been given by an SMD the judge must give the jury such warning (if any) as the judge considers necessary to ensure that the fact that the direction was given in relation to the witness does not prejudice the accused. It is possible that the jury will draw a prejudicial inference from the existence of special measures such as screens. Such warnings can be given in the judicial summing-up or during the trial. It should be pointed out also that the existence of SMDs makes it more likely, in cases like those in this problem where there are frightened witnesses, that the case will come to trial.[4]

Grace

If the case goes to trial it may be that Grace will be called as a witness.[5] Under **s. 96 of the Children Act 1989**, children are allowed to testify unsworn and the then existing common law test of competency was enacted to apply in civil proceedings. The test is that the child has sufficient understanding of the duty to tell the truth to justify the reception of her evidence. A 'child' is any person who has not reached the age of 18. The judge will question Grace before she gives any evidence to see if she shows sufficient understanding of the solemnity of the oath. Dennis (2013, p. 553) points out that the '. . . the first condition of **s. 96 of the Children Act** is certainly stricter than the criminal law'.[6] This is because it retains the requirement, now dropped by the criminal law, that the child understands the duty of truth-telling. He considers that whether such strictness is justifiable is debatable since its effect may be to exclude the testimony of very young children in civil cases. The relevant section specifies that where a child who is called as a witness in civil proceedings does not, in the opinion of the court, understand the nature of an oath, the child's evidence may be heard by the court if in its opinion the following apply:

[3] By referring to **Sch. 1A** you will demonstrate to the examiner a wide reading of the legislative provisions.

[4] See Home Office Report, Home Office Research Study, 'Are Special Measures Working?' (2004), http://www.popcenter.org/problems/witness_intimidation/PDFs/Hamlyn_etal_2004.pdf.

[5] The position of children as witnesses in civil trials is in some ways more strict than that in criminal cases.

[6] It is recommended that you try where possible to recall academic comment on these complex provisions since examiners will be expecting research skills and an understanding of the complexities of the law.

he understands that it is his duty to speak the truth and also he has sufficient understanding to justify his evidence being heard.

Keane and McKeown (2018, p. 136) states 'it is submitted that the court should be guided by the common law authorities which governed in criminal as well as civil cases prior to parliamentary intervention'. They refer (p. 138) to *R v Hayes* **[1977] 1 WLR 234** adding that the court adopted a 'secular approach' and appears to have accepted a concession made by counsel for the defence that 'the watershed dividing children who are normally considered old enough to take the oath and children normally considered too young to take the oath, probably falls between the ages of eight and ten'.

[7] The hearsay rule in civil cases has to all intents and purposes been abolished.

Grace may benefit from further provisions.[7] It is possible that some of her evidence may be heard as hearsay under the **Civil Evidence Act 1995**. **Section 5** of the 1995 Act makes it clear that the child will be a competent witness if he or she satisfies the requirements of **s. 96 of the Children Act 1989**, thereby making any hearsay evidence by the child admissible. A child for the purposes of this section is a person under the age of 18 years (**s. 105**). In *R v B, ex p P* **[1991] 2 All ER 65**, 72, Butler-Sloss LJ referred to the need to treat such evidence 'anxiously and consider carefully the extent to which it can properly be relied on'.[8]

[8] It is possible your course has included only a limited amount of civil law but it is important you familiarise yourself with the case law where relevant.

Conclusion

In relation to the criminal case, Freda as the alleged victim and, to a more limited extent Stacey as the defendant, may be eligible for special treatment by the court. In the civil case the claimants on behalf of Grace should also consult the **Civil Procedure Rules**. This covers the discretion the court has in the treatment of child witnesses. **Rule 32.3** provides that the court may permit a witness to give evidence through a video link or other means.[9] The court has a broad discretion to allow this.

[9] **Rule 29.9** contains Special Measures Directions for a young witness.

LOOKING FOR EXTRA MARKS?

- Questions on competence and compellability may appear to be deceptively straightforward but you have an opportunity to garner extra marks by including your knowledge of the details of the legislation, such as the implications for using SMDs of the offence being a 'knife crime'.
- Be fastidious in tracing the evolution of cases which have been referred back to the Court of Appeal, for example the two iterations of *R v Friend* in 1997 and 2004.
- In civil cases the **Civil Procedure Rules** play a crucial role so include relevant references.

Margaret, an accountant working at a hedge fund, is charged, along with others, with conspiracy to defraud. Part of the prosecution case against her is that it is alleged that at one meeting she and her partners agreed to send false VAT returns. She denies the charge. At trial she refuses to testify but claims through her counsel that she left the meeting early before the matters alleged were discussed. She had failed to respond to police questioning on this at interview before trial to the police investigators. Margaret had also failed to submit an alibi notice concerning her claim that she was on holiday at a time when another meeting of the alleged conspirators had taken place. Gary, a computer consultant hired by one of the partners, is prepared to give evidence for the prosecution anonymously. He has been told that Margaret is known to be violent and vindictive.

Advise Margaret.

CAUTION!

- Although Margaret is not testifying, note that you are told that her counsel is giving an explanation at trial of her whereabouts at a relevant time through her counsel. This raises the possible application of **s. 34 of the CJPOA** and permissible adverse comment by the prosecution.

- Do not attempt this question if you have not studied the complex arrangements which apply to possible anonymity for witnesses.

DIAGRAM ANSWER PLAN

Identify the issues	▓ The legal issues are: duty and procedure on disclosure and alibis; permissible judicial comment on failure to testify; witness anonymity.
Relevant law	▓ Criminal Procedure and Investigations Act 1996; Coroners and Justice Act 2009, s. 88; CJPOA 1994, ss. 34 and 35.
Apply the law	▓ Margaret may still present alibi evidence notice but court's comment on her failure to supply notice possible; comment on her failure to testify possible under CJPOA, s. 34; anonymity order unlikely to be granted to Gary.
Conclude	▓ Possible grounds of appeal.

Margaret: Failure to Give Explanation of Leaving the Meeting Earlier and to Disclose Alibi

The prosecution may argue that **s. 34 of the Criminal Justice and Public Order Act 1994 (CJPOA)** may apply to Margaret. We are told that Margaret's counsel gives an explanation at trial that she left a relevant meeting early and that she has an alibi for her whereabouts. In essence, explanations are offered at trial that Margaret had not offered earlier. It is immaterial that it is counsel and not Margaret who is offering the explanation. In *R v Webber* [2004] UKHL 1 the House of Lords held that where the defendant did not give evidence but his counsel put facts to prosecution witnesses which the defendant had not referred to at police interview that **s. 34** applied.[1] More information is needed as to whether Margaret had access to legal advice at the police interview.

The **Criminal Procedure and Investigations Act 1996 (CPIA)** requires the prosecution and the defence to disclose evidence prior to the trial. It imposes a duty on the defence, which goes further than previously required. **Section 5** requires the defendant to disclose evidence of the defence that will be raised at trial, after the prosecution has made primary disclosure and the defence has been served with relevant documents, including copies of the indictment and the prosecution's evidence.[2] **Section 11(2)** of the 1996 Act allows the court or any other party (with leave of the court) to make such comment on the defendant's failure to provide pre-trial particulars of alibi as appears appropriate. The court and jury may draw such inferences from such failure as appear proper in the circumstances of the case. Arguably, although **s. 5** is silent on the court's power to refuse to allow such evidence, the court retains its discretion under **s. 78 of the Police and Criminal Evidence Act 1984** to exclude evidence that would have an adverse impact on the fairness of the trial. Thus, even though Margaret may not have served particulars of alibi to support her claim that she was on holiday, in accordance with **s. 5** of the 1996 Act, she may be permitted to adduce evidence that she was not at a relevant meeting in connection with the alleged agreement to send false VAT returns. However, the court and the prosecution, with leave of the court, may comment on the failure to comply with the alibi requirements and the jury can draw such adverse inferences as are proper under **s. 11(2) of the CPIA**.

Margaret: Failure to Testify

By **s. 35 of the CJPOA**, adverse inferences can be drawn by the court from the refusal to give evidence at trial. It is not, however, contempt

---

[1] Note that the House stated (para. 28) that 'rarely if ever could a **section 34** direction be appropriate on failure to mention an admittedly true fact at interview'. Thus if the prosecution accepts the 'fact relied' as true, the section does not apply. You might have been tempted to consider s. 37 of the CJPOA also. However, this deals with 'presence at a particular place' rather than absence so on the facts it does not apply.

[2] Not all Evidence courses cover disclosure provisions. An outline of the law here is included. Disclosure provisions are strengthened under Part 5 of the Criminal Justice Act 2003 amending the 1996 Act.

of court for Margaret to fail to testify at trial. Under **s. 35(4)** of the statute the common law principle is retained that the accused is not compellable to give evidence on his own behalf. The prosecution is now permitted by **s. 35** of the 1994 Act to comment on Margaret's failure to testify but the section does not specify what kind of comment is appropriate and, unlike **s. 11(2) of the CPIA**, does not require leave of the court before such comment can be made. It may be some comfort to Margaret that under **s. 11(10) of the CPIA** and **s. 38(3) of the CJPOA** a person cannot be convicted of an offence solely on such inferences.

[3]Note that for this section to apply the statute does not specify that the accused should have had access to legal advice.

The procedure which must be followed by the court in relation to a defendant's refusal to testify is set out in **s. 35** and the Crown Court Compendium clarifies the process.[3] Before adverse comment may be considered the defendant must have pleaded not guilty, be physically and mentally fit to testify, and be aware of the risks attached to silence. Margaret should be aware that the same risks apply if she did decide to testify but then refused to answer some questions put to her. Under **s. 35(5)** a failure to answer questions is presumed to be 'without good cause' unless the accused is either entitled under statute not to answer particular questions or has a legal privilege not to answer or 'the court in its general discretion excuses him from answering'. Guidance on judicial comment where the accused does not give evidence is to be found in the Court of Appeal's judgment in *R v Cowan* [1996]. In three separate cases, heard together on appeal, defendants who had not given evidence appealed against conviction on the grounds of non-compliance with **ss. 35** and **38(3) of the CJPOA**. The court held that **s. 35(4)** had expressly preserved the right to silence but, that while the burden of proving guilt beyond reasonable doubt lay throughout on the prosecution, the court or jury might treat the defendant's failure to testify as a further evidential factor in support of the prosecution's case. The judgment stated that a Specimen Direction from the Judicial Studies Board was a sound guide and before any inferences from silence could be drawn the jury had to be satisfied that the prosecution had established a case to answer. In G and C's case misdirections had been made and the convictions were quashed. In C's case the judge had failed to tell the jury that

[4]*Cowan* is still the leading case and you will see it is given extensive coverage in most textbooks. It does improve your answer, however, to indicate that you are aware also of the official guidance given in the various iterations of practice directions which are freely available online.

they could not infer guilt solely from silence or to warn them that they could not hold his silence against him unless the only sensible explanation was that he had no answer to the case against him which could have stood up to cross-examination. In G's case there were also shortcomings in the summing-up. In R's case the judge had directed the jury correctly. The guidance given in *Cowan* is amplified in the Consolidated Criminal Practice Directions.[4] The direction is detailed and complex and underlines that jurors should take into account any evidence which might explain why the defendant elected not to testify. It is only if jurors are satisfied that the only sensible reason for Margaret not testifying is that she has no answer to the charge, or none that would stand up in cross-examination, that they can draw an inference which will support the prosecution case. The prosecution may argue that Margaret may reveal incriminating details about the meeting if she takes the stand.

A key question is the extent of the prosecution case against Margaret.[5] In *Doldur* **[2000] Crim LR 178**, Auld LJ set out the specific requirements of a **s. 35** direction which differ from those under **ss. 34**, **36**, and **37**. In the case of **s. 35** the jury should be directed to restrict its consideration to the prosecution case in deciding whether to draw adverse inferences. By contrast, in relation to **s. 34** the jury would have to consider both prosecution and defence cases since it was the contrast between the defendant's earlier silence and reliance on facts at trial that permitted the drawing of an adverse inference.

Margaret

Gary and Witness Anonymity

The prosecution may benefit from the **Coroners and Justice Act 2009** (incorporating the temporary provisions of the **Criminal Evidence (Witness Anonymity) Act 2008**), reversing *R v Davis* **[2008] AC 1128, HL** where the House of Lords held that a murder trial was unfair and a violation of **Art. 6(3)(d)** because an order preserved the anonymity of a witness. The Act which applies to civilian and police witnesses allows various measures to be taken to protect the identity of a witness such as the use of a pseudonym, screening, and voice modulation.[6] The court must be satisfied that:

- The measures are necessary, for example to protect the safety of the witness having regard to reasonable fear on his part if he were identified or to protect the carrying on of activities in the public interest (Condition A).

- The taking of the measures is consistent with the defendant receiving a fair trial (Condition B).

- The interests of justice require the order since it appears to the court that it is important the witness should testify and the witness would not testify if the order were not made (Condition C).

The Act sets out in **ss. 88–99** matters the court must consider. These include whether evidence given by the witness might be the sole or decisive evidence implicating the defendant. **Section 90** provides that, 'the judge must give the jury such a warning as the judge considers appropriate to ensure that the fact that [a witness anonymity order] was made in relation to the witness does not prejudice the defendant'.

[7] This is to date the leading case on the Act so you should refer to it although the answer goes on to explain that on the facts it may not apply.

The 2008 Act was applied in *R v Mayers* [2009] 1 WLR 1915, a series of conjoined trials.[7] The appeal was allowed in *Mayers* since the court could not be sure that the non-disclosure of the identity of the witness was fair to the defendant. In *Glasgow, Costelloe and Bahmanzahdeh* [2008] EWCA Crim 2989 the convictions were safe since the true identities of undercover police officers were rarely important to the defendant. The court stated that evidence given by an anonymised witness could not include anonymous hearsay.

[8] It is a good idea to refer to the principled grounds on which the courts will apply the Act, particularly so in this controversial area.

[9] His case is more directly relevant to the facts.

A key question which is not revealed in the facts is whether Gary is known to Margaret.[8] The prosecution should note the case of *R v Willett* [2011] EWCA Crim 2710. There the Court of Appeal held that Condition A cannot be met if the accused already knows the witness's identity.[9] Obviously in those circumstances an anonymity order will not help protect the witness and so would serve no purpose.

[10] The importance of the availability of cross-examination is central to the fairness of the trial as **Art. 6** and common law principles provide.

In any case, whether Gary is known or not to Margaret and in view of the reluctance of the courts to sanction witness anonymity, it is unlikely on the facts given here that Gary's identity will be kept secret. It is arguable that a fair trial requires that he be cross-examined.[10]

[11] The Conclusion should where possible avoid repeating points made already. Given the complex provisions in this question on admissibility and judicial directions, it is pertinent to point out that breaches may be grounds of appeal for Margaret.

Conclusion

The above account has highlighted the importance of correct application of the law on admissibility and on judicial directions to the jury. In particular, if the judge fails to give clear directions on the drawing of permissible inferences and she is convicted, Margaret may have strong grounds of appeal under **Art. 6** provisions (see *Condron v UK* [2000] Crim LR 679).[11]

LOOKING FOR EXTRA MARKS?

- You will need to cite quite a range of statutes including the **Criminal Procedure and Investigations Act 1996**; although some Evidence courses do not cover this in detail you should be familiar with the relevant section on alibis (**s. 5**).
- Note the similarities and differences between the possibility of adverse comment on failure to testify and comment on failure to provide an alibi notice.
- You are not told if Gary is known to Margaret. You will need to discuss whether this information is needed in order to assess the availability of the anonymity order.

TAKING THINGS FURTHER

■ Brabyn, J., 'A Criminal Defendant's Spouse as a Prosecution Witness' [2011] Crim LR 613.
A defence of spousal privilege as still socially valuable.

■ Home Office Research Study, 'Are Special Measures Working?' (2004), http://www.popcenter.org/problems/witness_intimidation/PDFs/Hamlyn_etal_2004.pdf.
Contains a review of the ways the Measures have improved the treatment of vulnerable witnesses.

■ Hoyano, L.C.H., 'Case Comment. *R v BA*' [2013] Crim LR 169.

■ Hoyano, L.C.H., 'Coroners and Justice Act 2009: Special Measures Directions Take 2: Entrenching Unequal Access to Justice' [2010] Crim LR 345.
The author is critical of the contrast between the treatment of vulnerable defendants and that applied to non-defendant witnesses.

■ Laudan, L., *Truth, Error and the Criminal Law: An Essay on Legal Epistemology* (Cambridge: Cambridge University Press, 2008), ch. 6.
A penetrating jurisprudential analysis of the way spousal privilege undermines the principle of free proof.

Online Resources

www.oup.com/uk/qanda/

Go online for extra essay and problem questions, a glossary of key terms, online versions of all the answer plans and audio commentary on how selected ones were put together, and a range of podcasts which include advice on exam and coursework technique and advice for other assessment methods.

Character

4

ARE YOU READY?

In order to tackle the questions in this chapter you will need to have covered the following:

● the codified framework on the admissibility of bad character in **ss. 98–112 of the Criminal Justice Act 2003**

● the evolving case law on the evidential value of bad character and how the judge should direct the jury

● an appreciation of the difference between relevance to issue and relevance to credit

● the common law on the admissibility and evidential value of good character and how the judge should direct the jury

● an outline of the historical development of the law on bad character

KEY DEBATES

Debate: is the non-defendant afforded better protection in terms of the admissibility of bad character than the defendant?

The change in the law on the admissibility of bad character for the defendant was prompted by Parliament's concern for victims and a programme of encouraging witnesses to testify. The definition of bad character is the same for defendants and non-defendants (prosecution and defence witnesses). There are two main differences on admissibility: the test for the non-defendant (see further **Chapter 9**) is higher (substantial probative value) and evidence must not be submitted without leave of the court.

Debate: should the defendant be protected from having his bad character revealed if his attack on another person is an integral part of his defence?

In *Selvey v DPP* **[1970] AC 304** (decided under the now repealed sections of the Criminal Evidence Act 1898) the defendant lost his 'shield' even though making an imputation against a prosecution witness was a necessary part of his defence. The Law Commission had recommended that imputations should not be defined to include evidence to do with the alleged facts of the defence. However, this provision was not enacted although the defendant in such a position does have a safeguard since the exclusionary discretion under **s. 101(3)** does cover **s. 101(1)(g)** which applies where the defendant has made an attack on another person's character.

Debate: is the definition of bad character in the Criminal Justice Act 2003 too broad?

The current definition of bad character (**ss. 98** and **112 of the Criminal Justice Act (CJA) 2003**) includes 'misconduct' which is defined in **s. 112** as 'the commission of an offence or other reprehensible behaviour'. Under the earlier law the courts rarely admitted bad character under the **Criminal Evidence Act 1898 (CEA)** that was not a criminal conviction. As Keane and McKeown point out (2018, p. 506), 'Whether particular awful behaviour involves culpability or blameworthiness will depend on the particular circumstances and is a question on which views are likely to differ'. One controversial area is the material on YouTube which shows gang membership as in *R v Lewis* **[2014] EWCA Crim 48**.

QUESTION | 1

There can be no doubt that it was the intention of parliament to relax the strictness of the common law by dropping any requirement for enhanced relevance for similar fact evidence.

(Dennis, *The Law of Evidence* (London: Sweet & Maxwell, 2013), p. 826)

Critically evaluate how far this observation accords with the operation of the provisions of s. 101(1)(d) of the Criminal Justice Act 2003.

CAUTION!

- A good answer will demonstrate a deep understanding of the intricacies of **s. 101(1)(d)** and of the leading cases. It is important that you do not simply give a factual account of the law in this area but develop an argument.

- Your answer should demonstrate in outline at least a critical awareness of the evolution of the law before 2003 and how the threshold of admissibility had been steadily lowered. You should refer to the Law Commission's proposals for change and indicate your awareness of the extent to which the legislation departed from them.

DIAGRAM ANSWER PLAN

> Introduction: common law background, Law Commission proposals, CJA 2003

> Examples of case law which suggests propensity evidence is more readily admitted; propensity to be untruthful

> Examples of case law suggesting a more restrictive approach

> Evaluation

SUGGESTED ANSWER

Why Propensity Evidence is to be Treated Carefully

One of the most complex questions in the law of evidence is the extent to which the prosecution may present evidence of the defendant's previous bad behaviour to suggest his guilt. The Law Commission in its Report in 1996 famously pointed out that evidence of previous misconduct or of discreditable propensity on the part of the defendant ran the risk of misleading a jury in two ways by what they identified as 'reasoning' or 'moral' prejudices. [1] The history of the law in this area demonstrates, however, the continuing difficulties the courts faced in devising tests to address such evidence. This essay will first outline the replacement of the common law tests by the statutory regime in 2003. It will be argued that the **Criminal Justice Act (CJA) 2003** continues the process previously demonstrated in the common law whereby social and political considerations have led to a presumption of admissibility of propensity evidence and the possibility of unfairness to defendants.

[1] First, it may be thought to be more relevant than it is and the jury then exhibits a 'reasoning prejudice'. Secondly, the actual relevance of the evidence to the facts in issue may be discounted and 'moral prejudice' may lead the jury to condemn the defendant as a disreputable person.

Evolution of Law on Propensity

Overall, historically the development of this aspect of law, originally known as the law of similar fact, has shown the difficulty of putting flesh on the key concept of relevance of previous behaviour to the issue in the case. [2] The Law Commission in its Report argued that the rules on similar fact were difficult to apply and proposed a codification of the law. However, the Government considered the Report too conservative and did not adopt its recommendation on more stringent tests for admissibility. Under **s. 101(1)(d)**, the successor to the similar fact common law rules, the defendant's bad character is admissible

[2] *Makin v A-G for New South Wales* [1894] AC 57 identified categories of admissibility, a test replaced by *DPP v Boardman* [1975] AC 421 by the emphasis on probative force. In *DPP v P* [1991] 2 AC 447 the test of 'striking similarity' was replaced by examining whether the evidence had sufficient probative value to outweigh its prejudicial effect.

if 'it is relevant to an important matter in issue between the defendant and the prosecution'. There is no reference to the need for the relevance to be 'substantial'.[3] **Section 103(1)** and **(3)** defines 'matter in issue between the defendant and the prosecution' as including '(a) the question whether the defendant has a propensity to commit offences of the kind with which he is charged, except where his having such a propensity makes it no more likely that he is guilty of the offence; (b) the question whether the defendant has a propensity to be untruthful except where it is not suggested that the defendant's case is untruthful in any respect'. **Section 112(1)** specifies that 'an important matter' means a matter of substantial importance in the context of the case as a whole. Further indication that the Government was determined, as Dennis points out, to increase the likelihood of admission of the defendant's prior bad character is that the statute specifies that where **s. 103(1)(a)** applies a defendant's propensity to commit offences of the kind with which he is charged should be established by evidence that he had been convicted of an offence of the same description as the one with which he is charged or an offence of the same category as the one with which he is charged. This approach appears automatically to allow admissibility of offences because they are of the same description rather than take into account more fully the surrounding circumstances.[4]

[3] As Dennis (2013, p. 826) points out, 'The Government rejected the conservative approach which would have imposed requirements for leave, substantial probative value and admission of the evidence in the interests of justice despite the risk of prejudice.'

[4] The increase in bureaucratic intervention is marked also by the provision that the Secretary of State may make orders for prescribing particular offences as offences of the same category.

Examples of a Broad Approach to Admissibility

The growing body of case law on **s. 101(1)(d)** supports the assertion made by Dennis quoted in the question.

It is clear that the courts are aware of Parliament's intention. In *R v Edwards (Stewart)* **[2006] 1 WLR 1524** the Court of Appeal stated '. . . it was apparent that Parliament intended that evidence of bad character would be put before juries more frequently than had previously been the case'. In *R v Weir* **[2006] 1 WLR 1885** it acknowledged that **s. 101(1)(d)** '. . . completely reverses the pre-existing general rule . . . the pre-existing one stage test which balanced probative value against prejudicial effect is obsolete'. If the evidence was relevant to an important issue between the prosecution and defence then, unless there was an application to exclude it, it was admitted. Furthermore in *R v Mitchell* **(2017)** the Supreme Court has held that propensity may be proved by a series of similar incidents which are not necessarily criminal convictions'. In that case also the court (para. 39) held that the jury may assess the incidents 'in the round' since 'obvious similarities in various incidents may constitute mutual corroboration of those incidents'.

Another argument to support the Dennis analysis is that propensity evidence may be admitted under other 'gateways'. Thus in *R v Highton* **[2005] EWCA Crim 1985** the defendant's previous convictions had been admitted under **s. 101(1)(g)**. However, the court held that the judge had been right to give a direction on propensity. Conversely, the broader range of convictions admitted under s. 101(1)(g) means that even if not so directed the jury might well consider the behaviour exhibits propensity as much as credibility. In *R v Clarke* [2011] EWCA Crim 939, the defendant was charged with sexual offences and his previous record for violent offences was admitted through s. 101(1)(g).[5] See also *R v D, P and U* [2012] 1 Cr App R 8.

The broad discretion available to the judge has meant that the Court of Appeal has been reluctant to overturn first instance decisions even where it might be argued that bad character evidence has been admitted too readily. In *R v Awaritefe* [2007] EWCA Crim 706 the court was ready to admit previous offences as showing propensity although they were less serious than the current charge and took place some time previously.[6] The Court of Appeal was of the opinion that some judges would not have admitted this evidence but it was within the range of discretionary action. However, the evidence from the case law is not exclusively pro-prosecution.

Examples of a Restrictive Approach to Admissibility

On the other hand, there are a number of indications that the courts may on occasion be more reluctant to admit propensity evidence. First, it is notable that the statute provides an exclusionary discretion for s. 101(1)(d), under s. 101(3) and (4). Secondly, in the leading case *R v Hanson* [2005] EWCA Crim 824, the Court of Appeal set out the way in which propensity may be demonstrated. It stated: 'A simple previous conviction for an offence of the same description or category will often not show propensity. But it may do so where, for example, it shows a tendency to unusual behaviour or where its circumstances demonstrate probative force in relation to the offence charged.'[7] Durston (2011, p. 193) suggests that although admissibility is more likely than under the common law, it is still restricted by statute. He writes, 'It is apparent that there is still a de facto, if not statutory, quality threshold on the admissibility of propensity evidence, albeit that it is set at a significantly lower level than was the situation at common law.' Furthermore, *Hanson* and *R v Campbell* [2008] Crim LR 303 both demonstrated a somewhat cautious approach to admitting evidence of a propensity for untruthfulness under s. 103(1)(b). The court distinguished between dishonesty and untruthfulness and stated in *Hanson*:

. . . the only circumstances in which there is likely to be an important issue as to whether a defendant has a propensity to tell lies is where telling lies is an element of the offence charged.[8]

This restrictive approach, however, is not uniform. First, a more expansive approach is taken when the evidence is defence evidence. Thus propensity to be untruthful is admissible under s. 101(1)(e) relating

[5] The Court of Appeal stated that it was not unreasonable to admit the whole of C's character under s. 101(1)(g) and for the judge in summing-up to remind the jury that none of these offences were sexual offences and they did not show he had committed the offences with which he was charged.

[6] Durston (2011, p. 196) cites this case as 'indicative of the range of the trial judge's discretion'.

[7] Durston (2011, p. 193) comments '. . . in *Hanson* the court was relatively conservative in its interpretation of s101, expressing a hope that application to adduce bad character evidence would not be made as a matter of course.'

[8] The effect of specifying that a propensity for being untruthful will only be rarely found is, as Mirfield put it (2008, p. 5), 'to render s. 103(1)(b) a dead letter'.

to a matter in issue between the defendant and a co-defendant. The section is not available to the prosecution. In *R v Lawson* [2007] 1 Cr App R 11, *Hanson* was distinguished. The judge had been correct in allowing the co-defendant to adduce evidence of L's conviction for unlawful wounding and his directions to the jury had been appropriate in directing them to use the conviction as evidence of untruthfulness. The appeal thus raised questions of L's propensity for truthfulness and credibility rather than his propensity to commit offences of the type charged.

Moreover in *R v N* [2014] EWCA Crim 419 the Court of Appeal departed from the restrictive approach in *Campbell* in interpreting s. 103(1). A further indication of the move away from the restrictive approach to propensity to untruthfulness was expressed by the Court of Appeal in *R v Jarvis* [2008] EWCA Crim 488. It stated (para. 30), 'We are quite satisfied that there is no warrant in the statute for restricting bad character evidence going to a propensity to untruthfulness to evidence of past untruthfulness as a witness. That would very largely and quite unwarrantably restrict the admission of very relevant evidence.'

Finally, a broad approach to admissibility of evidence on credibility is taken in s. 101(1)(g) as, for example, in *R v Singh* [2007] EWCA Crim 2140.

Conclusion

The *Makin* 'forbidden chain of reasoning' from propensity to guilt is the norm. The comment by Dennis is supported by the experience of the character provision of the CJA 2003. It should, however, be noticed that concepts of relevance, including what Dennis refers to as 'enhanced relevance' are subjective. The measurement of probative value is socially conditioned. This is not, however, a matter of semantics. In part the development of the law has reflected different social values on the part of the judiciary. Just as the notorious case of *Thompson* [1918] AC 221 reflects prejudice and ignorance, so the lowering of the threshold of admissibility in *DPP v P* [1991] 2 AC 447 and then even further in the CJA 2003 reflects a growing awareness of the needs of victims and of the potential value of children's evidence. Perhaps too much attention has been directed to relevance as an aspect of admissibility. Just as important perhaps are clear judicial directions on matters of prejudice as well as logic on how the jury should view such evidence. Zuckerman (1989, p. 248) suggested that: '[a] more effective way of combating prejudice would be to bring into the open the scope of prejudice created by evidence of past criminal record and strive to persuade jurors that the principles of criminal justice, which require resisting prejudice, reflect their own perception of justice'. Zuckerman suggested that 'the question of admissibility [would be] less important because the tools will be in place for counteracting prejudice'.

This is an argument to be made for his suggestion that the criminal record should be routinely admitted as in continental jurisdictions. This perhaps would avoid highlighting the criminal record as a matter of importance. But this proposition arguably underestimates the amount of prejudice juries draw from prior bad character and also presupposes that the judiciary are able to convey such complex ethical messages to a jury of differing experiences and moral standpoints.

LOOKING FOR EXTRA MARKS?

- Show your knowledge of the complexities of the subject by pointing out that propensity evidence may be admitted by joinder of similar charges; see, for example, *R v Freeman* [2008] **1 WLR 27**. In the latter case, evidence in relation to one count in an indictment was capable of being admitted as bad character evidence in relation to the others. The common law more restrictive approach no longer applied.

- Give an additional argument for defending the current law that the defendant in the face of the increased admissibility of bad character evidence has some statutory protection. Under **s. 101(3)** there is a test of fairness for admissibility and the court must not admit propensity evidence if, whether the defendant has made an application or not, it appears to the court that the admission of the evidence would have such an adverse effect on the fairness of the proceedings that the court ought not to admit it. This applies to **s. 101(1)(d)** and **(g)**.

QUESTION | 2

Andy, Ben, and Catherine are charged with theft of video machines brought to their shop for repairs by David. They all plead not guilty. Andy testifies in his own defence. He claims that Ben had asked him to help steal the machines but he had refused. Andy has several convictions for criminal damage. At the trial counsel for the prosecution and for Ben cross-examine Andy on these convictions. Ben gives evidence and claims he had nothing to do with the theft and that Andy had stolen the machines. He calls several witnesses to give evidence that he has done extensive charitable work for a local pensioners' club for many years. Catherine does not testify at trial but claims at interview that David was falsely implicating her out of resentment because she refused to have an affair with him. She also said at interview that Doris, David's girlfriend, had a grudge against her. David is a prosecution witness, Doris is not a witness. Catherine received a caution for shoplifting ten years ago. All the defendants' previous characters are admitted. In her summing-up, the judge tells the jury that they may take Ben's good character evidence as relevant to credibility and his propensity to commit offences and that the bad character of Andy and Catherine was evidence of their lack of credibility. Ben was acquitted. Andy and Catherine were convicted.

Advise Andy and Catherine whether they have any grounds of appeal on the grounds that evidence has been wrongly treated at trial.

CAUTION!

Do not attempt this question unless:

- you are familiar with the complex provisions in **ss. 98–113 of the CJA 2003** and the relevant case law, particularly the cases of *R v Hanson* **[2005] EWCA Crim 824** and *R v Highton* **[2005] EWCA Crim 1985**; on judicial directions you should be aware of the implications of *R v Hunter* **[2015] 2 Cr App R 116**;

- you are able to distinguish carefully the specific gateways of the admissibility of previous convictions and assess whether the court exercised discretion reasonably.

DIAGRAM ANSWER PLAN

Identify the issues	The legal issues are: (a) admissibility of previous bad character of defendants; (b) judicial direction on character; (c) whether same rules apply to testifying and non-testifying defendants; (d) good character evidence.
Relevant law	CJA 2003, ss. 98–112; common law on good character.
Apply the law	Consider definition of bad character in **s. 98** and whether **s. 101(1)(e)** and **(g)** apply; effect of direction on good character for Ben on Andy and Catherine see *R v Hunter*.
Conclude	Assess possible grounds of appeal on the admissibility of character evidence and on judicial directions.

SUGGESTED ANSWER

Admissibility of Andy and Catherine's Bad Character

[1] Note that previous convictions are of course included in the statutory definition of bad character but the definition is now wider.

Andy has previous convictions for criminal damage.[1] These convictions fall within the 'bad character' definition of **s. 98 of the Criminal Justice Act (CJA) 2003** as 'evidence of, or of a disposition towards, misconduct on his part, other than evidence which (a) has to do with the alleged facts of the offence with which the defendant is charged, or (b) is evidence of misconduct in connection with the investigation or prosecution of that offence.'

These convictions are admissible if, but only if, they are covered by one of the provisions in **s. 101**. Andy has given evidence against his co-defendant Ben in stating that Ben had asked him to help steal the machines. Ben denies this. **Section 101(1)(e)** permits bad character evidence to be admissible if 'it has substantial probative value in relation to an important matter in issue between the defendant and a co-defendant'. Note that under **s. 112** '"an important matter" means a matter of substantial importance in the context of the case as a whole'. In *R v Platt* **(2016)** the Court of Appeal, rejecting reliance on the common law precedents including *R v Randall* **(2003)**, held that 'substantial' 'should be given its ordinary unelaborated meaning'. In that case the accused's propensity did not have substantial probative value such as to be admitted under **s. 101(1)(e)**.

Section 109 provides that the relevance or probative value of evidence is a reference to its relevance or probative value on the assumption that it is true and that a court need not assume that the evidence is true if it appears that no court or jury could reasonably find it to be true. In other words, Andy will only trigger this gateway if his allegation against Ben that he set up the theft has some factual basis on which a jury could find it true.[2] If this is the case here, **s. 101(1)(e)** allows evidence of Andy's propensity and credibility. Arguably, only credibility is at issue here, since the question in the trial is who is telling the truth, Andy or Ben. The question then arises whether the convictions for criminal damage do have substantial probative value in helping the jury decide whether Andy is untruthful. The criminal damage convictions may therefore be admissible if they are relevant to Andy's lack of credibility. In *R v Edwards (Stewart Dean)* **[2006] 1 WLR 1524** the appellant claimed that a conviction for handling could not properly be regarded as evidence relevant to his propensity for telling the truth. The court acknowledged that a 13-year-old handling offence had marginal relevance to the question of whether the co-defendant was telling the truth. Relevant issues here will be how old the convictions are and whether Andy pleaded not guilty to them, thus suggesting lack of truthfulness.[3]

Here, from the facts we are given, it is very likely that Andy's evidence contradicts Ben's denial of involvement. There is no statutory discretion to prevent Ben's counsel questioning Andy on his previous offences but **s. 104** prevents the prosecution tendering such evidence. The statutory exclusionary discretion in **s. 101(3) of the CJA 2003** does not cover **s. 101(1)(e)**. Furthermore, the right to cross-examine is arguably only limited on grounds of relevance. It is likely that Andy's bad character will be held to have been rightly admitted and the judge rightly directed that the jury could take them into account in assessing his credibility. Therefore his grounds of appeal would be slim. The Court of Appeal is reluctant to interfere with the judge's discretion (see *R v Lawson* **[2007] 1 WLR 1191**).

---

[2] An allegation that has only marginal or trivial value would not be considered relevant.

[3] Note that Andy's convictions for criminal damage arguably did not involve deceit but note that in *R v Lawson* **[2006] EWCA Crim 2572** by contrast with *Edwards*, the court cited offences not involving dishonesty as potentially probative of the defendant's lack of credibility.

Catherine

Catherine has a previous caution for theft. The definition of bad character in **s. 98** refers to 'reprehensible behaviour'. The Explanatory Note refers to 'evidence where the charge is not prosecuted' and this arguably includes a caution. Her attack on David and Doris is arguably covered by **s. 101(1)(g)**: 'The defendant has made an attack on another person's character.'[4] The prosecution may therefore adduce evidence of her cautions although the court has discretion to exclude under **s. 101(3)** and **(4)**. **Section 101(4)** refers to the length of time which has passed since the bad character evidence was manifest so the fact that the cautions happened ten years previously would be a factor in exercising the discretion. There are three further issues to consider, namely that Catherine made the allegations at interview, does not give evidence at trial, and Doris is not a witness. **Section 106(1)(c)(i)** specifies that the 'attack on another person's character includes those where a suspect is being questioned under caution'. The prosecution therefore will try to argue that Catherine's comments at the interview have opened the gateway to admission of her caution. It will, however, on the authority of *R v Nelson (Ashley George)* **[2006] EWCA Crim 3412, [2007] Crim LR 709**, 709–711, have to convince the judge that a proper basis has been laid for putting Catherine's comments at interview in front of the jury.[5]

David is being called as a witness and if the defence counsel had referred to Catherine's claims in cross-examination that would provide a stronger ground for admitting Catherine's conviction.

In relation to the allegation against Doris who is not a witness, *R v Nelson* **[2006]** again gives some guidance. The defence argued that a victim and neighbour had conspired to fabricate allegations of violence. The defendant, in interview, had claimed that the neighbour was a liar who used illegal drugs. The neighbour was not a witness at trial. The judge ruled that there had been an attack on another person's character. Nelson was convicted and appealed on the ground that the comments in interview should not have been admitted. The Court of Appeal dismissed the appeal, holding that 'an attack on another person's character' did not confine that gateway to the situation where a defendant, personally or through his advocate, attacked the character of a prosecution witness. It had to be taken as Parliament's intention deliberately to widen the gateway in that fashion. The trial judge had a discretion, however, to exclude evidence of a defendant's bad character when he had merely made imputations about the character of a non-witness. That discretion could be exercised under **s. 78 of the Police and Criminal Evidence Act 1984 (PACE)** or **s. 101(3)** of the 2003 Act.[6] It is possible that Catherine's attack on Doris

[4]Section 106 explains that 'evidence attacking the other person's character' includes evidence that the other person 'has behaved or is disposed to behave in a reprehensible way' so it does not only need to refer to criminal convictions. This appears to cover the allegations Catherine has made.

[5]In *Nelson* the court considered that it would have been improper for the prosecution to seek to get such comments before a jury simply to provide a basis for satisfying gateway (g). However, in the event the requirements of gateway (g) were met by referring to the attack on the victim in cross-examination.

[6]The court stated that it would be a matter for the judge how he exercised that discretion but that it would be unusual for evidence of a defendant's bad character to be admitted when the only basis for so doing was an attack on the character of a non-witness who is also a non-victim.

[7] This is so even where, as in *Singh*, the relevant evidence included convictions for non-dishonesty offences such as violent disorder, assault, harassment, criminal damage, and driving while over the alcohol limit. Such evidence under this gateway may also be relevant to propensity, see Keane and McKeown (2018, p. 567).

[8] The comment on *Nelson* in the Criminal Law Review (2007, p. 711) states, 'the old law was criticised on the grounds that it made no exception to adduction of evidence of the defendant's bad character in cases in which the imputations that were cast were integral to the defence that was being run, e.g. that a confession had been fabricated. In this respect no change has been effected by the 2003 Act.' (Note, however, that allegations that evidence has been 'planted' are excluded from the definition in s. 98, see Explanatory Note.)

[9] Note that after 1898, when the defendant became capable of giving evidence at his trial, his good character was said to go primarily to his credibility: *R v Bellis* [1966] 1 WLR 234.

[10] See *Concentrate Evidence* (2017, p. 103) for a diagrammatic representation of the judgment.

should not have triggered **s. 101(1)(g)** but that on David rightly did so. If Catherine's bad character is rightly admitted under **s. 101(1)(g)**, it is well established that the jury should be directed that it is relevant to her lack of credibility (see *R v Singh* [2007] EWCA Crim 2140).[7] One further issue arises as to whether bad character evidence is admissible when the imputations made by the defendant are an integral part of the defence case. Academic comment has been critical that the answer still seems to be 'yes'.[8]

It is unlikely that Catherine has grounds of appeal on this issue.

Judicial Directions on Character

The defendant has long been entitled to adduce evidence of his good character with the aim of inducing the jury to conclude that a person with that character would not commit the alleged offence. Ben is likely to be able to adduce witnesses to testify on his charitable work. The general common law rule is that evidence of character is confined to evidence of general reputation (*R v Rowton* (1865) Le & Ca 520; *R v Redgrave* (1982) 74 Cr App R 10), though as an indulgence, a wider range of evidence is often admitted for the defendant.[9] Where a defendant of good character has given evidence, the judge is required to direct the jury about the relevance of good character to the defendant's credibility, but also to refer to the likelihood that a person of good character would act as charged. In *R v Vye* [1993] 1 WLR 471 the evidence is held to be relevant to both credit and lack of propensity. Problems arise where, as here, a person without a blot on his record (Ben) is tried alongside a defendant of bad character (Andy) and one of relative bad character (Catherine). By drawing the jury's attention to the fact that a person of Ben's good character is less likely than a person of bad character to have committed the offence, the judge inevitably suggests that Andy and Catherine are more likely to have committed it.

The leading case on good character and judicial directions where there is more than one defendant is *R v Hunter* [2015] 2 Cr App R 116(9).[10] Andy and Ben will be advised that the Court of Appeal reviewed the authorities in this area, including *R v Vye* [1993] 1 WLR 471 and *R v Aziz* [1996] AC 41 and took a restrictive approach. It drew a distinction between 'absolute good character' and 'effective good character'. Ben would fall into the former category since he has no previous convictions so he was entitled to directions on credibility and propensity. In the case of Catherine it is arguable that she exhibited 'effective good character' since she had a caution some years ago.

Catherine should be advised that the judge had discretion on whether to give the more limited effective good character direction.

She is not entitled to a good character direction and a failure to give one will not invariably lead to quashing the conviction.

Andy has previous convictions and therefore is not entitled to a good character direction. If his convictions were wrongly adduced at trial he could cite the case *R v Cain* **[1994] 1 WLR 1449**, which involved three defendants, one defendant had previous convictions, including an offence of dishonesty. The judge directed the jury as to the significance of one co-defendant's good character and said of another defendant only that he had 'had a spot of trouble with the police before'. However, the Court of Appeal dismissed the appeal of the latter on conviction. It accepted that the judge should have warned the jury to disregard the convictions as irrelevant to guilt but came to the conclusion that his dismissive language had reduced any adverse inferences which the jury might otherwise have drawn.

Conclusion

It is likely that Andy's and Catherine's previous bad characters were rightly admitted. It is unlikely also that they have grounds of appeal on the character directions. In relation to both they are reminded of Lord Steyn's observation in *Aziz* (para. 5) that 'A good starting point is that a judge should never be compelled to give meaningless or absurd directions.'

[11]It is pertinent to refer to the *Wednesbury* test as applied to exercise of judicial discretion.

Both Catherine and Andy should be warned that the Court of Appeal has indicated it will not readily interfere with the judge's discretion in this area (*Hanson* **[2005] EWCA Crim 824**, *R v Hunter* **[2015] 2 Cr App R 116(9)**).[11]

LOOKING FOR EXTRA MARKS?

- You will gain credit for thorough research if in answering questions on bad character you not only cite 'gateways' listed in **s. 101(1)(c)–(g) of the CJA 2003** but also cite the companion explanatory sections, **ss. 102–106, 109** and **112** and, where relevant, the Explanatory Note accompanying the Act.

- In the course of explaining judicial direction on the evidential worth of previous bad character, you should not only refer to the technicalities of the law but also the underlying principle, stated in *Cain* **(1994)** that the jury must not be misled.

Thelma and Louise are jointly charged with murdering Harry. Both plead not guilty to the charge. Their explanation is that Harry had tried to rape Thelma and in the course of protecting her they both were obliged to push him and he fell down some stairs. Both had fled the scene but later gave themselves up to the police. Louise chooses not to give evidence but her counsel calls her local vicar to state that Louise had been a Bible School teacher and sang in the church choir. Louise has two previous convictions for theft. Thelma elects to testify and in the course of giving evidence explains her flight from the scene of the incident by saying she was afraid of the police because she had cannabis in her pocket. Thelma is awaiting trial on a charge of violent disorder and has a conviction for cannabis possession. The police claim that when arrested Thelma had confessed to attempting to kill Harry but Thelma denies making such an admission.

Discuss the evidential issues involved.

CAUTION!

- It is important you consider the specific facts of the scenario and do not simply convey broad generalities about the law.
- Remember that the statutory discretionary exclusions may apply to the gateways.
- Make sure you cover both admissibility and evidential worth.

DIAGRAM ANSWER PLAN

Identify the issues	The legal issues are: bad character of non-testifying and testifying defendant; claim to be of good character; whether admissibility of bad character is triggered.
Relevant law	CJA 2003 gateways in s. 101(1)(b), (g), and (f); common law on good character, judicial directions.
Apply the law	Section 101(1)(g) will apply to Thelma and Louise and s. 101(1)(f) to Louise and s. 101(1)(b) to Thelma.
Conclude	Assess the likely outcome for both defendants.

Louise, Non-Testifying Defendant

The **Criminal Justice Act (CJA) 2003** applies to both testifying and non-testifying defendants and so both Thelma and Louise are covered by its provisions.

With regard to Louise's failure to testify, the scope of permissible comment by the judge and counsel for the prosecution is covered by **s. 35(3) of the Criminal Justice and Public Order Act 1994**, whereby the court or jury in determining whether the accused is guilty of the offence charged may draw such inferences as appear proper from the failure of the accused to give evidence. The prosecution can therefore now comment on her failure to testify but under **s. 35(3)** no conviction can be founded solely on the inferences drawn under **s. 35**. The Court of Appeal in *R v Cowan* **[1996] QB 373** laid down guidelines in this area. Provided an inference under this section is not the only evidence against the defendant, the section will usually operate.

Louise's Good Character

Under the common law the accused is entitled to adduce evidence of her own good character with the aim of persuading the jury that a person with that character is unlikely to have committed the alleged offence. The rule at common law, unaffected by the **CJA 2003**, is that evidence of character is confined to evidence of general reputation and not of specific creditable acts. *R v Rowton* **(1865) Le & Ca 520** and *R v Redgrave* **(1981) 74 Cr App R 10** are the leading cases.[1] It is likely that the court will accept that this evidence is admissible since the common law rule that it is, despite *Redgrave*, is not often strictly applied. The application of **s. 101(1)(f) of the CJA 2003** must then be considered.[2] The prosecution may be permitted to adduce evidence of bad character to correct any false impression that may have been created. In *R v Renda* **[2006] 1 WLR 2948** the defendant was held to be seeking to convey a misleading impression about his life and history by claiming that he had been a serving soldier in the Armed Forces, who had, while still employed, sustained serious head injuries, which had resulted in long-term brain damage. He said that at the date of his arrest he was in regular employment as a security guard. The court commented: 'For the purposes of **section 101(1)(f)** the question whether the defendant has given a false impression about himself and whether there is evidence which may properly serve to correct such a false impression under **section 105(1)(a)** and **(b)** is fact-specific.'

[1] In *Redgrave* the accused, who was charged with offences relating to homosexuality, was not allowed to prove his heterosexuality by evidence of past liaisons with members of the opposite sex.

[2] The section reads: 'In criminal proceedings evidence of the defendant's bad character is admissible if, but only if . . . it is evidence to correct a false impression given by the defendant.'

Louise's claim to be a Bible School teacher and sing in the church choir is likely to fall under **s. 101(1)(f)**. The question then arises what is permissible evidence to correct this impression. **Sections 98** and **112** of **the CJA 2003** indicate what is meant by 'bad character'. The Explanatory Note to the Act (at para. 353) reads, 'the definition covers evidence of or a disposition towards misconduct. The term "misconduct" is further defined in **s. 112** as the commission of an offence or other reprehensible behaviour. This is intended to be a broad definition and recover evidence that shows that the person has committed an offence, or has acted in a reprehensible way (or is disposed to do so) as well as evidence from which this might be inferred.' Louise's two previous convictions for theft will be likely to qualify for admission under **s. 101(1)(f)** although much will depend on how long ago they were. Although this section is largely a reflection of **s. 1(3) of the Criminal Evidence Act 1898** the wording of the section makes it clear that evidence is only now admissible if it goes no further than is necessary to correct the false impression.[3] Louise may also take advantage of **s. 105(3)** in withdrawing or dissociating herself from the false or misleading impression given by her counsel. There is no statutory discretion to exclude otherwise admissible evidence under **s. 101(1)(f)** except the general discretion under **s. 78 of the Police and Criminal Evidence Act 1984**. In light of the above, Louise is not entitled to an absolute good character direction, *R v Hunter* **[2015] 2 Cr App R 116(9)**. The judge has discretion to give an 'effective' good character direction but there is no entitlement to one and if the convictions are adduced at trial it would arguably be absurd to do so (*R v Aziz*).

Allegation Against Harry

Louise and Thelma claim that Harry tried to rape Thelma. Their argument appears to be they acted in self-defence. This is likely to engage **s. 101(1)(g)**. In *Hanson* **[2005] EWCA Crim 824** the Court of Appeal stated that 'pre-2003 authorities will continue to apply when assessing whether an attack has been made on another person's character, to the extent that they are compatible with the [new legislation]'. In *R v Selvey* **[1970] AC 304** the House of Lords made it clear that the 'no stymie' principle did not apply.[4] In *R v Lamaletie* **[2008] EWCA Crim 314** the Court of Appeal applied similar reasoning.

Thus Louise's convictions may be admissible by the prosecution under this head also although here under **s. 101(3)** such evidence may be excluded 'if on application by the defendant to exclude it, it appears to the court that the admission of the evidence would have such an adverse effect on the fairness of the proceedings that the court ought not to admit it'. One factor is 'the length of time between

[3] This is in contrast to the draconian common law position in *R v Winfield* [1939] 4 All ER 164 that character was indivisible.

[4] The judgment in the House of Lords stated 'cross-examination of the accused as to character [is permissible] both when imputations on the character of the prosecutor and his witness are cast to show their own reliability as witnesses independently of the evidence given by them and also when the casting of such imputations is necessary to enable the accused to establish his defence'.

matters to which that evidence relates and the matters which form the subject of the offence charged'. In *R v Bovell* [2005] 2 Cr App R 401 the Court of Appeal made it clear that the trial judge was not expected to conduct an investigation into why the defendant made the attack: 'the impact on the fairness of proceedings had to be assessed by reference to matters other than what the defendant's particular intention may or may not have been'. Thus Louise runs the risk of her convictions being admitted under two gateways.

Thelma

Thelma has also arguably 'made an attack on another person's character' under **s. 101(1)(g)** by claiming Harry had attempted rape and by denying the police version of her alleged confession.

She has possible bad character within the meaning of **s. 98** in that she is awaiting trial on another charge. The Explanatory Notes which accompanied the Act specified that bad character included 'evidence relating to offences for which the accused has been charged'. However, Thelma is advised that the court will most likely protect her privilege against self-incrimination and not allow reference to the charge. In *R v Smith* [1989] **Crim LR 900** the Court of Appeal decided that the accused cannot be asked in cross-examination about pending charges since they may tend to undermine her privilege against self-incrimination. However, Thelma is also denying the police version of events. More information is needed whether she is simply denying that she had committed the offence, made the confession, or if she is accusing the police of lying. Arguably, a simple denial is not an attack on another person and thus may also engage **s. 101(1)(g)**. Presumably the exchange was not tape-recorded to establish what had happened.[5]

Thelma's Flight

Thelma's explanation of her flight from the scene of the alleged crime has introduced evidence of 'reprehensible behaviour' under **s. 98 of the Criminal Justice and Public Order Act 1994 (CJPOA)**, namely that she had cannabis in her pocket, which is unlawful. **Section 101(1)(b)** covers this point specifying that 'the evidence is adduced by the defendant himself or is given in answer to a question asked by him in cross-examination and intended to elicit it'.[6] It follows therefore that the prosecution may cross-examine Thelma on her previous conviction. One question which arises is may the prosecution cross-examine on the details of previous offences where they are admitted? Since the bad character evidence is likely to be admitted in the case of Louise under **s. 101(1)(f)** and Thelma under **s. 101 (1)(b)** rather than the propensity provisions under **s. 101(1)(d)**, it is arguable that the

[5] Note that under the 1898 Act it was immaterial whether the allegation by the defendant was true or false for the purposes of loss of shield; see *R v Bishop* [1975] Crim LR 665.

[6] It is important to note here that the accused must have intended to reveal the bad character and not be led into it by robust cross-examination.

details should not be given; the fact of the conviction even for non-dishonesty offences is sufficient to raise questions about credibility. In *R v Clarke* [2011] EWCA Crim 939 the court noted (para. 29) that 'all convictions are potentially relevant to assist the jury to assess the character of the accused and it is not necessary, or at least not generally so, for detailed facts about the nature and circumstances of those convictions to be put before the jury'.

Finally the judge should direct on the evidential value of the bad character. The Act is silent on the evidential value of evidence admitted through the 'gateways'.[7] However, there is authority that evidence admitted under (g) is relevant to credibility, see *R v Singh* [2007] EWCA Crim 2140. The court gave guidance that the purpose of the gateway was to enable the jury to know from what sort of source allegations against a witness (especially a complainant but not only a complainant) have come. The gateway does not depend upon evidence demonstrating propensity to offend as charged or propensity to be untruthful. Thelma and Louise should both be warned that in *Highton* [2005] EWCA Crim 1985 the Court of Appeal held that evidence which was admitted through one gateway, for example gateway (g), is nonetheless capable of being used according to the definition of another section.[8]

This approach also underlines the importance of the guidance that was given in the case of *Hanson* and others as to the care that the judge must exercise to give the jury appropriate warnings when summing-up. In *R v D, P and U* [2012] Cr App R 8 the Court of Appeal in a commentary on *Hanson* stated that the particular gateway through which the evidence is admitted will, however, be of great help in identifying the ways in which the evidence can be used. The key question is relevance.[9]

Conclusion

Thelma and Louise should be advised that the discretion to exclude admissible bad character exists under **s. 101(3)** which applies to **s. 101(1)(g)** but not **s. 101(1)(f)**.[10]

---

[7] The distinction between relevant to issue and relevant to credibility is one of the most difficult for juries (and Evidence students) to grasp. Note that propensity to be untruthful is not included in s. 101(1)(g).

[8] It stated (para. 10): 'In the case of gateway (g) for example admissibility depends on the defendant having made an attack on another person's character, but once the evidence is admitted, it may, depending on the particular facts, be relevant not only to credibility but also the propensity to commit offences of the kind with which the defendant is charged.'

[9] Evidence students sometimes forget that amidst all the technicalities of this area of law at heart lies the notion of relevance, which is a largely a matter of inferential reasoning based on reason and common sense.

[10] The criteria for exclusion includes the provision that '. . . the court is satisfied by reason of the length of time since the conviction or for any other reason, that it would be unjust for it to apply in this case'.

 LOOKING FOR EXTRA MARKS?

You could gain additional credit if you:

- extend your analysis of the application of the exclusionary discretion in **s. 101 of the CJA 2003** and also consider whether **s. 78 PACE** may apply to **s. 101(1)(f)**;

- consider, in relation to Thelma's defensive explanation about the cannabis, the reasoning in the case of *DPP v Jones* [1962] AC 635, decided under the **Criminal Evidence Act 1898**.

Nicholas, a taxi driver, is charged with criminally damaging a small plantation of rare palm trees in a country park. His fingerprints are found on a note which was pinned to the gate of the plantation which called for 'British trees only to be planted in British parks'. Nicholas denies the offence and claims that he had picked up a passenger who asked to be dropped at the park. He claims that the customer asked him to put the note in the glove compartment of the car and took the note away at the end of the ride. Nicholas denies having entered the park and claims he drove away after dropping the customer off. He denies he has an obsessive interest in trees.

Advise the prosecution on the following matters:

- Whether they can adduce evidence of two previous acquittals of Nicholas on charges of criminal damage of tropical trees planted in country parks. On each occasion his defence was mistaken identity claiming that he had driven a paying customer to the parks and left them there.

- Whether evidence is admissible that Nicholas has posted on YouTube a video showing him with other members of a group wearing T-shirts with the slogan 'Keep our Flora British' and hacking down trees at an undisclosed location.

- Whether evidence from his wife is admissible that on their honeymoon ten years previously on an island off the coast of Cornwall, Nicholas had insisted they went into a private woodland containing tropical plants and had been warned by the landowner that they were trespassing.

CAUTION!

In order to answer this question well you should:

- display knowledge of how propensity evidence is now admissible under **s. 101(1)(d) of the CJA 2003**;

- appreciate the significance of the concept of relevance in this area of law;

- have researched the new forms of exhibiting bad character such as social network postings.

DIAGRAM ANSWER PLAN

Identify the issues	▓ The legal issues are: whether propensity evidence is admissible and if so whether previous acquittals, and bad behaviour short of criminal convictions, would be relevant and admissible.
Relevant law	▓ CJA 2003, s. 101(1)(d) and Explanatory Note.
Apply the law	▓ The defences in the previous acquittals show propensity to commit offences such as to increase the likelihood that Nicholas's defence is not to be believed; the pattern of non-criminal behaviour suggests an excessive interest in British Flora.
Conclude	▓ Assess the likelihood of admissibility and the possible exercise of the statutory discretion.

A **SUGGESTED ANSWER**

Acquittals

In relation to the admissibility of the acquittals, the prosecution will be helped by the Explanatory Note on the **Criminal Justice Act (CJA) 2003** and the decisions in *Hanson* **[2005] EWCA Crim 824** and *Highton* **[2005] EWCA Crim 1985**. The Explanatory Note reads 'evidence might be relevant to one of a number of issues in a case. For example, it might help the prosecution to prove the defendant's guilt of the offence by establishing their involvement or state of mind or by rebutting the defendant's explanation of his conduct.' In *Hanson* Rose LJ set out a three-stage test in relation to propensity: first, does the history of conviction(s) establish a propensity to commit offences of the kind charged; secondly, does that propensity make it more likely that the defendant committed the offence charged; thirdly, is it unjust to rely on the conviction(s) of the same description or category; and in any event will the proceedings be unfair if they are admitted? **Section 103(2)** provides that propensity may be established by evidence of convictions for offences of the same description or of the same category as the one with which the defendant is charged. This is 'without prejudice to any other way of doing so'. **Section 103(4)** gives an explanation of the meaning of description and category. [1]

[1] Offences are of the 'same description' if the statement of the offence in a written charge or indictment would be in the same terms. Offences are of the same category if they belong to the same category of offences prescribed under the statute by statutory instrument.

[2] It points out that 'if there were a series of attacks and the defendants were acquitted of involvement in them, evidence showing, or tending to show that he had committed those earlier attacks could be given in a later case if it were admissible to establish that he had committed the latest attack'.

The Explanatory Note to the 2003 Act thus makes it clear that the definition of bad character is broad and may include involvement in earlier offences, even those leading to acquittals.[2] Here the fact that Nicholas had tendered a very similar defence on three occasions makes the evidence relevant to an issue in the case, namely whether his defence of mistaken identity is believable. In the pre-2003 Act case of *R v Z* [2003] 3 All ER 385 the House of Lords admitted previous acquittals on a charge of rape since they had a direct bearing on the question of consent in the current charge. The approach taken in *R v Z* has been confirmed by *R v Mustapha (Mohammed Amadu)* [2007] EWCA Crim 1702, decided under the CJA 2003. The prosecution will not be able to rely on the SI on the Categorisation of Offences.[3]

[3] The Criminal Justice Act 2003 (Categories of Offences) Order 2004 (SI 3346/2004) to date lists two categories, namely, theft and sexual offences against a person under the age of 16, on which it is not unjust to rely.

The court has discretion to exclude these acquittals under two sections. **Section 101(3)** reads: 'the court must not admit evidence under **subsection (1)(d)** if, on the application by the defendant to exclude, it appears to the court that the admission of the evidence would have such an adverse effect on the fairness of the proceedings that the court ought not to admit it'. On an application to exclude evidence under **subs. (3)** the court must have regard, in particular, to the length of time between the matters to which that evidence relates and the matters which form the subject of the offence charged.

[4] It sets out an interest of justice test whereby the offences would not be admitted if the court is satisfied by reason of the length of time since the conviction or for any other reason, that it would be unjust to do so.

Section 103(2) and (3) gives as one criterion the length of time since the offences.[4] Arguably this includes acquittals also. More information is needed as to how long ago the acquittals were. The fact that there were three, however, makes it more likely that they will be admitted. The prosecution will need to give notice in advance that they wish to put the acquittals in evidence and since they are likely to want to adduce similarities in the defence argument about dropping off customers they will need also to specify these surrounding details. In *Hanson* (para. 17) the Court of Appeal referred to the need to specify surrounding circumstances in the context of convictions but presumably the same point applies to acquittals with even more force, since it is the similarities of the defence which are at issue.

It is uncertain whether the prosecution will also be able to rely on **s. 103(1)(b)** which refers to 'the question whether the defendant has a propensity to be untruthful, except where it is not suggested that the defendant's case is untruthful in any respect.' It is clearly the prosecution case that the defendant is putting forward a lying defence and the fact that he had put forward the defence several times before increases the likelihood that his defence is not to be believed. The acquittals in themselves, however, do not appear to fulfil the requirement for admissibility under **s. 101(1)(b)** in that they do not in themselves demonstrate a propensity to be untruthful (see *Hanson*).

[5] Explain that *Hanson* took the
position that propensity to be
untruthful is not the same as
propensity to be dishonest and
should only be admitted in very
limited circumstances.

The judge may have to direct that the acquittals are relevant to his
guilt but not to his propensity for untruthfulness.[5]

Keep our Flora British

According to the Explanatory Note bad character can include 'evidence not related to criminal proceedings . . . might include, for example, evidence that a person has a sexual interest in children or
is racist.' It is possible that even if Keep our Flora British (KFB) is a
non-criminal organisation it will be discreditable to Nicholas to admit
evidence of it. Nicholas is claiming no involvement with the offence
of destroying the trees. The likelihood of his defence that he was in
the area but did not engage in the offence would be undermined by
evidence that he was a member of an organisation which probably
only has a small number of members. His membership of this could
be inferred from the video. Someone who is a member of the KFB is
more likely to be involved in direct action on this issue than someone
who is not. That evidence does not have to reach certainty but simply
increase the likelihood of guilt sufficiently to overcome the obvious
prejudice of admitting it. Nor does the evidence have to be a criminal
conviction.[6] In *R v Weir* **[2006] 1 Cr App R 19**, a caution for taking
an indecent photograph of a child was admitted against a defendant
on a charge of assaulting a girl under 13 years.

Arguably here, membership of the KFB is likely to be admitted
because it is relevant to the defence of non-involvement. It surely
defies coincidence that a person who belonged to such an organisation and who was in the area at the time was not involved in the
offence. The prosecution is likely to be allowed to put this evidence
to the jury.

Arguments in favour of admissibility on non-criminal behaviour
can be found in *R v Saleem* **[2007] EWCA Crim 1923**, which involved possessing disturbing rap lyrics; arguments against are found
in *R v Edwards* **[2006] 1 WLR 1524**, where lawfully possessing an
antique firearm was not reprehensible behaviour. However, the defence should be aided by the warning that the Court of Appeal made
in *Hanson* that bad character evidence must not be simply used to
bolster a weak case.

The question of whether a YouTube video should be admitted to
suggest membership of a quasi-criminal group has been the subject
of recent case law. In *R v Lewis* **[2014] EWCA Crim 48** the test
for admissibility of a YouTube video proclaiming gang membership
was set out: is the evidence relevant to an important matter in issue
between a defendant and the prosecution; is there proper evidence
of the existence and nature of the gang or gangs; does the evidence,

if accepted, go to show the defendant was a member of or associated with a gang or gangs which exhibited violence or hostility to the police or with links with firearms; if the evidence is admitted, will it have such an adverse effect on the fairness of the proceedings that it ought to be excluded?

More information is needed on Nicholas's role in the video but it seems he admits membership.[7]

It is arguable that Nicholas's membership of the KFB does not fall within the **s. 98(a)** definition. It might therefore be admitted on grounds of relevance as what was known under the common law as 'background evidence' and is now covered by **s. 101(1)(c)**. Under *R v Kilbourne* **[1973] AC 729** evidence is 'relevant' if 'it is logically probative or disprobative of some matter which requires proof'. However, this section of the statute is not commonly used to adduce bad character.

Munday (2015, p. 251) comments, 'It is important that gateway (c) is not employed as a means of admitting bad character evidence properly admitted through other gateways.'

Nicholas's Wife's Evidence

The evidence of the wife arguably is 'bad character evidence' in that trespassing could be regarded as 'other reprehensible behaviour'. It also seems to be a statement contradicting Nicholas's testimony that he is not interested in trees. In *R v Davis* **[2008] EWCA Crim 1156** the Court of Appeal made clear that such evidence could not be readily admitted.[8] In *R v Awoyemi* **(2017)** evidence of gang-related activities, including a YouTube video were admitted. It was held that this was permissible under several sections, namely **s. 98(a)**, **s. 101(1)(c)**, and **s. 101(1)(d)**. The case involved the murder of the defendant's long-term partner where prejudicial evidence from the defendant's former girlfriend was wrongly admitted under **s. 101(1)(c)** as 'important explanatory evidence'.

This is defined as admissible evidence if '(a) without it, the court or jury would find it impossible or difficult properly to understand other evidence in the case, and (b) its value for understanding the case as a whole is substantial'. It was not acceptable to admit propensity evidence which was not admissible under (d) because it was more prejudicial than probative. It was appropriate to consider admissibility under the more stringent requirements of **s. 101(1)(d)**. Here, it is likely that the evidence would not pass the test set out in *Hanson* and so should not simply be admitted to contradict the defendant in relation to his obsessive interest in trees.

Conclusion

The evidence of the acquittals and membership of the KFB are likely to be admitted through the gateway of **s. 101(1)(d)** but the evidence from the wife would be held to be too remote to be relevant.

LOOKING FOR EXTRA MARKS?

You would impress the examiners if you made the following points linking your knowledge of character with that of other areas of evidence such as hearsay:

- police officers may be called to give expert evidence based on their knowledge of gangs, see *Lewis* **(2014)**;
- there is conflicting authority on whether evidence from YouTube videos is admissible as an implied assertion/real evidence or inadmissible hearsay. Note that Glover (2017, p. 316) says that *R v Bucknor* **[2010] EWCA Crim 1152**, which held it was inadmissible hearsay, was wrong.

TAKING THINGS FURTHER

- Law Commission Report No. 273, Evidence of Bad Character in Criminal Proceedings (Cm 5257) (London: HMSO, 2001).
- Lloyd-Bostock, S., 'The Effects on Juries of Hearing about the Defendant's Previous Criminal Record: A Simulation Study' [2000] Crim LR 734.

  Reports on an experiment examining the effects of disclosing previous convictions of defendants to simulated jurors.
- Mirfield, P., 'Character, Credibility and Untruthfulness' (2008) 124 LQR 1.

  See references in text to answers.
- Mirfield, P., 'Character and Credibility' [2009] Crim LR 135.

  Explains that the case law shows at least three different approaches taken to the meaning of credibility under **s. 101(1)(d)**, **(e)** *and* **(g)** *and that the judge has a considerable margin of appreciation.*
- Munday, R., 'What Constitutes "Other Reprehensible Behaviour" under the Bad Character Provisions of the Criminal Justice Act 2003' [2005] Crim LR 24.

  Explores the uncertain meaning of 'reprehensible behaviour' in a legal context.
- Redmayne, M., 'Recognising Propensity' [2011] Crim LR 117.

  Given that evidence of propensity is now admissible, the article examines how the concept is understood in the **Criminal Justice Act 2003**.
- Tandy, R., 'The Admissibility of a Defendant's Previous Criminal Record: A Critical Analysis of the Criminal Justice Act 2003' [2009] Crim LR 203.

  Demonstrates how the bad character provisions of the 2003 Act were designed to rebalance the criminal justice system in favour of victims while also maintaining fairness for defendants.

Online Resources

www.oup.com/uk/qanda/

Go online for extra essay and problem questions, a glossary of key terms, online versions of all the answer plans and audio commentary on how selected ones were put together, and a range of podcasts which include advice on exam and coursework technique and advice for other assessment methods.

Hearsay

5

ARE YOU READY?

Preparation for effectively answering the questions in this chapter requires you to have studied:

- the rationale and historical evolution of the rule, giving you an understanding of why it has not been amended rather than abolished and the impact of the **European Convention on Human Rights**
- the effective codification of hearsay in the **Criminal Justice Act 2003**, the application of the inclusionary and exclusionary discretion, and the remaining common law exceptions
- the civil law framework in the **Civil Evidence Act 1972**
- the application of the exceptions to the rule against hearsay to enable frightened witnesses to submit written testimony

 KEY DEBATES

Debate: should the same rules on hearsay apply to defence and prosecution?

The current law applies the same rules of exclusion and exception to both defence and prosecution, and judicial discretion allows for flexibility in the interests of a fair trial. Some academics argue that since the biggest exception to the hearsay rule, confessions, assists the prosecution the defence is disadvantaged. Against this it is asserted that, since there is no constitutional right to confrontation in English law, such a change would be theoretically incoherent.

Debate: is it a breach of Art. 6 to convict where the sole or decisive evidence is hearsay?

Both the Supreme Court and the Strasbourg Court acknowledge that there may be exceptional cases in which a conviction is founded on hearsay evidence alone. There must, however, be strong procedural safeguards including a rigorous assessment of how reliable the evidence is and power-ful reasons for not calling the witness.

Debate: are third party confessions admissible?

The common law position is that third party confessions are not admissible but the exceptions allowed in the **Criminal Justice Act 2003** for admitting oral and written hearsay as well as the inclusionary discretion do allow theoretically for admissibility to be possible. In practice the courts are reluctant to admit such confessions where there is an opportunity to call the witness.

QUESTION | 1

Each question is worth equal marks.

(a) David is charged with murdering his wife Heather. She had been found bound and naked hanging from the garden shed. The prosecution wish to adduce evidence of a text message sent to Heather and recorded by David on his mobile phone two days before Heather's death. 'Thanks for agreeing to pose for me.' David claims Heather's death must have occurred during a sado-masochistic experiment which Heather had frequently indulged in and in which he took no part. He produced a mobile phone photograph on Heather's phone of Heather bound and gagged on an earlier occasion. He claimed she had taken it of herself. However, Heather's sister Jean is willing to testify that Heather had told her that David had persuaded her to pose for the photograph against her will. He had claimed, she said, that he needed it as part of his plan to produce a book on erotic photography.

Advise whether any of the above statements may be held inadmissible because of the operation of the rule against hearsay.

(b) Anna, Freda, and Monisha are charged with robbery from Henfield Building Society (HBS). Tracker dogs were used to trace them. Freda was arrested shortly after the robbery when she was identified in a nearby station by one of the HBS staff who had been at the scene of the robbery. She denies involvement and claims mistaken identity.

At an identification parade held a short time after the robbery, Anna was picked out as one of the robbers by Paul, the manager of the branch. As a result of a concussion later received in a road traffic accident, Paul is now suffering from amnesia and is unable to remember what happened at the identification parade. However, Detective Inspector Daniels was pre-sent at the identification parade and is able to testify that Paul picked out Anna during the parade. Monisha was identified by Edmund, the assistant manager, who recognised her when he viewed the video-recording of Monisha during the robbery. The recording was accidentally deleted by Edmund shortly afterwards.

A few months after the arrest of Anna, Freda, and Monisha, just before she died, Gertrude spoke to her mother and confessed to having been one of the robbers. Her mother, who knows Freda, reports what Gertrude said to the police.

Advise as to the admissibility of the evidence.

CAUTION!

- Note that the answer involves familiarity with the recent case law on implied assertions.
- You must be aware of the distinction between real evidence and hearsay statements.

 DIAGRAM ANSWER PLAN

Identify the issues	■ The legal issues are: (a) is the text message an implied assertion or hearsay; is the photograph real evidence; is the statement by Jean *res gestae*; (b) is the dogs' evidence hearsay; are Edmund's account of the video tape and Gertrude's confession admissible; identification evidence.
Relevant law	■ Definition of hearsay in CJA 2003, s. 115(2) and (3); CJA, s. 129 on photograph as evidence from mechanical device; common law exception for res gestae, CJA, s. 118; (b) CJA definition that only statements of persons may qualify as hearsay; identification evidence as exception to rule against hearsay, CJA, s. 118(1); third party confessions and CJA, ss. 116 and 114.
Apply the law	■ (a) Apply the above provisions to the photograph, Jean's statement, and text message; (b) apply the above provisions to the dogs, Daniels, and Gertrude.
Conclude	■ Assess the likely outcome for each item of evidence in (a) and (b). Consider what would be the effect if hearsay were the 'sole or decisive' evidence.

 SUGGESTED ANSWER

(a) The Photograph

The defence argument is that Heather caused her own death and so the photograph becomes relevant evidence to suggest that her death was consistent with her allegedly previous reckless behaviour. The question arises whether it is admissible as real evidence or is a hearsay statement and thus may be inadmissible. In *R v Maqsud Ali* **[1966] 1 QB 688**, where a tape-recording was admitted in evidence, the Court of Criminal Appeal noted that the courts had long admitted photographs. The photograph here is thus a piece of real evidence and admissible. No statement is being relied on here. In **s. 129 of the Criminal Justice Act (CJA) 2003** the common law presumption that a mechanical device has been properly set or calibrated is maintained.

Jean's statement

The prosecution will want to undermine the defence on this issue by calling Jean to testify what Heather had told her. Statements made by a person concerning his or her contemporaneous state of mind or emotion are admissible as evidence of his or her state of mind or emotion. In *R v Blastland* [1986] AC 41 the House of Lords acknowledged this.[1] The common law rule is preserved in **s. 118 of the CJA 2003**. The prosecution will argue that Heather's state of mind is of immediate relevance since it suggests that David had contrived to get her compromising photograph for his own purposes. In *R v Gilfoyle* [1996] 3 All ER 883 the accused on trial for murdering his wife produced what seemed to be suicide notes written by the wife. It was argued subsequently that the notes were manufactured by the accused. The Court of Appeal held that statements by friends of the wife in which she said the accused had asked her to write the notes as part of his study of suicide, should have been admitted at trial.[2] They had been excluded as hearsay. The conversations with the friends were original evidence of the wife's state of mind in that they increased the likelihood that the 'suicide notes' were not written when she was suicidal. An alternative explanation was that the statements of the wife to the friends were hearsay if tendered to show she was prompted to write the notes by her husband. They were admissible, however, as a *res gestae* exception covering statements about contemporaneous states of mind or emotions. In *Gilfoyle* the *res gestae* exception was stretched to cover evidentiary facts as well as facts in issue.[3] The *res gestae* exception is preserved by **s. 118(1), para. 4(a)**[4] and its continuing importance is shown in *Barnaby v DPP* [2015] 2 Cr App R 4. In that case a woman had named her son as her attacker in a 999 call but refused to sign a police statement. The prosecution did not call her as a witness, being aware that she feared her son. There was no need to apply the **s. 114(2)** safeguards. The court had, however, noted (para. 34) that 'this was not a situation in which the prosecution was seeking to resort to unfair tactics in order to avoid introducing evidence that was potentially inconsistent with the case against the defendant or because it simply anticipated that there was a risk the witness might give an untruthful account'.

An alternative approach is that the statement by Heather may be admissible as oral hearsay under **s. 116(2)(a)**, the reason for the non-appearance of the maker being that she is dead. The common law exception, however, may be preferred since the exclusionary discretion set out in **s. 125(1)** applies to this statutory exception.

[1] The judgment noted 'statements made to a witness by a third party are not excluded by the hearsay rule when they are put in evidence solely to prove the state of mind of the maker of the statement or of the person to whom it was made'.

[2] The court stated (per Beldam LJ at 323) that 'the possibility of invention or unreliability could be discounted and there was little room for inaccuracy in the reporting of the statements'.

[3] Note that the scope of the exception had already been extended in *R v Andrews* [1987] AC 281 in a ruling which had the effect of marginalising the element of contemporaneity which had previously been required.

[4] Glover (2017, p. 370) refers to the continued use of the common law as a 'troubling issue'. He points out that the effect is to undermine the extent to which the **CJA 2003** codifies hearsay.

Mobile phone text

In relation to the mobile phone text the prosecution may succeed in arguing that the messages are implied assertions and not hearsay and therefore admissible as relevant evidence. Presumably they want to suggest that the phrase suggests that David had persuaded Heather to take part in the erotic games which led to her death. This contradicts his defence that she acted alone. The effect of the definition of hearsay in **s. 115(2)** and **(3)** is that implied assertions are not hearsay since a statement is only hearsay if the purpose, or one of the purposes, of the person making the statement appears to the court to have been to 'cause another person to believe the matter'. The appeal in *Singh* **[2006] 1 WLR 1564** turned on whether the prosecution should have been allowed to adduce evidence of entries in the memories of a mobile phone. The inference was that S had taken part in the conspiracy. The court held that the evidence was an implied assertion and not hearsay; see, for example, *R v Leonard* **[2009] EWCA Crim 1251**.[5] More recent cases, although not overruling *Leonard*, have established that text messages of this sort are not hearsay. In *R v Twist* **[2011] EWCA Crim 1143** the Court of Appeal considered four unrelated cases in which text messages were used as non-hearsay evidence. The two questions which had to be addressed in most cases were: (a) what was the matter which it was sought to prove and (b) did the maker of the communication have the purpose of causing the recipient to believe or to act upon that matter? To say that a communication was evidence of a fact (i.e. tended to prove it) was not the same as saying that the fact was the matter stated in the communication for the purposes.[6] In *R v Midmore* **(2017)** a Whats App message was admissible as an implied representation of intention falling within **s. 115(2)**. On this reasoning David's text message is not making a statement of fact which is directed at causing another person to believe the matter and so may be admissible as non-hearsay so as it is arguably relevant it is admissible as non-hearsay.

(b) Tracker Dogs

The tracker dogs will have picked up the scent of the robbers and presumably their barking led to Freda being discovered. *R v Pieterson* **[1995] 1 WLR 293** established that an account of the behaviour of tracker dogs will be admissible provided there is evidence of its reliability, which doubtless those handling the dogs could give.[7] In addition, the prosecution will point out that the CJA statutory scheme for hearsay refers to statements by 'persons' only.

Identification

Detective Inspector Daniels may be able to testify that he saw Paul identify Anna as one of the robbers during the identification parade.

---

[5] You could elaborate on the incoherence of the law in this area. In *R v Leonard* [2009] EWCA Crim 1251, phone text evidence was held to be hearsay and admissible under **s. 114(1)(d)** of the CJA 2003. *Singh* was distinguished.

[6] See also *R v Mateza* [2011] EWCA Crim 2587 where the court held (at para. 22) that '*Twist* sets out all the relevant considerations and the correct approach'.

[7] The court referred to the need for safeguards including detailed evidence establishing the reliability of the dog in question. Secondly, the judge must, in giving his directions to the jury, alert them to the care that they need to take having regard to the fact that the dog may not always be reliable and cannot be cross-examined.

Prima facie, it could be argued that this would infringe the rule against hearsay. In *R v Osbourne; R v Virtue* [1973] QB 678, a witness could not recall what happened at an identification parade held some seven-and-a-half months earlier. A police officer who was present at the identification parade was permitted to testify that the witness picked out the accused. The Court of Appeal was of the view that the evidence was admissible as it sought to prove the fact of identification at the identification parade. The court did not deal satisfactorily with the point that the testimony of the police officer may be hearsay. If, which is likely, the details of the video identification parade had been recorded, the position may be covered by **s. 117 of the CJA 2003**. This preserves the common law provision in **s. 118, para. 4(b)**, namely that the statement was *a res gestae* one accompanying an act.[8] This is the principle applied in *R v McCay* [1990] 1 WLR 645.

[8] Glover (2017, p. 370) suggests that such a statement may also be admissible under s. 120(4) of the CJA 2003.

Video-recording

As regards the evidence of Edmund who identified Monisha from the video-recording, it is clear that the video tape itself, if it was still available, would be admissible in evidence as original evidence: *Kajala v Noble* (1982) 75 Cr App R 149 and *R v Dodson* (1984) 79 Cr App R 220. However, in this case, the video-recording has been accidentally erased. In *Taylor v Chief Constable of Cheshire* [1986] 1 WLR 1479, a video-recording which was alleged to show the accused in the act of committing the offence was erased before the trial. The court decided that it was proper for the police officers who had seen the recording to give oral evidence of the contents of the tape. Thus, it would appear that on the facts of the case, Edmund could give evidence of what he saw on the tape.

Gertrude's admission

The final issue that has to be considered is whether the admission by Gertrude is admissible into evidence. Her statement should be disclosed to the defence. Since she is unable to give evidence in court, her statement to her mother is clearly hearsay if adduced to suggest it is true. However, it could be argued that this evidence has probative value in that it may cast doubts on the prosecution's case that it was the defendants who committed the robbery. In *R v Blastland* [1986] AC 41, the House of Lords held that a confession by a third party that he committed the crime with which the accused was being tried, would be inadmissible because it was irrelevant evidence of a third party's state of mind. The statement here fulfils the definition of hearsay in **ss. 114(1), 115(2),** and **121(2)**. On the assumption that Gertrude's confession is inadmissible because of the hearsay rule, the next question is whether it now could be admitted under one of the statutory exceptions to the hearsay rule.

One possible route to admissibility is under **s. 116 of the CJA 2003**. This admits first-hand oral hearsay if there is a reason for not calling the witness. One of the possible reasons is that the witness is dead (**s. 116(2)(a)**). This would apply in the case of Gertrude. Finally, this statement may be admissible under the 'interests of justice' inclusionary discretion in **s. 114.**[9] Arguments against admissibility, however, are that the courts are reluctant to admit evidence from absent witnesses, see *R v Finch* **[2007] 1 WLR 1645.** In that case a statement by a former accused who had pleaded guilty was not admissible as exculpatory evidence for the defendant.[10] By contrast, in *R v Y* **[2008] 2 All ER 484** the statement by a third party inculpating the defendant was admissible under **s. 114(1)(d).** The leading case on absent witnesses is *R v Riat* **[2013] 1WLR 2592.** This was applied in *R v Drinkwater* **[2016] EWCA Crim 16.** Before his death, a third party had first confessed and then retracted his confession concerning one of the rapes for which D was convicted. The court, observing (at para. 38) that *Riat* provided 'highly persuasive guidance' and held that the evidence the defence wanted to adduce lacked probative value.

[9] Note should also be taken of the procedural requirements for the admissibility of hearsay in the Criminal Procedure Rules 2015.

[10] However, this case presents different facts than those in the problem since the witness was alive but unwilling.

Conclusion

(a) It is likely that the photograph, the text, and Jean's statement will be admissible.

(b) It is likely that the tracker dogs' barks, the video tape, and the identification evidence will be admitted. The authorities conflict on Gertrude's confession but in view of the fact that she is not able to appear as a witness the court will probably admit it.

LOOKING FOR EXTRA MARKS?

- You would gain credit by showing knowledge of the conflicting recent cases on text messages and implied assertions by referring to *R v Lam Hai Vo [2013]* **EWCA Crim 2292** where the court, without referring to *Twist*, held the statement to be hearsay.

- You might add a point in the Conclusion that if, which seems unlikely on the facts, hearsay is the only or decisive prosecution evidence, that would not be a bar to conviction see *R v Horncastle* **[2009] UKSC 14.**

QUESTION | 2

Rather than rely on precisely defined and technically complex, and at the same time, legally inconclusive exceptions, trial judges should have the power to admit hearsay whenever it is of sufficient probative value.

(Zuckerman, *The Principles of Criminal Evidence* (Oxford: OUP, 1989), p. 216)

Discuss in relation to criminal trials.

CAUTION!

- Do not attempt this question unless you have read some of the academic commentary on reform of the hearsay rule.

- This is a very wide topic. Make sure you do not simply give a narrative account of the inadequacies of the current law but structure your answer to argue the case for and against abolition of the rule against hearsay.

DIAGRAM ANSWER PLAN

> Introduction: why has the rule survived, what is the current regime on criminal hearsay?

> Arguments for maintaining the rule: assess the fairness and coherence of the CJA statutory framework which is based on maintaining the rule, increasing the exceptions, and introducing an inclusionary discretion

> Arguments for abolition: assess the weaknesses of the current law particularly in terms of undermining rights of defendants.

> Conclusion: assess whether reform is needed.

SUGGESTED ANSWER

Introduction: Why Has the Rule Against Hearsay Survived For so Long?

[1] It is good practice to address the specific question set in your first few sentences.

[2] Lord Bridge in *R v Blastland* [1986] AC 41, states that 'The danger against which this fundamental rule provides a safeguard is that untested hearsay evidence will be treated as having a probative force which it does not deserve.'

In order to assess whether the hearsay rule should survive it is necessary first to appreciate why it has shown such powers of survival.[1] The current position is that the rule is preserved in the codifying **Criminal Justice Act (CJA) 2003** but with an increased number of statutory exceptions and with an extended inclusionary and exclusionary discretion. There are a number of reasons for the retention of the exclusionary rule on hearsay. First, it has been argued that the person who made the statement may have wrongly perceived the events in question. Secondly, there is a risk that because of the fallibility of human nature, the memory of the person who heard the statement may be flawed. Thirdly, there is a risk of concoction or distortion of the events in question. Finally, the statement may have been misunderstood by the person who witnessed it and this may not be tested in questioning the witness in court. Zuckerman (1989, p. 178) acknowledges that the limitation on cross-examining the witness is the central reason for the exclusion of hearsay statements.[2]

Because it is clear that a risk exists that hearsay statements are unreliable on grounds of concoction, distortion, or fallibility, the extent to which the hearsay rule applied historically was much wider than is necessary. The rigidity of the rule which concentrated on the form rather than the quality of the evidence meant that, along with weak evidence, material evidence which was credible, reliable, and of probative value was excluded if it did not fall strictly within one of the exceptions.[3]

The Law Commission had recognised the case for reform but the approach taken in their 1997 Report was to preserve the rule but extend the range of exceptions alongside both an inclusionary and exclusionary discretion. This framework was based on erosion rather than abolition.

In Favour of Retention: (i) Preserving the Right to Confrontation

As the American academic Friedman (1998, p. 697) points out 'lurking within the rule against hearsay and often shrouded by its many excesses and oddities is a principle of magnificent importance, ... that a person may not offer testimony against a criminal defendant unless it is given under oath face to face with the accused and subject to cross-examination.' This principled argument in favour of the rule against hearsay is reflected, for example, in *R v Warnick* **[2013] EWCA Crim 2320** where the Court of Appeal held that the Crown should not have been allowed to tender evidence under **s. 114(1)(d)**.

In Favour of Retention: (ii) Law is Art. 6 Compliant

Secondly, it could be argued that the hearsay rule is recognised by the European Court of Human Rights; see, for example, *Trivedi v UK* **[1997] EHRLR 520**, as compatible with the Convention.[4] Thus **Art. 6(3)(a)** does not provide a defendant with an absolute right to examine every witness whose testimony was used against him. *Seton v UK* **[2016] ECHR 318** concerned the admissibility of evidence under **s. 114 (1)(d)**. The Court held that although there was not a good reason for non-attendance, there was no breach of **Art. 6(3)** in view of the strength of the other prosecution evidence.

In Favour of Retention: (iii) Statutory Provisions now Based More on Relevance and Common Sense

One almost universally welcomed recommendation of the Law Commission was that the decision in *R v Kearley* **[1992] 2 AC 228** would be reversed and more relevant evidence may be admissible. The definition of hearsay now specifies that implied assertions are not hearsay: see **s. 115(2)** and **(3)**. Similarly the admissibility of hearsay statements is extended by increasing the oral and written exceptions and the use of the inclusionary discretion. Emson has welcomed this.

[3] One example was that of *Myers v DPP* [1965] AC 1001 where credible evidence was held to be inadmissible because of the hearsay rule.

[4] In *Doorson v The Netherlands* (1990) 22 EHRR 330 the proceedings as a whole were fair although frightened witnesses gave evidence in a pre-trial hearing.

He (2010, p. 123) comments, 'If the judge is of the view that the evidence is relevant and ought to be admitted, he will be able to rule that the exclusionary rule does not apply, by virtue of **s. 115(3)** of the Act …'.[5]

In Favour of Retention: (iv) Pro-Prosecution Bias of Judiciary

The retention of the exclusionary rule might also be applauded in that abolition would extend the scope of judicial discretion which, some argue, is overly pro-prosecution. Munday (2017, p. 409) points out that 'what emerges in the reported case law is that **s. 114(1)(d)** appears to afford assistance to the prosecution more frequently than it does to the defence, and that the Court of Appeal shows itself ready to employ this provision as a second line of argument, buttressing rulings of which it is not otherwise entirely confident'. He cites as an example *R v Singh* [2006] 1 WLR 1564 at para. 15. From the defence point of view, further erosion of the rule might give more scope for judicial prosecutorial bias. Perhaps a rule against hearsay is safer.

In Favour of Retention: (v) Clear Rule-Based Procedure

Similarly, a rule-based framework provides a clearer structure within which the court exercises its discretion in regulating the cases where a conviction could be founded on hearsay alone. The dialogue between the Supreme Court and the European Court of Human Rights arising from *R v Horncastle* [2009] UKSC 14 where hearsay was the 'sole or decisive' evidence shows the wisdom of retaining the rule in that it provides a clearer test for reflecting on the ingredients of a fair trial; see, for example, *R v Riat* [2013] 1 WLR 2592.[6] Ormerod (2016, p. 649) in his commentary on *Drinkwater* (2016) argued that *Riat*, which was applied in that case, 'provides a practical framework for practitioners dealing with a complex and technical statute on a difficult topic'. As Dennis [2012] Crim LR 375 points out, where a conviction is based on hearsay evidence solely or decisively, the court 'must subject the proceedings to the most searching scrutiny'. The eventual rapprochement between the English and Strasbourg approaches suggests that the current hearsay framework now ensures the fairness and reliability that Zuckerman called for. Perhaps total abolition is not therefore needed.

In Favour of Abolition: (i) Quality not Form

There are thus a number of convincing arguments to support the view that the CJA framework is the best of all possible hearsay worlds. This has achieved the legitimisation of the inclusionary principle that trial judges have the power to admit hearsay evidence which is of probative value. However, there is also a powerful case for abolition of the rule altogether. Jackson (1998, p. 187) had concluded that 'there are no functional reasons why the hearsay rule is needed in criminal proceedings any more than in civil proceedings'.[7] He stressed that in deciding admissibility 'the key issue is whether the police have discharged fair and accurate standards during the course of their investigation … rather than the technical question of whether out of court statements fall within the scope of the hearsay rule'. Has this obsession with form survived the **CJA 2003** reforms? Ormerod (2009, p. 802) in an assessment of *R v Leonard* **[2009] EWCA Crim 1251** noted that the Court of Appeal appeared to have been more concerned with analysing the form of the evidence than its reliability. Many argue that the current position still privileges form over content.

The difficulty of identifying implied assertions, as in *Leonard*, and the often contradictory decisions of the courts in this area, as in *R v Bucknor* **[2010] EWCA Crim 1152**, illustrates the problems and confusion of an overly technical analysis of the evidence.[8] Other examples of the difficulty of definitions are the 'state of mind cases' where authorities have not agreed on whether evidence of state of mind or emotion is admissible as non-hearsay or as an exception to the rule against hearsay.[9]

A major criticism of the rule was that in order not to exclude potentially reliable and credible evidence, the courts have over the years used numerous devices in order to avoid excluding the evidence on the basis of hearsay. Evasions of the rule have been described by Birch as 'hearsay fiddles' (1987). Ormerod's (2011, p. 399) criticisms of the decision in *R v Thakrar* **[2010] EWCA Crim 1505** suggest that some contortions still prevail.[10]

In Favour of Abolition: (ii) Difficulty of Maintaining Defendants' Rights

Another argument of the abolitionists is that the framing of hearsay exceptions in the statute is based on social policy considerations, such as the need to protect victims, rather than the preservation of fair trial rights. For example, **s. 116** allows oral first-hand hearsay by extending the 'fear' exception to witnesses who are unavailable through fear of 'financial loss'. This section will generally help the prosecution. By contrast, the defence is less well served. A criticism of the rule as it evolved historically was that it excluded evidence which may prove the innocence of the accused.[11]

The biggest exception to the rule against hearsay—confessions—is clearly pro-prosecution but third party confessions which may help the defence may not be excluded although **s. 114** and **s. 116** provide a possible route. In *R v Finch* **[2007] 1 WLR 1645** evidence exonerating the defendant was held not admissible although in *R v Amin* **[2014] EWCA Civ 1924** inculpatory statements by a third party and tendered by the Crown were admitted. At best the law as it stands creates uncertainty of outcome. Similarly the continuation of the common law exceptions, such as *res gestae*, tends to undermine the intent of the **CJA** effectively to codify the law, see *Barnaby v DPP* (2015).

[8] Glover (2017, p. 316) suggests that in the light of *Twist* (text message admissible as implied assertion), *Bucknor* must be a wrong decision. The court held that the YouTube 'gangster film' was hearsay.

[9] In *Gilfoyle*, the state of mind exception was extended to cover proof of facts which exist independently of the maker's state of mind.

[10] He points out, for example, that in admitting D1's statement which incriminated D2 the court did not address the common law rule that D1's confession is not evidence against D2.

[11] See *Sparks v R* [1964] 1 All ER 727.

Conclusion: Neither the Status Quo nor Abolition

The above review suggests that the possible exclusion of defence evidence is a drawback of the current hearsay framework. Academic opinion on the matter presents no unanimous way forward. Choo (2018, p. 288) suggests an alternative approach, neither the status quo nor total abolition. He would maintain the rule but instead of recognising specific exceptions along with an interests of justice inclusionary discretion, simply recognise that as the only exception. At the same time (p. 294), prosecution pre-trial procedures should be reformed. Birch (2004, p. 572) concludes that the rule will survive for some time. But she points out that 'An inclusionary discretion is now an inevitable feature of a statutory package built on the concept of exclusionary rule plus fixed exceptions.' She stresses the importance of the 'safety valve': 'If we did not have a safety valve, the judges would have to invent one, if only by dint of the process of "reading down" under the **Human Rights Act 1998** in order to admit crucial defence evidence.' Arguably then Zuckerman's 1989 recommendation of a power to include hearsay evidence which is sufficiently probative, should be the distinguishing feature of a fair state of the ancient rule.

QUESTION | 3

Tom is charged with sexually assaulting Harriet at a residential university summer school. He denies the charge and claims that Harriet made it up because he had spurned her advances. Tom claims that in fact he was away from the summer school on the day in question on a bicycle trip. However, the computer records which list the bicycle hires contain no listing of his name and no one else can substantiate his alibi. Jane, the school bursar, had retained a record of the incident, based on information from Carol, a gardener at the school. She claims to have seen a couple she identified as Tom and Harriet struggling in the grounds. They had not seen her and she did not intervene but saw Harriet run off with her clothes dishevelled. Having thought about the incident later that day, Carol sent a text about the incident to Jane. Jane, considering that this might lead to internal disciplinary proceedings and possibly a criminal investigation, sent an email of the contents of the text to her manager, John. Carol is now working in Australia and has not been traced. John and Jane are still employed by the university.

Advise on the admissibility of the computer bicycle hiring records, Carol's text to Jane, and of Jane's text to John.

CAUTION!

▨ Note that the question involves first-hand and multiple hearsay and oral and written hearsay.

▨ The answer involves knowledge of the meaning of negative hearsay.

DIAGRAM ANSWER PLAN

Identify the issues	▦ Are the statements made by Jane and Carol admissible hearsay; is absence of entry in the bicycle hirings log admissible?
Relevant law	▦ CJA 2003, ss. 114, 115, and 117. Article 6(2) and cross-examination. *R v Horncastle* and ECHR jurisprudence.
Apply the law	▦ Admission of Carol's statement may create unfairness for Tom.
Conclude	▦ Assess whether identification evidence and absence of bicycle hire log are admissible and if the prosecution should proceed if sole evidence is hearsay.

SUGGESTED ANSWER

Carol's Evidence

The rule against hearsay provides that an assertion other than one made by a person while giving oral evidence in the proceedings is inadmissible as evidence of any fact charged (see **ss. 114, 115,** and **121 of the Criminal Justice Act (CJA) 2003**). Carol could give direct oral evidence of what she had seen and this would clearly be relevant to the facts in issue since Tom's defence is alibi and fabrication. Since she is not available, the only evidence of this is what she has told Jane which was recorded both in a text and an email.[1] Both of these appear to fulfil the definition of hearsay in that the purpose of the person making the statement (Carol) was to cause another person to believe the matter; that is, that Harriet was being assaulted by a person Carol identified as Tom.

The question then arises as to whether the evidence is admissible by virtue of the exceptions for documentary hearsay under the **CJA 2003**. Carol's statement may be admissible under **ss. 117** and **121**. Under **s. 117** in criminal proceedings a statement contained in a document is admissible as evidence of any matter stated if oral evidence given in the proceedings would be admissible as evidence of that matter and the requirements of **subs. (2)** are satisfied. **Subsection (2)** is satisfied if the document was created or received by a person

[1] The definition of a document in s. 134 of the CJA 2003 'means anything in which information of any description is recorded' so it includes text messages and the emails.

in the course of a trade, business, profession, or other occupation, the person who supplied the information (the relevant person) had or may reasonably be supposed to have had personal knowledge of the matters dealt with, and each person (if any) through whom the information was supplied from the relevant person to the person mentioned in **subs(2)(a)** received the information in the course of a trade, business, profession, or other occupation. The creator of the document may be the person who supplied the information.

Carol was acting in the course of a trade and also might reasonably be expected to have had personal knowledge of the matters dealt with.

The general common law rule is that a party who wishes to tender evidence must prove any necessary preconditions by admissible evidence. Proof must be to the appropriate standard, namely proof beyond reasonable doubt in the case of the prosecution and proof on the balance of probability in the case of the defence. Some forms of documentary hearsay are admissible as an exception to the general hearsay rule. Jane's emailed note of what Carol told her is likely to be treated as a statement in a document.

The series of statements constitutes multiple hearsay in different forms, namely text and email. Here the creator of the original document is Jane. It so happens that Carol satisfies two criteria in that she is the supplier of the information with, she claims, some first-hand knowledge of the circumstances of the alleged incident involving Harriet and Tom. She is also as an employee acting in the course of trade etc. although it could be argued that the information she gathered did not fall within her responsibilities as a gardener. Her evidence might support any identification of Tom made by Harriet (see **Chapter 7**).

Whether or not the email is admissible, then, depends on Carol's and Jane's status. Carol's evidence is identification evidence and she is not available to be cross-examined, factors which constitute two arguments the defence could put forward to object to the text and email. On the other hand, the prosecution can argue that **s. 117 of the CJA 2003** may be satisfied and that there is supporting evidence in the non-entry of Tom's name in the bicycle records. Carol had personal knowledge of the facts as she perceived them. Jane received the text in the course of her occupation as bursar.[2] John received the email as part of his occupation as Jane's manager.

It is also necessary to consider the purpose for which the text and email was made. A statement prepared for the purposes of criminal proceedings or investigation, for example a witness statement, is not admissible under **s. 117** unless either one of the reasons for non-appearance of the witness in **s. 116** is met, or the maker of the statement (the 'relevant person') cannot reasonably be expected to have any recollection of the matters dealt with having regard to the time

[2] Note the implications for the admissibility of hearsay evidence originating from an absent witness of *R v Adeojo* [2013] EWCA Crim 2398 concerned a witness who did not give evidence through fear and the court stressed that there should be safeguards and counterbalancing measures where the witness could not be cross-examined.

which has elapsed and all the circumstances. The maker here is Carol. In *R v Bedi* **(1991) 95 Cr App R 21** the prosecution had been allowed to adduce evidence of bank reports concerning lost and stolen credit cards.[3] The judge had not considered as he should have done the purpose for which the reports were prepared. Here, the Court of Appeal held they were business documents which had not been made in connection with criminal proceedings **(s. 117(4))** and the judge, if he had considered the question, would have taken that view. This was a matter of fact to be determined by the judge in the light of the surrounding circumstances.

On the facts, it does appear possible that Jane made the statement with possible criminal proceedings in mind; however, in interpreting this section Munday (2017, p. 371) points out that 'most commonly, the provision contemplates statements that witnesses have made to the police'. We are told that internal disciplinary reasons were also the impetus.[4]

Credibility

Section 124 of the Act enables the opposing party to test the credibility of the absent 'maker' of the statement. The purpose is to put the absent maker in as close a position as possible to a witness who testifies in person. Thus, for instance, with leave of the court the other side may call evidence that could have been put to the 'maker' in cross-examination as relevant to his credibility, as if he had given oral evidence.

The party seeking to rely on **s. 117 of the CJA 2003** must satisfy the court that the requirements of the section have been met. Here it is the prosecution which wishes to use the statement and the criminal standard of proof will apply (see *R v Case* **[1991] Crim LR 192**). The judge must generally hear oral evidence in a voir dire. The court has a discretion to exclude the statement even if it is technically admissible under **ss. 117(7), 125, and 126(1) of the CJA 2003** and **s. 78 of the Police and Criminal Evidence Act 1984 (PACE)** and at common law.

Under **s. 117(6) and (7)** the court has power to exclude otherwise admissible business and other documents.

All possible effort should be made to find Carol. If, however, Carol will not be available to be cross-examined on the identification, which is a fact in issue, it may be argued this would create unfairness to Tom. **Section 120** is not available to the prosecution because this only applies to prior statements of witnesses who are called to testify.[5]

The defence may try to argue that particular care must be taken since the statement involves evidence of identification. It will not necessarily be excluded, however. Much depends on the strength of the evidence. Thus, in *R v Setz-Dempsey and Richardson* **(1994) 98 Cr App R 23** the Court of Appeal held that statements ought not to have been admitted since medical evidence undermined the quality of the evidence and the evidence of identification might have been further undermined by cross-examination.[6] Much will depend here then on whether the

[3] This case is still authority for documentary hearsay since it was decided under a statutory provision (CJA 1988, s. 24) which was the precursor to the 2003 Act.

[4] Carol's absence probably is one of the acceptable reasons for non-appearance, following the Court of Appeal in *R v French and Gowhar* (1993) 97 Cr App R 421. In this regard, in examining whether it was 'not reasonably practicable' to secure the attendance of Carol the court will question whether the prosecution have done their best to produce her as a witness.

[5] This refers to previous consistent statements.

[6] However, in *R v Greer* [1998] Crim LR 572 the evidence was admissible. It was held that the fact that there was other live identification evidence was not a reason for preventing the absent witness's evidence of identification from being read.

court is convinced that the defence is disadvantaged on the facts from being denied the opportunity to cross-examine Carol. It may be possible to take her evidence on commission. Thus in *R v Radak* [1999] 1 Cr App R 187, where the prosecution failed to do this, it was held that the statement should have been excluded under s. 26 of the CJA 1988.

Article 6

The defence will also argue that the court will have to take into account the provisions of **Art. 6 of the European Convention on Human Rights** following the implementation of the **Human Rights Act 1998.** Article 6(3)(d) of the Convention states that a person charged with a criminal offence has the right 'to examine or have examined the witnesses against him and to obtain the attendance and examination of witnesses on his behalf under the same conditions as witnesses against him'.[7] However, the prosecution will be helped by recent case law. In *R v Horncastle* [2009] UKSC 14 the Supreme Court held that hearsay alone could found a conviction, and this was accepted by the Grand Chamber in *Al-Khawaja and Tahery v UK* (2011) 54 EHRR 23 but with strict safeguards, see *R v Riat* [2012] EWCA Crim 1509. Thus in considering whether Carol's statement is admissible much will depend on the strength of the other evidence, particularly the testimony from Harriet and the strength of her identification of the alleged assailant. Harriet's defence of fabrication is undermined by Carol's evidence.

Computerised Bicycle Records

The prosecution may wish to show the computer printout from the bicycle hirings to suggest that Tom's alibi is false. The first issue is whether it is hearsay. There was a historic conflict of authority on whether absence of a record constituted hearsay but recent case law will help the prosecution here. The prosecution will want to adduce this evidence and may succeed in arguing that it is non-hearsay since it is not an express statement. They could rely on a decision which Glover (2017, p. 317) says 'is to be welcomed'. In *DPP v Leigh* [2010] EWHC 345 (Admin) the absence of a record was held to be non-hearsay in accordance with s. 115 (2) and (3).[8]

The 'non-statement' here is in documentary form generated by a computer but it seems there is an absence of human input for that day. Under s. 129 where a representation of any fact is made otherwise than by a person but depends for such accuracy on information supplied (directly or indirectly) by a person, the representation is not admissible in criminal proceedings as evidence of the fact unless it is proved that the information was accurate.

[7] It is good practice to refer to the Art. 6 right to 'examine and have examined' but note that this does not give a 'right to confrontation'.

[8] The defendant's failure to provide evidence of the identity of the driver of his vehicle was held to be the absence of a record.

Conclusion

The computer hiring records are likely to be admissible as non-hearsay, the text may also be admissible under **s. 117 of the CJA 2003** but here there has to be a reason for not calling Carol, if **s. 117(4)** applies.

LOOKING FOR EXTRA MARKS?

- Analyse the evolution of the courts' stance on 'negative hearsay'; see *R v Patel* [1981] **3 All ER 94**, and *R v Shone* (1982) **76 Cr App R 72**. Even though *Leigh* has resolved the inconsistency to some extent, Glover (2017, p. 317) points out that some problems remain. To give one example, absence of a record may be deliberate.

- It is relevant to develop your analysis that the hearsay provisions do not violate fair trial rights. The issue was decided under the earlier law. In *Trivedi v UK* [1997] **EHRLR 520** the Commission decided that the provisions of **ss. 23–26** of the 1988 Act were not contrary to **Art. 6**. In *Gokal* [1997] **2 Cr App R 266** the Court of Appeal considered that the rights of defendants under this statute were safeguarded by **s. 26**.

QUESTION | 4

Henry is charged with causing grievous bodily harm to James. The prosecution case is that he attacked James with a knife after a row in a public house. James has been disfigured as a result of the wounding. Henry denies the attack, claiming he was elsewhere at the time and that he has never met James. James was taken to hospital by ambulance. As he travelled there he gave an account of the incident to PC Green. PC Green read it back to James and he nodded his agreement, not being able to sign because of the drips in his arm. After an operation he has not regained consciousness.

Tom and Gerry were eyewitnesses to the incident and both made statements to the police which they subsequently signed. However, Tom has told the police he is too afraid to tell the court about what he saw and Gerry's mother has told police he also is too scared to give evidence. Henry's alibi is that he was having dinner in his club with Freda, a Brazilian student, at the time of the attack. Freda subsequently wrote a letter to Henry thanking him for the dinner. Freda has now returned to Brazil. Henry also wants to submit in evidence a note he found on his car in the car park of the club when he left after the dinner. The note gave the number of a car whose driver had allegedly damaged Henry's wing mirror. Henry passed the note to the police in reporting the accident. He alleges this note is relevant to confirm his alibi.

Advise on evidence.

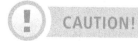

CAUTION!

- It is not enough simply to summarise the relevant sections of the **CJA 2003**. In this question you need also to be aware of how the courts have interpreted these somewhat overlapping provisions and how their requirements can be proved.

- You need to be familiar with case law on what is meant by 'fear' originally found in **s. 23(3) of the CJA 1988**, now included in **s. 116 of the CJA 2003**. Note that this question is an illustration of how evidential issues are closely related to procedural ones.

- Note that the question involves first-hand and multiple hearsay and oral and written hearsay.

DIAGRAM ANSWER PLAN

Identify the issues	■ The legal issues are: are out-of-court oral or written statements, first-hand and multiple, admissible if witnesses are unavailable; what are acceptable reasons for unavailability?
Relevant law	■ CJA 2003, ss. 116–126; difference between 'business' and other hearsay; case law on acceptable reasons for non-appearance of witness.
Apply the law	■ Section 116 may apply to the statements from James, Tom, Gerry, and Freda; s. 117 may apply to the note on the car; possibility of inclusionary discretion, s. 114.
Conclude	■ Advise on evidence.

SUGGESTED ANSWER

James

James makes a statement to a police officer but is not available as a witness at the trial because he is unconscious. **Section 116 of the Criminal Justice Act (CJA) 2003** provides that a statement by a person is admissible in criminal proceedings as evidence of any fact of which direct oral evidence would be admissible. Thus 'first-hand' hearsay evidence is admissible provided certain conditions are met (see **R v Kamuhuza [2008] EWCA Crim 3060**).

The maker of the statement must be unable to attend court as a witness for one of the reasons set out in **s. 116(2)**.[1]

[1] Note that in *R v Kamuhuza* [2008] EWCA Crim 3060 the court stated that first-hand documentary statements made to the police could in principle be admissible under **s. 116** if there is a statutory reason for not calling the witness.

Here, **s. 116(2)(b) of the CJA 2003** will apply, since the witness is unfit to attend. Further conditions are that the statement must be first-hand hearsay and the person making it would be a competent witness. Thus, Green can testify about what James said to him.

'Fear' Exception

With regard to Tom, the prosecution may seek to rely on **s. 116(2)(e)** that he does not give evidence through fear. **Section 116(3)** provides that 'fear' is to be 'widely construed' in line with the statute's objective of addressing the problem of witness intimidation.[2] The prosecution may cite the pre-2003 case *R v Martin* **[1996] Crim LR 589** for the proposition that the fear does not have to be reasonable or be causally linked with the offence charged. Protection for the defendant is provided now by **s. 116(4)** which applies an 'interests of justice' test; see *R v Doherty* **[2006] EWCA Crim 2716**. In *R v Boulton* **[2007] EWCA Crim 942** the Court of Appeal considered the sort of evidence required to establish fear. The facts of the offence, although not sufficient reasons, could constitute the conditions in which to evaluate the evidence. It was not relevant that fear was not the only reason for not testifying if fear was a significant ingredient. The court under **s. 116(4)** has to give leave to allow such a statement.[3] It may be difficult to prove that a witness who is not present in court is fearful.

[2] The earlier provision in the **CJA 1988** had been directed at meeting the problem of witness intimidation.

[3] **Section 116(4)** provides that the admission of the statement must be considered by the court to be 'in the interests of justice'.

If the witness attends, the fear may be visible (*R v Ashford and Tenterden Justices, ex p Hilden* **(1992) 96 Cr App R 93** and *R v James Greer* **[1998] Crim LR 572**). In *Neill v North Antrim Magistrates' Court* **(1993) 97 Cr App R 121** there was an inadmissible third-hand hearsay statement.

A problem may arise if the jury asks why a witness was not called.[4] In *R v Churchill* **[1993] Crim LR 285**, where the judge told the jury he had decided circumstances applied in which a crucial witness who claimed to be in fear need not give evidence, the Court of Appeal said the judge should have discussed with counsel how to handle the question. The judge's 'explanation had amounted to something in the nature of a pat on the back for a witness whose testimony had been disputed but had not been tested in cross-examination'. The jury might wrongly have inferred that the failure to testify could be a matter to the discredit of the accused. In the circumstances the judge should simply have said he could not answer the question. In *Neill v North Antrim Magistrates' Court* **[1992] 1 WLR 1220**, a case arising under a similar Northern Ireland provision, namely **art. 3(3)(b) of the Criminal Justice (Evidence, etc.) Northern Ireland Order 1988**, the House of Lords held that the fact that a witness was absent

[4] The judge decides the issue of whether the witness is in fear in a voir dire.

through fear had to be proved by admissible evidence. There, the evidence of the police officer as to what he had been told by the mother of the two youths about their apprehensions had been hearsay and could not be admitted under the exception to the hearsay rule that enabled the court to receive first-degree hearsay as to state of mind.[5]

Accordingly, the statements of the youths in that case should not have been admitted in evidence. *R v O'Loughlin* [1988] 3 All ER 431 was applied. The court held (obiter) that a statement by a witness who is afraid of appearing through fear would be admissible as a *res gestae* statement of present state of mind, the common law exception. Thus, the police officer may here give evidence of what Tom said directly to him but not what Gerry's mother told him, in explaining to the court why the witnesses will not give evidence. We are not told the reasons for Tom's fear. In *R v Sellick* [2005] 1 WLR 3257 the Court of Appeal held that a defendant's rights under **Art. 6(3)(d)** of the Convention could not be infringed where he kept a witness away from a trial through fear as he was the author of his own inability to examine the witness and deprived himself of his only opportunity to do so. This principle is now enshrined in **s. 117(5)**.[6]

Freda's Letter

The defence will want to adduce Freda's statement in order to give the defendant an alibi. Her letter to Henry is first-hand documentary hearsay and may be admissible under **s. 116(2)(c)**. An earlier authority under the **CJA 1988** may be cited. In *R v Case* [1991] **Crim LR 192** the trial judge had admitted witness statements by two Portuguese tourists, including the victim. The Court of Appeal held that they had been wrongly admitted because the court should have been presented with evidence on non-availability other than the contents of their statements. Thus, the defence may be required to produce additional evidence that Freda cannot attend. The court may take account of the costs of Freda's travel in deciding what is reasonably practicable. In *R v Gonzales* [1992] **Crim LR 180**, the Court of Appeal held that the trial judge had been wrong in concluding that it was not reasonably practicable to secure the attendance of two booking clerks from Bogota. Further steps could have been taken, such as offering to pay their fares. In *R v Gyima* [2007] **EWCA Crim 429** the Court of Appeal considered whether the prosecution should have employed a video link at the trial to enable a child witness to give evidence live from America. One of the factors was the expense. The court found 'the prosecution had proved that they had taken all reasonable steps to secure the witness' attendance'.

The prosecution in objecting to the admissibility of Freda's statement may cite *R v CT* [2011] **EWCA Crim 2341**. In that case the appeal against conviction was allowed since the prosecution's attempts to locate a complainant had fallen well below what was considered reasonable. Arguably, however, the court will be reluctant to exclude defence evidence.[7]

[7] Note, however, that the rule against hearsay applies equally to both parties.

Note Passed to Police

The question is raised whether the note left on Henry's car which he wants to submit to confirm his whereabouts is admissible. In *Maher v DPP* [2006] EWHC 1271 (Admin) a bystander left a note for the driver of an allegedly damaged car, and he passed it to the police, whose record was admitted at trial.[8] This was a case of multiple hearsay, only admissible under s. 121(1)(a) if s. 117, 119, or 120 were fulfilled. Section 117 was not fulfilled since neither the supplier of the information nor the first intermediary were acting under a duty. Here neither the writer of the note nor Henry are acting under a duty. The only routes to admissibility are s. 121(1)(b), if the parties agree, or s. 121(1)(c) 'the court is satisfied that the value of the evidence in question, taking into account how reliable the statement appears to be, is so high that the interests of justice require the later statement to be admissible for that purpose'. Section 114(1)(d) should also be considered. The defence might still find support in the decision in *Maher*, however, where it was held that since the trial judge did not express any concerns about the statement's reliability under s. 117, the statement could be considered to be properly admitted.

[8] Section 117 did not apply since there had been a breach in the chain in passing the information in the course of business, trade, etc.

For all of these statements, even if these preliminary requirements are met, the court will only admit in the light of the discretion afforded under s. 126(1) of the CJA 2003 which applies to defence as well as prosecution evidence.[9] With regard to Tom and Gerry's statements, the fact that Henry may have to give evidence to controvert them is not in itself unfair, as the Court of Appeal held in *R v Moore* [1992] Crim LR 882. In each case, the court must conduct a balancing exercise between the interests of the public as represented by the prosecution and the interests of the particular defendant.[10] It may thus be unfair to admit the evidence of Tom and Gerry and not Freda's letter because Henry requires this to back up his alibi.

[9] As Emson put it (2010, p. 412), 'Whatever the precise scope of s 121(1), as a matter of practical reality few trial judges are likely to feel confident about excluding defence evidence, even if the provision empowers them to do so, for the simple reason that the evidence might well be true.'

[10] Although in that case it was the actions of the defendant which had caused the non-appearance of an elderly witness.

LOOKING FOR EXTRA MARKS?

- The question of not appearing witnesses is so important you could spend more time on it. You could refer here to *R v Finch* [2007] 1 WLR 1645 on the distinction between witnesses who are unwilling and witnesses who are unavailable.

- Make it clear that the exclusionary discretion in s. 126(1)(b) applies to hearsay statements proffered by the defence as well as the prosecution, unlike s. 78 PACE. You should therefore refer to this when discussing statements which the defence want to submit.

■ You would gain marks for adding a procedural point that the Court of Appeal in *R v Montgomery* **[1995] 2 All ER 28** confirms that a witness who does not give evidence through fear and whose evidence is admitted in documentary form may still be sentenced for contempt of court. So Tom and Gerry may be punished on those grounds.

TAKING THINGS FURTHER

▨ Birch, D., 'Hearsay-Logic and Hearsay-Fiddles: *Blastland* Revisited' in P. Smith, (ed.), *Criminal Law: Essays in Honour of JC Smith* (London: Butterworths, 1987).
The law in this article is out of date but it is still worth reading for a penetrating analysis of the concepts of relevance and third party confessions.

▨ Birch, D., 'The Criminal Justice Act 2003. (4) Hearsay; Same Old Story, Same Old Song?' [2004] Crim LR 556.
See reference in answer to questions.

▨ Dennis, I., 'The Criminal Justice Act 2003, Part 2' [2004] Crim LR 251.
A comprehensive analysis of the statutory changes.

▨ Friedman, R.D., 'Thoughts from Across the Water on Hearsay and Confrontation' [1998] Crim LR 697.
A powerful defence of the right to confront one's accuser and a critique of how the hearsay rules may erode this.

▨ Jackson, J.D., 'Hearsay: The Sacred Cow that Won't be Slaughtered' (1998) 2 E & P 166.
See reference in answer to questions.

▨ Law Commission Report No. 245, *Evidence in Criminal Proceedings: Hearsay and Relevant Topics* (London: TSO, 1997), http://www.lawcom.gov.uk/app/uploads/2015/03/lc245_Legislating_the_Criminal_Code_Evidence_in_Criminal_Proceedings.pdf.

▨ Ormerod, D., 'Case Comment: *R v Leonard*' [2009] Crim LR 802.
A contribution to the discussion on implied assertions.

▨ Ormerod, D., 'Case Comment: *R v Drinkwater*' [2016] Crim LR 648.
*Explains the importance of the test for admissibility set out in **R v Riat**.*

▨ Tribe, L., 'Triangulating Hearsay' (1974) 87 Harv LR 957.
A classic study of the psychology of the rule against hearsay.

Online Resources   www.oup.com/uk/qanda/

Go online for extra essay and problem questions, a glossary of key terms, online versions of all the answer plans and audio commentary on how selected ones were put together, and a range of podcasts which include advice on exam and coursework technique and advice for other assessment methods.

Confessions, the defendant's silence, and improperly obtained evidence

6

ARE YOU READY?

In order to tackle the questions here you must have covered:

- the statutory rules for excluding confessions on grounds of oppression or unreliability framework in **ss. 76** and **76A of the Police and Criminal Evidence Act 1984 (PACE)**
- the procedural difference between exclusion by rule and exclusion by judicial discretion under **s. 78 PACE** or the common law
- the application of **s. 78 PACE** to improperly obtained evidence other than confessions
- the law on permissible inferences from a suspect's pre-trial failure to respond to questions by investigating officers in **ss. 34–38 of the Youth Justice and Criminal Evidence Act 1999** and the importance of access to legal advice
- the impact of the **Human Rights Act 1998** in these areas

KEY DEBATES

Debate: should the test for drawing inferences from silence under s. 34 of the Criminal Justice and Public Order Act 1994 be amended?

Under the current test the defendant's claim that he failed to respond to police questions at interview must have been genuinely accepted by him and there should be reasonable objective grounds for his reaction. In other words, the defendant cannot hide behind legal advice. Critics argue that this requires the jury to speculate about the state of mind of the defendant and also that in giving his explanation to the court the defendant is forced to waive legal professional privilege.

Debate: is there a need for tougher legislation to control undercover policing?

There are uncontroversial areas of undercover operations such as test purchases of alcohol and cigarettes to reveal shopkeepers breaking the law. Recent scandals have erupted, however, where undercover agents have infiltrated lawful citizens' organisations, such as environmental groups. In some cases they have engaged in love affairs with members and entrapped others into committing offences. Miscarriages of justice have resulted. Some argue that **Part 11 of the Regulation of Investigatory Powers Act 2000** has proved inadequate to control such abuses.

Debate: is the test for applying s. 76(2)(b) PACE too narrow?

This test allows the exclusion of a confession, if as a result of something said or done any confession obtained under those circumstances would be unreliable. Two criticisms are made of the interpretation of the courts. It is argued that it is too narrowly applied, only to suspects who are regarded as vulnerable in some way, and also that in a number of cases the 'something said or done' cannot be self-induced. The latter appears to treat drug addiction as a moral not a medical problem.

QUESTION | 1

The curtailment of the right to silence in the police station is objectionable because of the risk of abuse of state power associated with custodial interrogation. **Section 34 of the Criminal Justice and Public Order Act 1994** ought to be repealed as a matter of principle.

(Dennis, The Law of Evidence, 5th edn (London: Sweet & Maxwell, 2013), p. 208)

How far, in your view, does the provision in s. 34, specifying that the suspect must have been allowed an opportunity to consult a solicitor before the section applies, provide a safeguard against the risk of abuse of state power to which Dennis refers?

CAUTION!

- Be careful here to answer the specific question set which requires you to assess whether the availability of legal advice to the suspect is a sufficient counterbalance to the extension of state power enshrined in **s. 34**.

- Note that the question is about the relative advantages to the defendant in the interview situation rather than an invitation to recite all the arguments for and against the abolition of the right to silence.

- The current position is enshrined in the decision in ***R v Beckles (No. 2)* [2005] 1 WLR 2829** but you should show some understanding of the evolution of the law and criticisms made of it.

DIAGRAM ANSWER PLAN

Introduction: explain inequality of arms and the legislative erosion of the privilege against self-incrimination.

Discuss arguments to support the analysis by Dennis, including the judicial direction on the reasonableness of legal advice and effect on legal professional privilege.

Discuss arguments critical of Dennis including ECtHR decisions that right to silence is not an absolute right.

Assess the arguments and other possible alternative protective measures such as increased disclosure.

SUGGESTED ANSWER

Inequality of Arms

The risk of abuse by state power referred to by Dennis is inherent in the very nature of police interrogation. Inevitably there is an imbalance of power, or inequality of arms, between the suspect and the state actors who conduct the questioning. Historically, therefore, the common law provided that a refusal to give an explanation in the face of official questioning could not be proffered as prosecution evidence.[1] Pressure, particularly from the police, led to the changes to this aspect of the privilege against self-incrimination in the **Criminal Justice and Public Order Act 1994 (CJPOA)**. The targets were said to be a small number of hardened criminals but the new provisions of course applied to all suspects and have generated considerable controversy and unease that they are disproportionately eroding defendants' rights.[2]

[1] Apart from the special circumstances outlined in *R v Parkes* [1976] 1 WLR 1251.

[2] Galligan (1988, p. 70) quotes the former Metropolitan Police Commissioner Peter Imbert as saying that the protection of silence had 'done more to obscure the truth and facilitate crime than anything else in this century'.

Strasbourg Decisions

An early indication of this unease was the reaction to the Strasbourg Court's decision in *John Murray v UK* (1996) 22 EHRR 29, a case arising from the introduction of the erosion of the right to silence into Northern Ireland. The Court determined that the right to remain silent under police questioning and the privilege against self-incrimination were generally recognised international standards which lay at the heart of the notion of fair procedure. However, disappointingly for the critics of the new legislative provisions, these immunities were not absolute. Whether the drawing of adverse inferences from an accused's silence infringed **Art. 6** was a matter to be determined in the light of all the circumstances of the case, having particular regard to the situations where inferences might be drawn, the weight attached to them by the national courts in their assessment of the evidence, and the degree of compulsion inherent in the situation.

Amendment to the Statute

[3] The European Court of Human Rights held that it could not be said that the drawing of reasonable inferences from the applicant's behaviour had the effect of shifting the burden of proof from the prosecution to the defence so as to infringe the principle of the presumption of innocence.

This judgment thus gave support to Dennis's argument that **s. 34** exhibits excessive state power over the individual.[3] However, Dennis's analysis gains some support from another aspect of the judgment which was that denial of access to legal advice for 48 hours did infringe **Art. 6**. In the light of this, the UK amended the law. **Sections 34 and 36–38 of the CJPOA** are not operative if the defendant had not been allowed an opportunity to consult a solicitor prior to being questioned, charged, or officially informed he was to be prosecuted. As the question suggests, access to legal advice has not proved a safeguard against what the Strasbourg Court saw as the risks to the defendant in the new provisions.

Genuine Reliance on Legal Advice not Sufficient

The legal advice must be reasonable in the circumstances. Subsequent case law determined the nature of direction the judge should give the jury in order to maintain the fairness of the trial. In **Condron v UK [2000] Crim LR 679** the trial judge was held to have violated **Art. 6(1)**. In that case the accused had been advised by his solicitor to be silent and the judge failed to direct the jury that only if, despite the evidence or lack of it, the jury concluded that the failure to answer questions at interview could only sensibly be attributed to the accused's having no answer, or none that would stand up to cross-examination, might they draw an adverse inference. The Court of Appeal had accepted that there had been a misdirection but nonetheless the guilty verdict should stand.

[4] Earlier case law held that the issue was whether the suspect genuinely relied on legal advice: see *R v Betts and Hall* [2001] EWCA Crim 224.

Dennis's reservations about **s. 34** are to that extent confirmed in that legal advice to remain silent in itself will not preclude the possibility of adverse inferences being drawn. The jury must be directed to consider if it was reasonable to rely on the advice or if the accused remained silent because it suited his purposes.[4] The leading case is *R v Beckles (No. 2)* [2005] 1 WLR 2829 where the court held that even if the accused genuinely relied on his solicitor's advice to remain silent, it was nevertheless permissible for the jury to draw an adverse inference under **s. 34**, if it was not reasonable to rely on that advice. In *R v Hoare* [2005] 1 WLR 1804, Auld LJ stated (at 1821): 'Legal entitlement is one thing. An accused's reason for exercising it is another. The belief in his entitlement may be genuine, but it does not follow that his reason for exercising it is.'

Suspect has to 'Second-Guess'

Thus the right of access to a solicitor may be undermined in that the court will conduct an examination about the suspect's state of mind. Commenting on the decision in **Beckles** that the reliance on legal advice has to be reasonable and genuine, Malik (2005, p. 216) argues that 'Effectively the accused is required to 'second-guess' the advice of his solicitor and determine whether its quality would convince a jury that it was "the true reason for his silence".'

The approach of the courts in interpreting the legislation therefore appears to confirm Dennis's concern about **s. 34**. In particular, it means that in effect the trial is commencing at the interview stage which is where the suspect is expected to disclose his innocent explanation, if he has one.

Waiving Legal Professional Privilege

Further, it is clear that if the suspect gives his reasons at trial for his earlier silence he is thereby waiving his legal professional privilege and the solicitor can be cross-examined. In **Bowden [1999] 2 Cr App R 176** the Court of Appeal held that if the court is to examine the reasons for the legal advice there will be an implied waiver of the privilege. To prevent adverse inferences being drawn it may be necessary to provide reasons for the advice, yet this may be interpreted as a waiver of legal professional privilege, so the accused, or the legal adviser, may be cross-examined on whether there were additional, tactical reasons for the advice.[5]

The courts have acted somewhat cautiously and in **R v Bresa [2005] EWCA Crim 1414** a conviction was overturned when the judge had failed to emphasise the importance of the defendant's right to privilege in relation to communications between him and his solicitors. On the other hand, there are difficulties for the defendant in giving reasons for deciding not to answer questions at interview because he is subject to the hearsay rule which might limit how he repeated what his solicitor had told him (**R v Davis [1998] Crim LR 659**).

Complex Directions to Jury

Dennis's concern is supported by the resulting complexity of the directions the judge must give to the jury in relation to reliance on legal advice to remain silent. The Specimen Direction of the Judicial Studies Board is, as a result of these considerations, very complex. Roberts and Zuckerman (2010, p. 571) comment that Specimen Direction No. 40 on **s. 34 of the CJPOA** 'is easily one of the most lengthy and complicated sets of judicial instructions in the entire Crown Court Bench Book'. However, they note that a misdirection will not automatically lead to rendering a conviction unsafe.[6]

[5] As Choo points out (2018, p. 129) 'The possible consequences of waiver would seem to place the accused in an unenviable "catch-22" situation'.

[6] You could point out, as the authors do, that there is a common-sense or rational basis for **s. 34** that suspects who are innocent would be reasonably expected to give an explanation at interview.

Compensatory Protections Afforded to Defendant

There are nonetheless some reservations that could be expressed about the objections Dennis has put to **s. 34**. Some cases illustrate a pro-defendant stance on the part of the Court of Appeal. One example is the case law on the status of prepared statements read out by a solicitor at the beginning of the police interview and the failure of the suspect to answer consequential police questions. As long as the prepared statement is a full account of the defence later relied on at trial, **s. 34** is not engaged. (See *R v Knight* **[2004] 1 WLR 340** and *R v Turner* **[2003] EWCA Crim 3108.**) Another pro-defendant stance is that the court will take into account whether there had been insufficient disclosure by the police in directing whether it is reasonable for the suspect to rely on legal advice to remain silent (see *R v Argent* **[1997] 2 Cr App R 27** and *R v Nickelson* **[1999] Crim LR 61**).

Conclusion

In the light of the above case law, the question of the extent of the protection against abuse of state power afforded by **s. 34**'s right of access to legal advice is a complex one.[7] On the one hand, it is an important manifestation of the need to address inequality of arms between the citizen and the state. On the other hand, there are stringent requirements upon the assessment of this advice. The jury have to look at the context in which the advice was given.[8] Since Parliament went to the lengths of amending the original statute to make provision for access to a solicitor, it seems perverse for the courts to hold that it may be unreasonable to act on what he or she advises. If Dennis is right and the current situation is an example of an excess of state power there are arguably two possible alternatives to the status quo. Zuckerman (1994, p. 117) argues that the principle of natural justice requires the suspect to have full notice of the evidence against him. In Zuckerman's view the right way to deal with an 'ambush' defence at trial is to institute a proper system of pre-trial pleading in which prosecution and defence set out in writing the essence of their cases. In those circumstances common sense might allow comment on silence.[9] The other alternative, as Dennis says, is to repeal **s. 34**.

[7] The vulnerability of the UK's protection of the privilege against self-incrimination is suggested by the Government's proposal to opt out of the new EU Directive, due to be in force in April 2018 which aims at strengthening defendants' rights. See MacPartholan (2016).

[8] Keane and McKeown (2018, p. 468) point out that 'if the accused has stayed silent on legal advice and his silence is objectively unreasonable, it will not become reasonable merely because the solicitor's advice was ill-judged or bad'.

[9] He adds, 'Once the courts have evolved parameters of fairness they would benefit not only the suspects who maintain silence but all suspects' questions by the police' (1994, p. 139).

 LOOKING FOR EXTRA MARKS?

- Your answer would be enhanced by reference to the need for corroborative evidence to found a conviction, thereby which qualifying Dennis's observation. Under **s. 38 of the CJPOA** the defendant cannot be convicted or brought to trial on their silence alone.

- Depending on the content of your specific Evidence course, you could refer to the even more stringent provisions in relation to access to legal advice for those suspected of presenting immediate danger to the public, see *Ibrahim v UK* **[2016] ECHR 750**, which concerned the aftermath of the 2005 terrorist attack in London.

QUESTION | 2

Police are puzzled by a series of thefts of valuable greyhounds from kennels and suspect the perpetrators are involved in a gambling scam. They call on Gerry and Cliff, noted professional gamblers, as part of their routine inquiries. Gerry invites them in and agrees to answer any questions, although he is clearly upset because he has just heard his mother is dying in hospital with cancer. As they are talking, Gerry's 14-year-old son, Tom, comes in and says: 'I hope they arrest you for cruelty to animals. It's horrible leaving that greyhound tied up in the shed. Grandma will cry her heart out when I tell her.' Gerry breaks down in tears and says: 'What a fool I have been. I said I'd mind the brute but I didn't know it was stolen. Cliff made me take it in.' He is arrested and cautioned and taken to the police station for questioning. There the custody officer asks him if he has his own solicitor. Gerry replies that he has but since he owes him money for arranging the sale of his house he doesn't like to call him. The police do not offer a duty solicitor and proceed to question Gerry further. Gerry tells them that he doesn't know any details of the thefts but the police persist in questioning him. The police then produce photographs of Tom on animal rights demonstrations and say to Gerry, 'You know we could take this further if you don't play ball.' Gerry then confesses that he, Cliff, and several others had organised the thefts. He tells them that they had been forced to kill some of the dogs and they are buried on Hackney Downs. The police visit Cliff and ask him to come down to the station to help with their inquiries. He agrees but at the station asks for a solicitor. They reply that there is no need for that at this stage. They then leave him alone for about two hours. Cliff, who is 18 years old, suffers from claustrophobia and when they return is in a very distressed state. Cliff is cautioned and told he is under arrest; he begins to sob violently and admits that he had stolen the greyhounds. At the trial he argues that he was forced to make the confession due to his mental distress.

Advise Gerry and Cliff.

CAUTION!

- In a question of this sort it is important not to miss any of the issues. The visit to Gerry is described as 'routine' initially, so you need to discuss if and when it becomes an 'interview', and thus whether the requirements of the statute and Codes of Practice apply.

- The information on legal advice given by the police to Gerry must be checked against the Code requirements.

- Do not overlook the issue of the incriminating of a third party, namely Cliff, and whether, even if the confession is inadmissible, the trial may still consider the discovery of real evidence which it prompted, the buried dogs.

DIAGRAM ANSWER PLAN

Identify the issues	▓ Identify the legal issues: the definition of a police interview; status of mixed statement; information on legal advice; confessions incriminating others; 'fruits of the poisoned tree'.
Relevant law	▓ PACE, ss. 76–82 and Code of Practice C.
Apply the law	▓ Gerry: admissibility of statements, Cliff admissibility of Gerry's inculpatory statement.
Conclude	▓ Possible outcomes for defendants.

SUGGESTED ANSWER

Initial Statement by Gerry

Gerry's initial statement in his house is clearly incriminating, although he is also trying to excuse himself. Since it is partly adverse to the maker it falls within the definition of 'confession' in **s. 82(1) of the Police and Criminal Evidence Act 1984 (PACE)**. If it is admitted, the whole statement may be evidence of the truth of its contents, as the House of Lords held in **R v Sharp [1988] 1 WLR 7.** There is no evidence of oppression here and therefore **s. 76(2)(a) PACE** is not applicable.[1] However, it is necessary to consider the possible application of other sections of **PACE** and the Code of Practice. We are told the police are engaged in 'routine' inquiries; that is they are not conducting an interview, which is questioning of a person regarding his involvement in an offence, but rather questioning to obtain information. The state of mind of the police is the key question, but, on the facts as they are given, it seems the exchange was not an interview.[2] The words uttered by Tom may amount to something said or done which was likely in the circumstances existing at the time to render unreliable any confession Gerry might have made. The Court of Appeal held that it is not necessary for the words or action which prompted the statement to come from the police (**R v Harvey [1988] Crim LR 241**). There are two limbs to the test under **s. 76(2)(b) PACE**. First, circumstances existing at the time and here Gerry's emotional state concerning his mother's condition may be applicable; see also

[1] There is no need routinely to consider statutory sections where the facts do not merit it.

[2] Explain that it follows that Gerry does not get the protection outlined in **PACE**; e.g. caution, legal advice, etc.

R v McGovern (1990) 92 Cr App R 228. Secondly, as regards anything said or done, can Tom's words be sufficient? The main question is to find a causal connection between these words and the confession such as to make any confession in such circumstances unreliable.[3] This does not appear to be the case here.

[3] On the facts, there does not appear to be anything in Tom's remark which would have made any confession unreliable, unless it could be argued that Gerry confessed in order to stop Tom's tirade and painful remarks about his dying mother.

Interview at Police Station

At the station, Gerry appears to have been properly cautioned. However, there may be inadequacies in the information given about access to legal advice which may, inter alia, render his confession inadmissible: see **s. 58 PACE** and para. 11.2 of Code C.[4] It appears that, when Gerry is asked whether he has a solicitor and he replies that he is worried about owing him money, Gerry is not told of his entitlement to free legal advice. However, access to legal advice may be lawfully delayed for up to 36 hours in the case of indictable offences (**s. 58 PACE**). Thus, the failure in Gerry's case may well be permissible as long as the police can convince the court that they reasonably feared one of the contingencies referred to in **s. 58(8) PACE** would arise. In any case, a wrongly authorised delay in obtaining legal advice does not render the confession automatically excluded under either **s. 76** or **s. 78 PACE**. In *R v Alladice* (1988) 87 Cr App R 380, the court stressed that influential factors in excluding under **s. 78 PACE** were whether or not the police acted in bad faith and whether the presence of a solicitor would have made any difference, particularly to a seasoned offender.

[4] Immediately prior to the commencement of any interview at a police station or other authorised place of detention, the interviewing officer must remind the suspect of his entitlement to free legal advice.

Oppression Test

However, there are arguably other pressing grounds to exclude the confession here under **s. 76 PACE**. Has this confession been obtained by oppression?[5] Does the implied threat to Tom amount to oppression of Gerry? Oppression is only partly defined in **s. 76(8) PACE** as including 'torture, inhuman or degrading treatment and the use or threat of violence whether or not amounting to torture'. Showing the photograph and the threat to 'take things further' probably does not fall within this partial statutory definition. The court in *R v Fulling* [1987] QB 426 found that psychological pressure did not fall within the definition.[6] However, Gerry might be able to rely on *R v Paris* (1992) 97 Cr App R 99 where the police questioning was oppressive in that in the presence of a solicitor they shouted at the suspect to tell them what they wanted to hear after he had denied the offence some 300 times.

[5] Once the defence raises the issue and it is accepted by the judge as a possibility, the burden is on the prosecution to prove beyond reasonable doubt that it has not been so obtained.

[6] The main requirement is misuse of power or authority.

Reliability and Fairness Tests

Section 76(2)(b) PACE may be applicable in that in such circumstances any confession made by the defendant would be likely to be unreliable since he was offered an inducement to confess. This test is an objective one and does not require bad faith.[7] **Section 78 PACE** is also widely applied to confession evidence (*R v Mason* **[1988] 1 WLR 139**) and the combination of factors, particularly police bad faith over the threat, could lead to exclusion here. Even if the confession is excluded, the court may still allow evidence of finding the greyhounds, although clearly their evidential worth will be less considering that it may not be possible to admit its source (**s. 76(4) PACE**). One final point is that even if the confession is admitted will it be evidence against Cliff and should it be edited before the trial?[8]

[8] See *R v Spinks* [1982] 1 All ER 587.

Confession Evidence Against Maker

If the defence do not succeed in getting Gerry's confession excluded, the question then arises whether it is admissible as evidence against Cliff. One possibility is for it to be edited so that Cliff's name is excluded but the court will have to bear in mind fairness to Gerry. In *R v Silcott* **[1987] Crim LR 765** Hodgson J ruled that where the interviews of some of the defendants implicated others, names should be replaced by initials. This did not overcome the prejudicial effect since prosecutors were permitted to cross-examine over the meaning of the initials. One possibility would be to order separate trials. If this is not ordered the judge must give very clear instructions that Gerry's statement is not evidence against Cliff. Cliff should be warned, however, that it may be permissible for the jury to use Gerry's confession as the basis for establishing his guilt and then use that finding of guilt in determining whether Cliff is guilty (see *R v Hayter* **[2005] 1 WLR 605**).[9]

[9] Note that in that case there was scant other evidence against H which seems also to be the case here in relation to Cliff.

Cliff's Initial Statement

With regard to Cliff's position, it is arguable that the police were wrong not to treat their initial exchange with him as an interview under the definition in Code of Practice C para. 11.1A. There were already reasonable grounds to suspect him because of Gerry's confession. He should therefore have been cautioned and told of his right to free legal advice, although it is arguable that this is an indictable offence and access to a solicitor could be delayed on appropriate grounds. There is, perhaps, a breach of the Code also in leaving him for two hours, since under para. 1.1 of Code C, persons in custody should be dealt with expeditiously. As someone not under arrest, Cliff was free to leave but clearly had not appreciated this. There are possible grounds for unreliability given that the 'something said or done' could be leaving him for two hours and the circumstances of his claustrophobia. For exclusion on grounds of **s. 76(2)(b) PACE**, there is no need for police impropriety. In *R v Crampton* **(1990) 92 Cr App R**

369 according to the court it was a matter for those present at the interview to decide whether a drug addict was fit to be questioned in the sense that his answers could be relied upon to be true. The series of breaches could also, especially if bad faith was found, amount to exclusion on grounds of unfairness under **s. 78 PACE**. Since *R v Ward* **[1993] 1 WLR 619** the courts have taken an increasingly open stance on allowing expert evidence of a psychiatrist or psychologist on the reliability of a confession if the accused was suffering from a mental disorder that fell short of mental illness. In *R v O'Brien* **[2000] Crim LR 676** the Court of Appeal stated that admissibility of expert evidence depended on the satisfaction of three conditions: first, the disorder must be such that it would affect the reliability of the confession; secondly, the accused's condition must depart significantly from the norm, and, finally, there must be an earlier history of his mental disorder. In that case expert evidence should have been admitted, since the accused's mental disorder was associated with the making of false confessions. Cliff might be able to rely on the case of *R v Blackburn* **[2005] EWCA Crim 1349**. The suspect was a vulnerable teenager, aged 15 years, who did not have a mental disorder at the time of his interview when he made what was alleged to be a 'coerced compliant' confession. The Court of Appeal held that evidence of a forensic psychologist was admissible as relevant to the reliability of the confessions under **s. 76(2)(b)**. The issue fell outside the jury's normal knowledge and experience. The court noted that the evidence of the expert was that 'the key feature giving rise to a coerced compliant confession is fatigue, which, together with an inability to control what is happening, may induce the individual to experience a growing desire to give up resisting suggestions put to him'. [10] It added, 'normal people, not suffering from any personality disorder or abnormal disorder, could be rendered compliant by prolonged interrogation'.

The defence will therefore have to examine whether the circumstances of Cliff's interrogation, combined with his claustrophobia and mental vulnerability and his age, make it arguable that an expert witness should be called.

Conclusion

If admitted, Gerry's inculpatory statements are not evidence against Cliff, although if the jury find Gerry guilty they may use this evidence in considering Cliff's guilt. Cliff's statements may have been improperly obtained and there may be a stay of prosecution: the defence may be assisted by a landmark ruling by the Grand Chamber. In *Ibrahim v UK* **[2016] ECHR 752** the pre-trial procedural conditions for the admissibility of confessions were considered and list of ten relevant factors specified.

[10] Young and otherwise vulnerable people may be affected (see Glover (2017, p. 417)).

LOOKING FOR EXTRA MARKS?

▨ You will gain credit if you add that the interviewing officer should have given Gerry the opportunity to confirm or deny his incriminating unprompted statement made before the interview.

▨ You could expand your analysis of the effect of *Hayter*, a controversial majority judgment where there was scant other evidence against H. Lord Rodger in a dissenting speech stated (para. 47) that the Crown was 'in substance asserting that the jury have a power to turn inadmissible evidence into admissible evidence, and to convict a defendant by using evidence that is inadmissible against him'.

QUESTION | 3

Arnold and Brenda were summonsed on charges of criminal damage of a wine shop in Boxfield High Street. The incident occurred at 3.00 a.m., when the window was smashed and the alarm sounded. Arnold was stopped shortly afterwards in the next street, where police suspicions are aroused because he is not wearing shoes. He is stopped and questioned in the street. He refuses to say why he is in the area at that time. He also refuses to explain why he is not wearing shoes. An abandoned pair of wine-covered sandals, which the police believe were Arnold's, were found in a bin near the scene of the burglary. Arnold was arrested and questioned in the police station about his whereabouts and the absence of shoes. He had, on his request, a solicitor present on this occasion. His solicitor, however, considers that he is under the influence of drink and advises him not to answer questions at this stage. At the trial Arnold puts forward the explanation for his failure to respond to questioning that his solicitors had so advised him. He explains that he had not volunteered why he was in the area because he had been drinking with his girlfriend and did not want his wife to find out. He also says he had passed by the wine shop and seen the damaged window. Some wine from a broken bottle had spilt on his sandals. When he heard the police car coming he took off the sandals and threw them away because he feared he would be implicated since he used to work at the shop. He denied involvement in the criminal damage.

Brenda worked at the wine shop at the time of the offence and when she turned up for work the next day and saw the debris, she asked the manager, 'What happened here?' He replied, 'I think you know all about this, don't you? Your friend Arnold and you smashed my window.' Brenda said nothing in reply. She was interviewed by police with a solicitor present and again said nothing. At the trial Arnold and Brenda plead not guilty. She refuses to testify but her counsel cross-examined Arnold and put it to him that he knew Brenda was at the cinema with his wife that evening and therefore knew that she was not involved in the offence.

Advise on the evidence.

CAUTION!

- The defendants here have acted in different ways in the face of questioning about their involvement in the offence. You will need to examine whether their reactions and behaviour amount to confessions; if so, what is their evidential worth and if there are grounds to exclude them by rule of law or exercise of discretion.
- Arnold's behaviour raises several issues under **ss. 34, 36, 37,** and **38 of the CJPOA.**
- You need therefore to discuss Brenda's behaviour in relation to common law provisions on silence. You are only given information about questioning outside the police station so do not speculate about other possible interviews.

DIAGRAM ANSWER PLAN

Identify the issues	The legal issues are: silence when questioned but not under arrest; silence at police station; legal advice on silence.
Relevant law	CJPOA, ss. 34–38, common law on silence, legal professional privilege.
Apply the law	Arnold's silence at interview may lead to inference of guilt if the legal advice was not genuinely and reasonably relied upon. Brenda's silence when questioned by manager may be admissible under the common law; possibility of inferences from silence at interview (s. 34) and in court (s. 35).
Conclude	Advise on the evidence.

SUGGESTED ANSWER

Questioning in Street

[1] Note that **s. 34** may apply after caution and before arrest, but **ss. 36** and **37** only apply after arrest.

The first question is whether Arnold's silence when first questioned in the street is admissible and whether **s. 34** is engaged.[1] The prosecution may try to argue that **s. 34** does apply. Arnold gives an explanation at trial which he might reasonably have given when first questioned. It is unlikely that Arnold will be able to rely on **s. 34(2A)**, in that he has not had an opportunity to consult a solicitor; that provision only applies if he was at an authorised place of detention at the time of the failure. He does give an explanation at trial for his whereabouts and his lack of shoes, so **s. 34** may be engaged on those grounds. The prosecution will have difficulty, however, in successfully arguing that evidence from the interview 'at the scene of the crime' is admissible. A preliminary matter is that Arnold should have been cautioned (Code C para. 10.4). Even if he had, it is doubtful that the failure to respond to police questions will be admitted.

It is unclear from the facts whether the police have reasonable suspicion of Arnold's involvement. His proximity to the scene of the crime and the lack of shoes do, however, appear to be significant. The issue is whether the questioning amounts to an interview. If it does then the statute and Code of Practice apply. The Code defines an interview as the questioning of a person regarding his involvement in an offence, but that questioning to obtain information or in the ordinary course of duty does not constitute an interview.[2] This does leave some doubt, however, as to when questioning to obtain information turns into questioning about involvement in an offence. *R v Park* **[1994] Crim LR 285** upholds the principle that 'at the scene' interviews are not admissible. In that case, it was held that exploratory questions at a roadside could give rise in due course to a well-founded suspicion that an offence had been committed. So what started out as an inquiry could become an interview.[3]

In the instant case the police already know of the offence and so there might be more grounds for considering their questions to Arnold as an interview. Arnold will thus be advised that even if he has been cautioned it is possible that the prosecution cannot make use of **ss. 36** and **37**, because he should not have been questioned away from the police station. It is, however, appropriate that 'emergency' provisions should be considered. It does not appear on the facts that any of these do apply to Arnold and so it is unlikely his silence in the street will be admissible.

Interview at Station

The prosecution may more successfully argue that **s. 34**, **36**, or **37 of the CJPOA** may apply in the circumstances arising from the interview in the police station. Arnold is allowed access to a solicitor, so **ss. 34(2A)** and **36(4A)** and **37(3A)** are satisfied. He should in addition have been given an opportunity to confirm or deny his earlier silence outside the police station, and for **ss. 36** and **37** to be operative he should have been given the special warning set out in Code C paras 10.10 and 10.11. The prosecution may seek to rely on **ss. 34, 36,** or **37**, although Arnold may argue that **s. 36** specifies the failure to account for the presence, not absence, of objects, namely his shoes. The plethora of case law which has been generated in this area is applicable to

[2] The case law is primarily based on the admissibility of confessions, but is arguably relevant also to the suspect's silence.

[3] However, the Court of Appeal upheld the judge's decision not to apply s. 78 PACE.

all three sections (as well as **s. 35**, see *R v Cowan* **[1996] QB 373**). In *Argent* **[1997] 2 Cr App R 27**, the Court of Appeal set out the conditions which have to be met before a jury can draw an adverse inference. In particular it will be a matter for the jury to determine whether in the circumstances existing at the time the defendant could reasonably be expected to mention a fact. Relevant factors to be considered include the particular circumstances of the defendant and the state of his knowledge, including information from the police. Arnold is only expected to account for or to mention facts he could reasonably have been expected to mention but it is certainly arguable that these included his absence of shoes and why he was in the area.[4] It is not necessary, however, that Arnold should be told the precise details of the alleged offence. *R v Compton* **[2002] EWCA Crim 2835** also established that 'section **36**, unlike section **34**, invites no comparison between the statement in interview and the evidence at trial since **section 36** contains no parallel to the question under **section 34(1)** of whether it was reasonable for the defendant to mention a particular fact: reasonableness usually being judged from the starting point of whether the fact was mentioned at trial'.

Legal Advice

Arnold may argue that he had remained silent on legal advice. That in itself is not sufficient to preclude the operation of **ss. 34**, **36**, or **37** but it would be one of the circumstances that the jury should take into account in deciding if it was reasonable for him to rely on this. Here drunkenness may be a justification (*R v Beckles (No. 2)* **[2005] 1 WLR 2829**). Arnold should be warned that if he goes beyond a bare assertion of the solicitor's advice he risks breaching legal professional privilege (*R v Bowden* **[1999] 1 WLR 823**).

What constitutes a proper inference for the court or jury in any particular case is a matter of fact. However, Arnold may gain some comfort from **s. 38(3)** of the 1994 Act.[5] Here there does appear to be other circumstantial evidence, such as the finding of the sandals.

Silence and Common Law

Is Brenda's failure to respond to the manager's allegation admissible? Under **s. 82(1) PACE** a confession includes any statement wholly or partly adverse to the person who made it, whether made to a person in authority or not and whether made in words or otherwise. It is by no means clear that silence would fit such a definition. The common law rule is that a statement made in the presence of the accused is not evidence against him except insofar as he accepts what has been said (*R v Christie* **[1914] AC 545**). It may be that a reply or indignant rejection of the accusation could reasonably be expected from Brenda

[4] The phrase 'in the circumstances' should not be construed restrictively. Arnold's actual qualities, knowledge, state of mind, degree of drunkenness should be considered.

[5] This provides that 'A person shall not have the proceedings against him transferred to the Crown Court for trial, have a case to answer or be convicted of an offence solely on an inference drawn from such a failure or refusal.'

and thus her failure to do that may be an implied acceptance of the truth of the accusation. Thus in **Parkes v R (1977) 64 Cr App R 25**, the defendant's silence when accused by a mother of stabbing her daughter was held by the Privy Council to have been properly admitted as evidence going to guilt. The courts have applied this principle to situations where the parties are on even terms.[6] Brenda's accuser is her manager and she may have been quiet from considerations other than guilt. If her failure to reply is admitted, the jury should be directed to consider, first, whether the silence indicates acceptance of the accusation and, secondly, whether guilt could reasonably be inferred from what she had accepted. A failure to leave both these issues to the jury led to the quashing of a conviction by the Court of Appeal in **R v Chandler [1976] 1 WLR 585**. **Section 34 of the CJPOA** does not apply to Brenda because it is only relevant in relation to silence when being questioned by the police or others charged with investigating offences. The shop manager does appear not to fit this definition.

However, in relation to her silence at the police interview **s. 34** may well apply. She has a solicitor present, thus satisfying one of the statutory requirements. Is she at trial relying on a fact she could have referred to earlier? Arguably this is the case since the defence that she was at the cinema with Arnold's wife could have been said to the police earlier. Similarly, the fact that she presents the fact through her counsel does not per se preclude telling the jury that they may draw an adverse inference. In **R v Webber [2004] UKHL 1** the House of Lords held a party relies on a fact, for example, when his counsel conducts questioning in such a way that he puts a positive case to the witness as counsel does in relation to Brenda's alibi.[7]

Conclusion

The standard Judicial Studies Board Specimen Direction to be found in the Crown Court Bench Book should be given.[8] Brenda's failure to testify engages **s. 35** and the judge should give a **Cowan** warning. Further assistance in relation to Arnold is given in **R v Beckles**. If the defendant testifies that he relied on legal advice to remain silent, did he genuinely rely on that and were there soundly based objective reasons such that it was also reasonable for him to rely on that advice? Arnold may plead that under the **Human Rights Act 1998** the absence of such a direction is a violation of **Art. 6(1) of the European Convention on Human Rights (Condron v UK [2000] Crim LR 679)**. However, each case depends on its own specific facts.[9]

[6] Note that Munday (2015, p. 421) suggests that it may be better to concentrate on the second limb of the test in *Chandler*: 'whether, in the circumstances, an accusation might reasonably be expected to elicit a response from a suspect'. See also *R v O (Stevie)* [2005] EWCA Crim 3082.

[7] It is clear from the case law that the word 'fact' should be given a broad meaning.

[8] See http://www.judiciary.gov.uk/publications/.

[9] Note that in *Condron* the Strasbourg Court stressed the importance of carefully worded judicial directions on the permissibility of drawing inferences from silence.

LOOKING FOR EXTRA MARKS?

▨ Add that it may not be necessary for the judge to direct the jury that they must find a case to answer against Arnold before drawing any adverse inference under **ss. 34, 36**, or **37**: *R v Doldur* **[2000] Crim LR 178**.

▨ Stress it is no bar to drawing an inference from a failure to mention a fact earlier that the fact goes to the heart of her defence: see *R v Milford* **[2001] 2 All ER 609**.

QUESTION | 4

Evidence is the basis of justice: to exclude evidence is to exclude justice.

(Jeremy Bentham, *A Rationale of Judicial Evidence* (1827), bk. 9, ch. 3, p. 490)

Discuss this statement in the light of the current approach of the courts to the use of illegally or improperly obtained evidence other than confessions and the defendant's silence.

CAUTION!

In order to prepare this area you should have:

▨ read some at least of the leading academic commentaries on access to evidence;

▨ reviewed the considerations which the courts bring to bear on exclusion of evidence obtained by police impropriety, such as entrapment or unauthorised undercover surveillance, or by breaches of primary or delegated legislation such as Codes C and D of **PACE**;

▨ demonstrated your understanding of the terms of **s. 78 PACE** which refers to 'the circumstances in which the evidence was obtained' as a ground for non-admissibility but only if the evidence would have 'such an adverse effect on the fairness of the proceedings that the court ought not to admit it'. In other words, there has to be a causal connection between any impropriety and the trial proceedings;

▨ noted that the question refers to the 'use' of evidence obtained by improper means. You should distinguish between those situations in which a stay of prosecution is appropriate and those in which the prosecution may go ahead but the evidence may be excluded.

DIAGRAM ANSWER PLAN

Outline of current law from *R v Sang* to PACE, s. 78; stay of prosecution.

▼

Arguments in favour of inclusion: Laudan, Bentham.

▼

Need to distinguish exclusion of evidence and stay of prosecution, importance of *R v Looseley*.

SUGGESTED ANSWER

This question raises one of the most controversial questions in Evidence law, namely how far should relevant and reliable evidence be excluded if there has been some impropriety in the way it was obtained? Bentham for one argued for a system of free proof; that is, that all relevant evidence should be admitted. Others, however, maintain that the integrity of the trial is undermined if those gathering evidence, particularly if they are state actors, have acted illegally or improperly.[1] The case law demonstrates, however, that, confessions aside, the courts have traditionally been reluctant to exclude evidence because of some impropriety in the way it was obtained. Arguably, however, the **Human Rights Act 1998** has, as *R v Looseley; Attorney General's Reference (No. 3 of 2000)* [2000] **1 WLR 2060** demonstrates, brought about a significant change in recent years. The essay will first outline the evolution of the law in this area and then examine the arguments for and against a robust exclusionary doctrine.

Evolution of Law on Excluding Improperly Obtained Evidence

At common law, courts have a general discretion to exclude evidence, albeit relevant, to ensure a fair trial. In *R v Sang* [1980] AC **402** the House of Lords acknowledged that this had two aspects, namely the exclusion of evidence if it would be likely to have a prejudicial effect outweighing its probative value, and a more limited discretion to exclude unfairly or illegally obtained evidence. But the general rule of English law was that, apart from confession evidence, impropriety in obtaining evidence has no relevance to admissibility.[2] Their Lordships in *Sang* limited the exercise of the discretion to exclude evidence obtained after the commission of the offence, likening the general exclusionary approach to that on

[1] The essence of this stance is expressed in **s. 76(2)(a) PACE** which provides that confession evidence obtained by oppression, notwithstanding that it may be true, should not be admitted.

[2] This is illustrated in cases such as *Kuruma v R* [1955] AC 197.

[3] In *R v Christou* [1992] QB 979 Lord Diplock pointed out that the only case brought to their Lordships' attention in which the appellate court had actually excluded evidence on the ground that it had been unfairly obtained by a trick was *R v Payne* [1963] 1 WLR 637.

[4] It should be pointed out that it is getting increasingly difficult to argue that investigations are unlawful in the sense of not authorised by statute: see particularly **RIPA**. In *Re McE* [2009] 1 AC 908 in a majority judgment the House of Lords held that **RIPA** permits covert police surveillance of a suspect's confidential interview with a lawyer. Of course any material gained may not necessarily be admissible at trial.

[5] There the trial judge had admitted evidence of secret tape-recordings obtained in breach of **PACE** and the civil law of trespass, and in violation of **Art. 8 of the European Convention on Human Rights**.

unfairly obtained confessions. In fact the courts rarely exercised the common law discretion to exclude. [3]

The **Police and Criminal Evidence Act 1984 (PACE)**, while preserving the common law discretion, introduced an additional statutory discretion, **s. 78**, which applies to non-confession as well as confession evidence, on which the prosecution proposes to rely if it appears that 'having regard to all the circumstances, including the circumstances in which the evidence was obtained, the admission of the evidence would have such an adverse effect on the fairness of the proceedings that the court ought not to admit it'. Two features of this provision are relevant to the question under discussion: first, that there is no automatic exclusion for impropriety, there has to be a causal connection between the impropriety and the fairness of the proceedings; secondly, the courts have to consider the interests of the prosecution and the defence when applying the discretion. Cases concerned with impropriety at the investigative stage fall into two groups, namely those concerned with alleged entrapment by the police and, secondly, those involving some breach of procedure, such as unauthorised surveillance or an illegal search. [4]

Arguments in Favour of Inclusion

Arguments in favour of maintaining an inclusionary approach to admissibility can be categorised as follows: first, the evidence exists and if it is relevant it should be admitted: see *R v Chalkley* [1998] **QB 848** for an example of this approach. [5] The tape-recordings were highly probative of guilt and not affected by the unlawful police activity. This case thus supports the Benthamite argument about truth-seeking being the prime purpose of the trial. Similarly in *R v B (Attorney General's Reference (No. 3 of 1999))* [2001] 2 AC 91 the House of Lords held that in connection with retention of DNA samples, which was then unlawful, the sample could be used in the subsequent trial of the same defendant on another charge. Lord Hutton (at 590) stated that it was necessary to consider the interest of the victim and the public as well as the defendant. Thus the key test was relevance. Laudan, upholds this argument (2008, p. 190): 'it is perfectly clear that the exclusion of germane inculpatory evidence on account of the way in which it was obtained, significantly increases the likelihood of false acquittals'. He gives two further reasons for privileging truth-seeking above other considerations, namely the economic waste of court time in deciding on admissibility and public perception of injustice over wrongful acquittals. It is also arguable that exclusion of evidence where the offence is a serious crime is a disproportionate response to police transgressions.

Lord Nolan commented in *R v Khan* **[1997] AC 558** at 573, 'It would be a strange reflection on our law if man who has admitted his participation in the illegal importation of heroin should have his conviction set aside on the grounds that his privacy has been invaded'.[6] It is significant that the House of Lords' stance was supported by the Strasbourg Court which held that there had been no breach of **Art. 6** although there was a breach of **Art. 8**. There was no absolute rule of exclusion.

Support for an inclusionary approach may also be based on the argument that if the objective is to discipline the investigative authorities, there are other means than exclusion of evidence to do this. These might include disciplinary proceedings against the police or civil suits on the part of the defendant. On the other hand, **s. 67(10) PACE** makes it clear that a breach of the Codes of Practice will not of itself render the officer liable to criminal or civil proceedings.[7] Finally, in favour of a flexible approach, it could be argued that an absolutist exclusionary approach avoids the difficulties faced in deciding whether minor improprieties should lead to evidence being excluded.

[7] It is open to the defendant to pursue other means of redress against investigatory impropriety; however, it is acknowledged that such avenues are limited. Roberts (2004), writing in relation to breaches of Code D of **PACE**, points out: although **s. 67(8) PACE** originally provided that an officer would be liable to disciplinary proceedings for any breach of the codes of practice, this provision was repealed by **s. 37 of the Police and Magistrates' Court Act 1994**.

Arguments in Favour of Exclusion or Stay of Prosecution

There are counter-arguments to those outlined earlier. In relation to entrapment there has been an increased adoption of the exclusionary approach deplored by Bentham. Thus in *R v Smurthwaite* **(1994) 98 Cr App R 437** the Court of Appeal considered applying **s. 78** to exclude evidence of a police 'sting' but decided on the facts not to do so. Here **Art. 6** considerations also prompt exclusion of evidence or stay of prosecution as in *Teixeira de Castro v Portugal* **(1998) 28 EHRR 101**. The leading case in the area is *R v Looseley*, conjoined appeals involving undercover police officers soliciting drugs. The judge stayed the proceedings on one case on the grounds that the police had incited the commission of the offence and that otherwise the accused would be denied his right to a fair hearing under **Art. 6(1)**. The stay was lifted, the prosecution offered no evidence, and the accused was acquitted. The Attorney General referred to the Court of Appeal the question whether in cases of entrapment the judicial discretion conferred by **s. 78 PACE** and the power to stay proceedings as an abuse of process had been modified by **Art. 6(1) of the European Convention on Human Rights**. The Court of Appeal held that it had not and that the trial judge had been wrong to stay the proceedings. The defendant in the first case appealed and reference was made from the Court of Appeal in the second. The House of Lords stated that the court must ask the central question which was whether the actions of the police were so seriously improper as to bring the administration of justice into disrepute.[8] If there was an abuse of state power

[8] This judgment demonstrates strong judicial recognition of the dangers of excessive police behaviour in cases of entrapment. Lord Nicholls stated that *R v Sang* [1980] AC 402 had been 'overtaken' by statute and case law. In terms of criminal procedure, it is notable that the decision paid more attention to stay of prosecution than it did to exclusion of evidence.

then the appropriate remedy was a stay of the indictment, rather than exclusion of evidence. The appeal of the defendant in the first case was dismissed since the undercover officer did no more than present himself as an ordinary customer to a drug dealer. The judge had been correct in the second case to stay the proceedings. The decision of the Court of Appeal was reversed in part. The test was the integrity of the criminal justice system.

It is significant that a number of academics applaud this principled approach. Dennis (2013, p. 51) is one of a number of academics who applaud this principled approach to exclusion. He sees the overriding reason to be that of protecting the moral legitimacy of the verdict. Ashworth (2000) argues for an underlying principle of fidelity to legal values which should guide the exercise of the exclusionary discretion. He also identifies particularly the importance of compliance with Convention rights under the **Human Rights Act 1998.** He lists (2002, p. 35) 'the right to trial on evidence not obtained in violation of a fundamental right' as one of the procedural rights for persons accused of potentially serious crime.[9] There are indications that this principled approach is being increasingly embraced by Strasbourg as well as the English courts. Examples are *Allan v UK* **(2002) 36 EHRR 12** and the landmark judgment *A v Secretary of State for the Home Department (No. 2)* **[2006] 2 AC 221.** Evidence obtained by torture abroad, including that by non-state actors, may be contaminated and should not be admitted.

Nonetheless it is arguable that the Benthamite inclusionary approach is still more the norm than exclusion on grounds of impropriety although it is difficult to identify a coherent approach by the courts. Breaches of the **Regulation of Investigatory Powers Act 2000 (RIPA),** for example, rarely lead to exclusion. *Warren v Attorney-General of Jersey* **[2011] UKPC 10** held that the misconduct (illegal surveillance) had not influenced the defendants' behaviour and a stay had not been ordered.[10] Stays are, on the other hand, however, apparently now applied in some cases where the 'trick' is perpetrated by a non-state actor. In *Council for the Regulation of Health Professionals v GMC* **[2007] 1 WLR 3091** sufficiently gross misconduct by a non-state agent was potentially an instance where the use of evidence could be a breach of **Art. 6.** Such developments are significant in view of the increased involvement of lay people and individuals in forensic activity through social networking and the growth of what O'Floinn and Ormerod (2012, p. 506) call 'private entrapment'.

Conclusion

In conclusion, it is acknowledged that there are powerful moral arguments in favour of excluding improperly obtained evidence and that Bentham's utilitarian stance is ethically unattractive. Bronitt

[9] He points out (p. 36) that 'whereas a breach of **art. 3 [ECHR]** will make it unfair to rely on a resulting confession, it seems that a breach of a defendant's **art. 8** rights (for example by listening in to his conversation without authorisation to do so) will not necessarily render it unfair to rely on the resulting evidence'.

[10] In *Warren* Lord Dyson observed that a stay was correct in cases of abduction and entrapment but not illicitly intercepting privileged conversations (disapproving of the judgment in *R v Grant* [2006] QB 60).

and Roche (2000) argue that the consequence of tolerating abuse of the criminal justice process is the erosion of the rights of citizenship. Doubtless there is a need for undercover policing but there are dangers in upholding the view that secrecy and lack of accountability are paramount objectives, or ends justify means in policing and in investigating alleged criminal activity as recent scandals concerning police infiltration of protest groups have shown. Hyland and Walker (2014) give a very full account of serious abuses by undercover police leading to miscarriages of justice. An exclusion of evidence gathered in violation of human rights encourages public participation in the criminal justice process, a necessary ingredient of a healthy democracy.

LOOKING FOR EXTRA MARKS?

- ▦ *Allan v UK* deserves deeper analysis, particularly since it shows the close connection between confession gathering, impinging on the privilege against self-incrimination, and improper police practices.

- ▦ You could extend your examination of the Strasbourg cases in particular by reference to *Teixeira v Portugal* **(1998) 28 EHRR 101** whose importance the House of Lords recognised in *Looseley*.

- ▦ Another development with socio-legal implications for modern policing and legitimate protest movement is the increased use of undercover police infiltrating activist groups which may include entrapment: see *R v Barkshire* **[2011] EWCA Crim 1885**.

TAKING THINGS FURTHER

- ▦ Ashworth, A., 'Testing Fidelity to Legal Values: Official Involvement and Criminal Justice' (2000) 63 MLR 633.

  See reference in text to answer.

- ▦ Ashworth, A., *Human Rights, Serious Crime and Criminal Procedure* (London: Sweet & Maxwell, 2002).

  See reference in text to answer.

- ▦ Bronitt, S. and Roche, D., 'Between Rhetoric and Reality: Sociological and Republican Perspectives on Entrapment' (2000) 4 E & P 77.

  See reference in text to answer.

- ▦ Brooks, P., *Troubling Confessions* (Chicago: University of Chicago Press, 2001).

  A historical examination of the powerful place of confessions in culture, religion, and literature as well as legal systems.

- ▦ Dennis, I.H., 'Miscarriages of Justice and the Law of Confessions: Evidentiary Issues and Solutions' [1993] PL 291.

  A powerful review of the notorious miscarriages of justice which led to the appointment of the Royal Commission on Criminal Justice in 1991.

Galligan D.J., 'The Right to Silence Reconsidered' [1988] CLP 70.

See reference in text to answer.

Hartstone, J., 'Defensive Use of a Co-Accused's Confession and the Criminal Justice Act 2003' (2004) 86 E & P 165.

*Argues that the provisions in **s. 76A PACE** are unsatisfactory and may be in violation of **Art. 6 ECHR**.*

Hyland, K. and Walker, C., 'Undercover Policing and Underwhelming Laws' [2014] Crim LR 555.

Discusses concerns that undercover officers on occasion overstep the boundaries of fairness and gives examples of recent abuses.

Jackson, J.D., 'Silence and Proof: Extending the Boundaries of Criminal Proceedings in the United Kingdom' (2000) 5 E & P 145.

Jackson reviews the legislation which eroded the right to silence and illustrates how the police interview is now a formal part of the proceedings against the accused.

Laudan, L., *Truth Error and Criminal Law* (Cambridge: Cambridge University Press, 2008).

See reference in text to answer.

MacPartholan, C., 'Silencing Silence? The Right to Silence and the "Opt Out" of the New EU Directive on Criminal Proceedings' (2016) 180 Criminal Law and Justice Weekly, 26 November.

A perceptive summary of the Directive and reservations of UK and Ireland.

Malik, B., 'Silence on Legal Advice: Clarity But Not Justice, *R v Beckles*' (2005) 9 E & P 211.

See reference in text to answer.

O'Floinn, M. and Ormerod, D., 'Social Networking Material as Criminal Evidence' [2012] Crim LR 486.

See reference in text to answer.

Roberts, A., 'The Problem of Mistaken Identification. Some Observations on Process' (2004) 8 E & P 100.

See reference in text to answer.

Zuckerman, A., 'Bias and Suggestibility: Is There an Alternative to the Right to Silence?' in D. Morgan and G.M. Stephenson (eds), *Suspicion and Silence: The Right to Silence in Criminal Investigations* (London: Blackstone Press, 1994), p. 117.

See reference in text to answer.

Online Resources

www.oup.com/uk/qanda/

Go online for extra essay and problem questions, a glossary of key terms, online versions of all the answer plans and audio commentary on how selected ones were put together, and a range of podcasts which include advice on exam and coursework technique and advice for other assessment methods.

7

Supporting evidence: lies, identification evidence, and suspect witnesses

ARE YOU READY?

In order to prepare for the questions in this chapter you will need to have covered the following areas:

- identification evidence including **Turnbull** warnings, Code D of the **Police and Criminal Evidence Act 1984 (PACE)** on Identification of Persons by Police Officers and the relevant hearsay provisions of the **Criminal Justice Act 2003**
- the application of **s. 78 PACE** to improperly obtained identification evidence in breach of Code D
- lies by the defendant and discretionary ways of supporting such hazardous evidence

KEY DEBATES

Debate: should confessions be corroborated?

Forced confessions have been a major source of wrongful convictions. Some argue that the risk is all the greater since, by contrast with the position in Scotland, a confession alone is sufficient to found a conviction. Others doubt whether including a corroboration requirement would be sufficient and a better way forward would be the introduction of a **Turnbull**-style warning in situations where the conviction depends wholly or substantially on a disputed or retracted confession.

Debate: what additional measures could be introduced to address the continuing problem of mistaken identification?

Research suggest that one of the flaws in identification procedures is the way a witness's memory is vulnerable to distortions because of involvement in the pre-trial procedures after the initial encounter. This is too often seen as predominantly a question of evidential procedures whereas an interdisciplinary approach, including using insights from psychology, would achieve better results.

Despite the demise of the technical rules of corroboration, it remains an important part of a suspect witness warning to draw the attention of the jury to the existence or absence of evidence capable of confirming the evidence of the witness.

(Glover, *Murphy on Evidence*, 15th edn (Oxford: OUP, 2017), p. 287)

Critically evaluate this observation in the light of the current position on corroboration.

 CAUTION!

- You are required here to demonstrate an understanding of how and why the former corroboration rules have been replaced by the system of care warnings.

- You will need to demonstrate knowledge of the statutory changes made in 1988 and 1994 and the developing case law which has prompted Glover's comment, suggesting new practices are becoming systematised.

- As in all essay questions, you will be expected to have read some of the leading texts, such as those by Pattenden and Dennis and the theoretical arguments about the concept of corroboration put by Roberts and Zuckerman.

- By breaking down the question into smaller propositions you will develop a framework for your answer. As always, it is important to realise that the examiner in essay questions is not only requiring you to demonstrate up-to-date knowledge but also skilled legal analysis.

DIAGRAM ANSWER PLAN

Introduction: abolition of the old law: end of categorisation of witnesses and overly technical rules.

⬇

The current position: discretion not rule.

⬇

Anomalies of the current position.

⬇

Possible new areas for reform: confessions, expert evidence.

⬇

New areas: legislation on silence and case law on hearsay.

⬇

Conclusion: need also to improve pre-trial procedures.

Introduction: Abolition of the Old Law and End of Categorisation of Witnesses and Technical Rules

Glover's observation on the recent history of corroboration in English law suggests that it followed this trajectory: abolition of the overly technical old law and its eventual (i.e. not immediate) replacement by corroboration requirements to suit the modern age. This essay will analyse this development and suggest also that the observation suggests that further developments in this area may still be necessary.[1]

The law on corroboration had been very formal and included a rigid categorisation of witnesses. A major weakness was the mandatory requirement of a corroboration warning for certain groups of witnesses, irrespective of their specific individual characteristics. Historically, the three categories of witnesses were, first, child witnesses, the need for a formal warning having been abolished by **s. 34(2) of the Criminal Justice Act (CJA) 1988**. Particular criticism was directed at the mandatory requirement of a corroboration warning for the second category, complainants in sexual cases, who were predominantly women. The third category was accomplices testifying for the prosecution. The latter two categories were removed in **s. 32 of the Criminal Justice and Public Order Act 1994 (CJPOA)**.

Current Position: Discretion Not Rule

Glover's comment suggests that the courts here eschewed an absolutist stance on corroboration. While recommendations were made to abolition of formal categorisation of witnesses, there was a parallel argument that there should be acknowledgement of the need to maintain the already existing discretionary power. This allowed for a residual class of cases where some form of warning should be given because the testimony of the witness may be suspect or tainted for some reason which might include honest mistake. An important example of this was the introduction of **Turnbull** warnings in identification cases. Other areas of discretionary warnings also had developed. This could be because the witness may have a grudge against the defendant, or is malicious, or has some other purpose of his or her own to serve.[2]

Apart from the categorisation of a witness, another major criticism of the corroboration rules had been the complex definition of corroboration, as set out by the Court of Appeal in **R v Baskerville [1916] 2 KB 658**. This definition looked at the accumulation of testimony rather than its quality. By requiring 'independent evidence implicating the accused', rather than independent evidence that confirms the suspect witness is telling the truth, the definition concentrated on guilt rather

---

[1] The Law Commission Report, *Corroboration in Criminal Trials* (Cmnd 1620, 1991) had described the law as 'arcane, technical and difficult to convey'.

[2] An example of the existing 'care warnings' is *R v Beck* [1982] 1 WLR 461 in relation to defendants suffering from a mental disorder.

than the witness's credibility. In *R v Makanjoula* [1995] 1 WLR 1348 the Court of Appeal rejected the need for a 'full old style direction' in cases where the trial judge decided that some form of warning may be necessary. Lord Taylor CJ said (at 1351) '[it] was in our judgment, partly to escape from the tortuous exercise which juries must have found more bewildering than illuminating, that parliament enacted **s 32**'.

The birth of the new regime for corroboration was not immediate and it slowly became clear that discretionary warnings rather than abolition was the result. The warnings now, however, were to be applied mostly when the evidence not the characteristics of the witness appeared to prompt it. The value of introducing discretionary warnings was illustrated in the case of *Pringle v R* [2003] **UKPC 9**. Lord Hope's speech referred to the need to consider a discretionary warning 'where an untried prisoner claims that a fellow untried prisoner confessed to him that he was guilty of the crime for which he was then being held in custody'. Cell confessions have proved a fertile area for the development of the type of case where discretionary warnings are more or less expected. Guidance on these is given in *R v Stone* [2005] **EWCA Crim 105**. In *Benedetto and Labrador v R* [2003] 1 WLR 1545 the prosecution case rested largely on a cell confession. The Privy Council stated that in these circumstances the prisoner would normally have an interest in providing information to the authorities and there should be safeguards in place. A judicial warning as to possible dangers in relying on the confession was normally required.

Anomalies of the Current Position

It could be argued that the current approach has its failings. In the first place some commentators see an unwelcome return of rigidity in relation to warnings concerning accomplices testifying for the prosecution. Thus in *R v Jones and Jenkins* [2002] **EWCA Crim 1966** the Court of Appeal required a discretionary care warning in a case where co-defendants operated a 'cut-throat defence'. Some argued that this achieved too close an affinity with the abolished practices. Thus Choo (2018, p. 349) writes, '. . . there is a danger that trial judges may in fact be continuing to give strong warnings in relation to alleged accomplices testifying for the prosecution and complainants in sexual cases, even if a warning is not warranted in the circumstances of the particular case'.[3] On the other hand, perhaps some approaches are arguably not strict enough. For example, there is some pressure to make warnings in the case of cell confessions compulsory. As Leake and Ormerod (2005, p. 571) comment on *R v Stone* [2005] **EWCA Crim 105**, 'the especially damning nature of the evidence' together with other dangers renders cell confessions 'a qualitatively more dangerous category of evidence in all cases'.[4]

[3] He points out that particularly in sexual assault cases there may be a danger of wrongful acquittals.

[4] This was felt to be particularly important if the confession was very short.

[5] She rejected the proposal for
corroboration along the lines of
Scots law.

[6] Dennis points out that 'The use
of caution warnings has become
the preferred technique of both
the courts and Parliament in recent
years.'

Others argue that forced confessions made in the interview room also require support. Pattenden (1991) recommended a *Turnbull*-type warning should be introduced.[5] Dennis (2013, p. 654) writes, 'there remains a good case for the introduction of such a warning but to date no legislation has implemented the recommendation and the courts have shown no inclination to give effect to it'. The tendency thus, or the 'contemporary posture', is to favour warnings which are, as Dennis puts it, 'less formal and less technical'.[6]

An indication of the reluctance to return to the earlier state of affairs is the current controversy over flawed expert scientific testimony. In *R v Cannings* [2004] 1 WLR 2607 the Court of Appeal called for 'additional cogent evidence, extraneous to the expert evidence' where there was a dispute between experts over the cause of sudden infant deaths. This was not, however, applied in *R v Kai-Whitewind* [2005] EWCA Crim 1092 where there was a previously admitted urge on the part of a parent to kill the infant.

Identification and the Defendant's Lies

In two particular well-established areas, identification evidence and to a lesser extent lies as evidence, there are suggestions that further official intervention is needed. With regard to the latter, Kennedy LJ in *Burge and Pegg* [1996] Cr App R 163 stressed the danger of overuse of *Lucas* directions: 'if a *Lucas* direction is given where there is no need for such a direction (as in the normal case where there is a straightforward conflict of evidence) it will add complexity and do more harm than good'. The risk is the jury might be confused (see also *R v Middleton* [2001] Crim LR 251). It seems here there is a return to elements of the former rigidity. Identification evidence is a more complex matter. Here the risk perhaps is that the emphasis on discretionary warnings detracts from other means of treating this area of evidence which is a notorious cause of miscarriages of justice. Roberts and Zuckerman (2010, p. 689), although acknowledging that *Turnbull* can hardly be said to have eliminated the risk of mistaken eyewitness identification leading to wrongful conviction, argue that the guidelines have probably achieved all that can be achieved in this regard without fundamentally rethinking the basic adversarial structure of English criminal procedure and trial practice. The courts are addressing the new forms of identification through social media. In *R v Alexander and McGill* [2013] 1 Cr App R 26 suspects were initially informally identified by the alleged victims through Facebook pictures. The Court of Appeal, although it did not declare an abuse of process, was critical of the practices of the police and CPS. It stated (para. 22), 'It seems to us, for the future, that if, as is to be anticipated, identifications occur in the way in which this identification occurred, namely by looking through Facebook, it is incumbent upon the police and the prosecutor to take steps to obtain, in as much detail as possible, evidence in relation to the initial identification. For example, it would be prudent to obtain the available images that were looked at and a statement in relation to what happened'.

Glover's reference to 'suspect witness' needs some amplification. In the case of identification evidence, mistakes can of course be made by honest members of the public who have no reason to be biased. Thus some commentators call ambitiously for a broader approach to developing new frameworks to avoid miscarriages of justice. Roberts (2004) advocates an interdisciplinary path to reform which imports safeguards beyond the rules of evidence in areas such as cognitive psychology.[7]

[7]This would aid understanding of how a witness's memory is open to distortion by encounters in pre-trial procedures.

New Areas: Legislation on Silence and Hearsay

Glover indicates how the concept of corroboration has been given a new lease of life particularly in the case law on discretionary warnings. Parliament also has played a part in extending the practice of seeking supportive evidence. It has legislated to prescribe corroboration practices, as in **s. 38 of the CJPOA** for example.[8] Finally, one further point could be made to set the context for Glover's analysis. Overall, English law remains wedded to the doctrine that one piece of evidence may be sufficient to convict. New areas of jurisprudence on the extent of the need for supportive evidence are emerging as *R v Horncastle* **[2009] UKSC 14** has demonstrated in the case of hearsay.[9]

[8]The defendant's silence alone admitted under **ss. 34–37** cannot found a conviction.

[9]In rare circumstances a conviction can be founded on hearsay alone.

Conclusion

Glover's analysis highlights the flexibility of the current law which replaced an overly rigid framework. Discretionary care warnings allow the courts greater flexibility. There seems to be little appetite to return to the former rigidity. However, it is important that the concept of corroboration as a theoretical device should be kept alive. As Roberts and Zuckerman point out (2010, p. 663), 'Abolishing the law of corroboration no more dispenses with epistemic standards assessing evidential support than abolishing the law of hearsay would curb the inherent infirmities of second-hand evidence.' It is crucial, they argue, to put in place pre-trial procedures as well as directions on corroboration to deal with evidence that is suspect.[10]

[10]Examples they give include identification procedures, meetings of expert witnesses, and pre-trial interviewing of witnesses.

LOOKING FOR EXTRA MARKS?

■ You could gain credit by extending your analysis of *R v Spencer* **[1987] AC 128** where the House of Lords, overturning earlier authority, held that where the prosecution relied on the evidence of a witness who because of his mental condition and criminal background may give suspect evidence, the judge should warn the jury that it is dangerous to convict on the uncorroborated evidence of the witness. However, the House of Lords stressed that the judge need not give the full corroboration warning required in the established categories.

- Another example of judicial acceptance of the need to temper the technical rules was *R v Chance* [1988] QB 932 where the Court of Appeal decided that where the only issue was one of identity in a rape case, only a *Turnbull* warning was required. Of course, *R v Turnbull* [1977] QB 224 had set, albeit lengthy, 'guidelines' for identification cases rather than setting a requirement for a formal corroboration warning.

- You would impress the examiners by exhibiting a deeper knowledge of the Strasbourg jurisprudence, for example point to *Khan v UK* (2001) 31 EHRR 45 where the only prosecution evidence in securing the conviction was uncorroborated evidence obtained by undercover activity which breached **Art. 8**.

QUESTION | 2

Sam and Alan are charged with the attempted rape of Amy. The case against them is that Amy met Sam and Alan in the local wine bar and they started chatting. She had not known them before. After a short while Amy, who was feeling drunk, went outside to an alleyway for some fresh air. The alleyway was very dark at the time. Two men approached her and attempted to rape her. She thought she recognised them as the men in the wine bar but she is unsure. As a result of her screams, the two men stopped and ran away. A passer-by, Mandy, saw two men running away. She saw the face of one of them under a street lamp and the police made a photofit to her description. Giles, a police constable, recognised the photofit picture as being that of Alan whom he had previously arrested on suspicion of criminal damage. Amy is taken to the wine bar the next day by police and picks out Sam, a customer, as one of the men who tried to rape her. The police had failed to take a description of the attackers from Amy before they took her to the wine bar. At first Sam claimed he was at work on the night of the alleged attempted rape but later admitted this was a lie and that he was in the wine bar with a girlfriend. He claims he lied to protect the girlfriend because she was married. Mandy was killed in a road traffic accident shortly after the alleged attempted rape. Tony, a cleaner at the wine bar, is visually impaired but claims he recognised Alan's voice in the bar. Alan denies he was at the wine bar on the night in question. Both Sam and Alan deny any involvement in the attempted rape and demand that identification procedures are held.

Evaluate the difficulties which the prosecution may face with the evidence.

CAUTION!

- This question requires a discussion of the rules relating to the treatment of identification evidence in court and also the use of lies told by the defendant as prosecution evidence. As regards the victim's evidence, it is clear that because of her state of intoxication and the bad lighting conditions, a *Turnbull* direction will have to be given.

- The other issue revolves around the photofit picture and how the court should treat this evidence.

- Another difficulty that will be encountered is with regards to the identification of Alan by Giles. The basis of Giles's recognition of Alan and whether that is admissible in evidence will have to be considered.

- There is also the point in relation to corroboration in this case in that it needs to be made clear that no corroboration warning is required as a result of the **CJPOA 1994**. And the controversial area of voice recognition is also in issue.

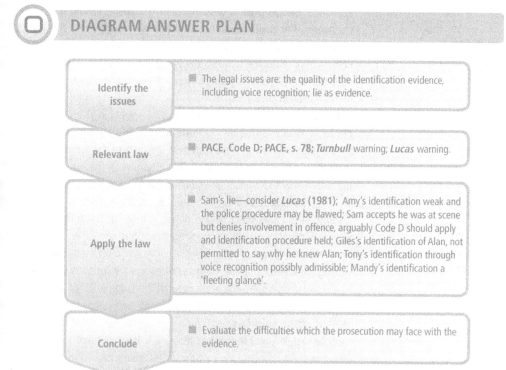

DIAGRAM ANSWER PLAN

Identify the issues
- The legal issues are: the quality of the identification evidence, including voice recognition; lie as evidence.

Relevant law
- PACE, Code D; PACE, s. 78; *Turnbull* warning; *Lucas* warning.

Apply the law
- Sam's lie—consider *Lucas* (1981); Amy's identification weak and the police procedure may be flawed; Sam accepts he was at scene but denies involvement in offence, arguably Code D should apply and identification procedure held; Giles's identification of Alan, not permitted to say why he knew Alan; Tony's identification through voice recognition possibly admissible; Mandy's identification a 'fleeting glance'.

Conclude
- Evaluate the difficulties which the prosecution may face with the evidence.

SUGGESTED ANSWER

Amy's Identification of Sam: *Turnbull* Warning

The problems faced by the prosecution counsel start with the identification of Sam by the victim, Amy. In effect, her identification evidence is weak both because of her intoxicated condition and the bad lighting. In *R v Turnbull* **[1977] QB 224**, the Court of Appeal laid down guidelines for the treatment of identification evidence where the case depends wholly or substantially on the correctness of the identifications. The guidelines state, inter alia, that the judge should warn the jury of the special need for caution, before convicting the accused in reliance on the correctness of the identification evidence which the defence alleges to be mistaken. The judge should draw the jury's attention to the possibility that an error was made and should invite them to examine closely the circumstances in which the observation took place. The guidelines go on to provide that the jury should also examine closely the conditions under which, and the length of time for which, the observation took place. Factors such as whether the witness knew the accused, or whether there was any particular reason for the witness to remember the accused, or how soon after the event the witness gave a description to the police, should also be considered. The guidelines state that the judge should remind the jury of any weaknesses in the identification evidence and that where the identification evidence is weak, the judge should withdraw the case from the jury unless there is any other evidence which will support the identification evidence.

It has been made clear by the Court of Appeal in *R v Oakwell* **[1978] 1 WLR 32**, that the *Turnbull* guidelines are not to be interpreted inflexibly. It is thus clear that on the facts of the present case, the judge will need to draw the jury's attention to the weaknesses present in Amy's identification evidence, namely that it was dark, that she was intoxicated, and the fact that she may have remembered him because of the time spent talking to him in the wine bar. If the judge considers that the quality of the identification is good then he may allow the case to proceed in the absence of any other evidence supporting the identification, as long as he delivers the *Turnbull* warning in the summing-up. On the other hand, if the judge is of the opinion that the quality of Mandy's or Amy's identification is poor but sees there is other evidence which could support the two identifications then he should point this out to the jury. It is for the jury to decide whether the evidence does support it. He should also warn the jury about any evidence which, it is felt, they might wrongly believe is supportive.[1]

[1] The possible supporting evidence is Sam's admitted lie which is covered below.

No Video Identification Procedure

The defence may suggest that the police should have held a video identification rather than take Amy to the wine bar for the identification. However, it may be argued that they had no information whereby they could make an arrest of Sam. Code D of the **Police and Criminal Evidence Act 1984 (PACE)** including Annex B governs the procedure for obtaining identification evidence. Code D para. 3.2 and Annex C provides that where the identity of a suspect is not known a police officer may take a witness to a particular neighbourhood or place to see whether he or she can identify the person allegedly seen on the relevant occasion. Before doing so however, and, where practical, the police should take a record of any description given by the witness of the suspect (Code D para. 3.2(a)). Here the police have failed to do this. They should also have made a video of the general scene if practicable, to give a general impression of the scene and the numbers present. One question is whether a video identification should have been held. In *R v Forbes* [2001] **1 AC 473** the appeal turned on whether the street identification of the defendant could be admitted. It was held that the breach of Code D did not require the evidence to be excluded under s. 78. The facts are similar here to *Forbes* and it is arguable that the judge will not exclude the evidence of the identification.[2]

Sam's Lie

The identification evidence against Sam is arguably weak and the prosecution may seek to rely on his admitted lie as supportive evidence of his guilt. If they do so the judge will have to warn the jury about the dangers of relying on this evidence. In *R v Goodway* **(1994) 98 Cr App R 11** Lord Taylor CJ stated that 'where lies told by the defendant are relied on . . . as support for identification evidence, the judge should give a direction along the lines indicated in *Lucas* [1981] QB 720'. In *R v Burge and Pegg* [1996] **1 Cr App R 364** the Court of Appeal summarised the circumstances in which a *Lucas* direction should be given. Sam has admitted the lie so it is therefore unnecessary for the judge to direct that the jury must find it proved beyond reasonable doubt. The lie can support the prosecution case only if the jury is sure Sam did not lie for an innocent reason. There is thus a significant amount of case law. The jury must be satisfied that there is no innocent motive for the lie, as here there may be. It may be that Sam did lie to protect his girlfriend.[3]

Mandy

Mandy does not appear to have seen Sam but only Alan. Since the evidence against Alan is weak and in view of the *Turnbull* guidelines, it is possible that the judge will withdraw the case against him and direct the jury to acquit him. If, however, there was another eyewitness who saw Alan running away, albeit in a fleeting glimpse-type situation, whilst the judge may leave the evidence to the jury, he would need to give the *Turnbull* warning and direct them specifically that even a number of honest persons can be wrong: *R v Weeder* **(1980) 71 Cr App R 228** and *R v Breslin* **(1984) 80 Cr App R 226**.

The other difficulty that the prosecution may have with the evidence is Mandy's testimony. If Mandy was still alive and gave testimony in court, her testimony would be subject to the *Turnbull* direction, as it could be argued that her evidence falls within the situation which the *Turnbull* guidelines were intended to cover. Again, arguably an identification parade should have been held, although clearly Mandy's death was unforeseen. However, now that she is dead the question is whether the photofit is admissible into evidence. In *R v Smith* **[1976] Crim LR 511**, a photofit picture was held not to offend the rule against hearsay. However, the Court of Appeal in *R v Cook* **[1987] 1 All ER 1049** went a step further. The Court of Appeal decided that photofit pictures were in a class of evidence of their own. Neither the rule against hearsay nor the rule against previous consistent statements had any application to such evidence.[4] The Court of Appeal's approach in drawing an analogy between a photofit or sketch and a photograph is arguably surprising in view of the acknowledged differences between them. Thus, on the facts of this case, it is clear that the photofit picture would be admissible in evidence notwithstanding that Mandy is not able to give evidence.

However, in view of the fact that Mandy's identification originally was as a result of a fleeting-glance situation, it seems probable that the judge will have to give the ***Turnbull*** direction with respect to this evidence and may have to withdraw the case from the jury unless there is some other evidence to support it.

Giles and Tony

The third problem with the evidence is with regards to Giles's identification of Alan. Whilst it is likely that he can say that he identified Alan from the photofit picture, he is not allowed to say why he knew Alan. It is not permissible to tell the jury that the reason why Giles recognised Alan was because he had previously arrested Alan for criminal damage.[5] Tony may also be called as a witness. He may be able to identify the voice of Alan, one of the two suspects. It is now accepted that a ***Turnbull*** warning should be given in the case of voice recognition, see *R v Hershey* **[1998] Crim LR 281**. The police should have given Tony an opportunity to hear recordings of the voices of the suspects before the trial but this is an area which is as yet subject to scant regulation leading to possible mistaken identification. Since then *R v Flynn and St John* **[2008] 2 Cr App R 266** has given guidance.[6]

Conclusion

Thus, on the facts of the present case, it is likely that the case against Sam will be withdrawn from the jury and the ***Turnbull*** direction will, at the very least, have to be given with respect to the identification of Alan. It is not altogether clear whether the case against Alan will be withdrawn or not. This would depend on whether there was any other evidence available to support it, for example if Tony's voice recognition evidence is admissible.

[4] The photofit pictures are, according to the Court of Appeal, manifestations of the seeing eye, translations of vision onto paper through the medium of a police officer's skill of drawing or composing which a witness does not possess.

[5] If he did so it would reveal bad character.

[6] In that case the evidence against the defendants had included covert police recordings from a probe placed in the van used in a robbery. Police officers claimed the voices on the recording matched those of the defendants which they had heard following arrest. The defendants successfully appealed to the Court of Appeal. The court held that it was desirable but not mandatory for voice recognition to be carried out by experts.

LOOKING FOR EXTRA MARKS?

▧ Sam accepts he was present at the scene but denies involvement in the offence. You could
make reference to the disputed authority as to whether the police are required to conduct
a video parade when a suspect accepts he was present but denies involvement. In **K v DPP**
[2003] EWHC 351 (Admin) it was held that the judge was wrong not to hold a procedure
but in **Chen [2001] EWCA Crim 885** it was held that this was not necessary.

▧ If Amy cannot recall at the trial who she identified, the accompanying police officer may
give details of her identification evidence (**R v McCay [1990] 1 WLR 645**). The common law
exception to the rule against previous consistent statements allowed evidence of out-of-court
identification to be given by the witness or a third party who had witnessed the identification.
The **Criminal Justice Act 2003** extends this exception. **Section 120(4) and (5)** allow a
witness's previous statement which 'identifies or describes a person, object or place to be
admissible of any matter stated if the witness indicates that to the best of his belief he made
the statement, and that to the best of his belief it states the truth'.

TAKING THINGS FURTHER

▧ Costigan, R., 'Identification from CCTV: The Risk of Injustice' [2007] Crim LR 591.
*Demonstrates that research by psychologists reveals that the high level of confidence in CCTV
evidence is based on questionable assumptions, with insufficient awareness of the dangers of
identification from images.*

▧ Leake, S. and Ormerod, D., 'Case Comment. *R v Stone*' [2005] Crim LR 569.
*Questions whether the trial judge is obliged to give a special warning to the jury before
convicting the accused on the basis of a cell confession to a fellow untried prisoner.*

▧ Ormerod, D., 'Sounds Familiar—Voice Identification Evidence' [2001] Crim LR 595.
*A detailed examination of ways of addressing the risks in pre-trial and trial procedures of
using voice identification.*

▧ Pattenden, R., 'Should Confessions be Corroborated?' (1991) 107 LQR 317.
*Considers and rejects the introduction of a corroboration warning for confession evidence and
suggests alternative ways to prevent false confessions causing miscarriages of justice.*

▧ Roberts, A., 'The Problem of Mistaken Identification' (2004) 8 E & P 100.
*Identifies a serious problem of mistaken identifications leading to miscarriages of justice and
argues for an interdisciplinary approach, in particular the employment of insights from psychology.*

Online Resources
www.oup.com/uk/qanda/

Go online for extra essay and problem questions, a glossary of key terms, online versions of
all the answer plans and audio commentary on how selected ones were put together, and a
range of podcasts which include advice on exam and coursework technique and advice for
other assessment methods.

8 Opinion evidence

ARE YOU READY?

To perform well in these questions you will need to be familiar with recent developments in civil and criminal law including:

- the occurrence of miscarriages of justice caused by flawed expert evidence and allegedly poor scientific and statistical understanding by juries and lawyers
- the differences between expert and non-expert opinion evidence
- the statutory framework for civil law including the **Civil Evidence Act 1972** and the **Civil Procedure Rules 1998**
- the provisions of **s. 30 of the Criminal Justice Act (CJA) 1988** on expert evidence and hearsay and **s. 118(8) of the CJA 2003** preserving the common law rule that an expert witness may draw on the body of expertise relevant to his field
- the relevant sections of the **Criminal Procedure Rules 2015**

KEY DEBATES

Debate: should changes to the use of expert evidence in criminal trials be implemented by statute?

The Law Commission 2011 Report recommended a statutory admissibility test to be applied in appropriate cases. Under this, expert opinion would be admissible in criminal proceedings only if it is sufficiently reliable to be admitted ('the reliability test'). The judges would be provided by statute with a single list of generic factors to help them apply the reliability test. These proposals have not been accepted on grounds of cost. Instead amendments have been made to the **Criminal Procedure Rules**. Defenders of this approach argue that the common law precedents are sound but in some cases not adequately applied.

$\circlearrowright$

Debate: is the adversarial form of trial suitable to determine questions of expert evidence?

Some commentators argue that there is an overly deferential perception of expert witnesses and that this has led to miscarriages of justice such as *R v Clark* [2003] EWCA Crim 1020 and *R v Cannings* [2004] EWCA Crim 1. Note that the role of juries has been challenged by the decision in *R v Brennan* [2014] EWCA Crim 2387 holding that juries must have a good reason for refusing to accept uncontradicted expert evidence.

QUESTION | 1

Sarah (a minor) is suing Henfield Health Authority for damages for pain and suffering and loss of earnings as a result of negligent treatment she received as a patient in Henfield Hospital. It is alleged that the surgeon who operated on her was negligent in that what was supposed to be a simple surgical procedure resulted in some intermittent paralysis of her left side. Her solicitors have sought the opinion of John Williams, who worked in the same hospital as the surgeon and who produced a written report concluding that, in his opinion, the surgeon had not followed conventional and well-established procedures. Williams is relying in part on published reports of research by US surgeons. Williams, who had also acted for other claimants who had had a similar experience to Sarah in the same hospital, has been slow to respond to a court order that the experts from both parties set out areas of agreement or disagreement. The defence wishes to call evidence of Joan Soap, a psychiatrist, to the effect that Sarah is not to be trusted to speak the truth.

Advise the parties.

CAUTION!

- You need to consider the application of the **Civil Evidence Act 1995** providing for the making of new rules governing the admissibility of expert opinion evidence.

- A working knowledge of the procedural rules governing the admissibility of expert reports under the **Civil Procedure Rules 1998** will need to be shown.

DIAGRAM ANSWER PLAN

Identify the issues	▨ The legal issues are: the admissibility of expert medical and psychiatric evidence in civil cases; use of hearsay evidence, impartiality of expert.
Relevant law	▨ Application of **Civil Evidence Act 1972, s. 3(1)** and **CPR, r. 35.1.**
Apply the law	▨ Judge must establish expertise of Williams and Soap and admissibility of their evidence; experts may rely on work of others. Williams's impartiality may be questioned since he had acted for others in similar cases. He may be disqualified for failure to comply with the **CPR**.
Conclude	▨ Both witnesses' evidence may be admitted although the court may be critical of Williams's possible lack of objectivity and failure to respond to the court order.

SUGGESTED ANSWER

General Rule

The general rule is that a witness cannot give his or her opinion on a fact in issue. To allow a witness to do so would be to usurp the function of the court, which is to draw an inference from the facts put before it. A witness should therefore only be allowed to give evidence of facts and that which he or she has observed. However, there are exceptions to this and the important exception that applies here is the admissibility of expert opinion evidence where it would assist the court in reaching its decision.

John Williams

First, it should be noted that the expert evidence is admissible even though the expert may give an opinion on the ultimate issue.[1] On the facts of the present case, it is arguable that Williams, by concluding that the surgeon was negligent, is offering an opinion as to the ultimate issue. This is not a problem in civil trials because **s. 3(1) of the Civil Evidence Act 1972** provides that where any person is called as a witness, his opinion on any relevant matter (which by **subs. (3)** includes an issue in the proceedings in question), on which he is

[1] In criminal law the rule technically still exists, although in practice ignored. Choo observes (2018, p. 323). '. . . the express abolition of any ultimate issue rule in criminal proceedings must be regarded as long overdue'.

qualified to give expert evidence, is to be admissible in evidence. It is for the judge to decide on the admissibility of this medical evidence of Williams.

The **Civil Procedure Rules (CPR) 1998** made sweeping changes as to the admissibility of expert evidence in civil cases. **Rule 35.1** of the 1998 Rules restricts expert evidence to that which is reasonably required to resolve the proceedings. One of these fundamental changes that the Rules have made is that in accordance with **r. 35.3** the duty imposed on the expert is to assist the court on those matters in which he has expertise.

Impartiality

The fact that the expert is employed by one of the parties is dealt with by the rule that makes it clear that the duty to the court overrides any obligation to the person who instructed him. This is reinforced by the fact that the written expert reports must be addressed to the court.

The court will have to be satisfied that the experts are independent—in other words, that although they are retained by the parties they give opinions in an objective and fair way and place their duty to the court beyond that to the parties. **Rule 35.3 of the CPR 1998** provides: '(1) it is the duty of an expert to help the court on the matters within his expertise. (2) This function overrides any obligation to the person from whom he had received instructions or by whom he is paid'.[2] Williams should be reminded that the courts have given much attention to the ethical considerations involved in the use of expert witnesses. *Vernon v Bosley (No. 1)* **[1997] 1 All ER 577**, for example, had stressed the requirement of objectivity, and the duty owed to the court.[3] It is possible that Williams's impartiality may be called into question since **r. 33.2 of the CPR 2015** specifies the requirement of an 'objective and unbiased' opinion.

The **CPR** specify how expert evidence is presented to the court. **Rule 35.5** provides that expert evidence shall be given by way of a written report in all cases unless the court orders otherwise. In this, Williams appears to be following procedure.[4] **Rule 35.10** states that the report should contain a statement that the expert understands his duty to the court and has complied with it. Williams must verify that the facts and opinions stated in the report are true and correct.

Joan Soap's Evidence

The submission of evidence from Joan Soap would raise difficult issues. Psychiatrists are generally less well received than other medical practitioners.[5] The defence will be aided, however, by *Re M and R (Minors) (Sexual Abuse: Video Evidence)* **[1996] 4 All ER 239**.

[2] The court held that a QC should not act as an expert witness on behalf of a member of his chambers. The latter was a defendant in an action for professional negligence and the proposed expert witness had expressed his sympathy for his colleague.

[3] In that case the court observed that the plaintiff was not assisted by disinterested evidence from the medical professional witnesses.

[4] For cases that are on the fast track the court will not permit oral expert evidence unless the interests of justice require such oral testimony.

[5] Note also that as Glover puts it (2017, p. 623), in civil cases the CPR 1998 'effectively supersede the right of the parties at common law to present expert evidence as they see fit'.

In that case Butler-Sloss LJ held that a suitably qualified expert could give evidence as to the credibility of a child witness who had given evidence by way of a video-taped interview. The expert evidence fell within the ambit of **s. 3 of the Civil Evidence Act 1972.** Glover (2017, p. 626) argues that this analysis is inaccurate but can be understood on the basis that this was expert psychiatric and psychological evidence.[6] He points out that the 'ultimate issue in such a case is not whether the child's evidence is credible but whether the alleged abuse occurred (though obviously the question of the child's credibility is of great importance in resolving the ultimate issue)'. He goes on, however, to point out that the decision in the case can be defended on the basis that although expert opinion is not admissible on the issue of credibility since that is a lay matter, psychiatrists and psychologists may form an opinion about credibility because their assessments are often based on what their clients told them. The issue for the defence is relevance. If Sarah's testimony is disputed then arguably her credibility is a collateral issue and evidence may be taken on it.

[6] Note the differing stances in criminal and civil cases. In *R v MacKenney* (1981) 76 Cr App R 271 a psychologist's evidence was not admitted since he was not medically trained.

Necessary Expertise

It will be necessary to establish that Williams and Soap have the requisite expertise in the area in order to give their opinions on these matters. The Supreme Court addressed the factors which suggest the need for skilled evidence in *Kennedy v Cordia Services Ltd UK* **[2016] UKSC 6.**[7] The court set out four: (i) whether the proposed skilled evidence will assist the court in its task; (ii) whether the witness has the necessary knowledge and experience; (iii) whether the witness is impartial in his or her presentation and assessment of the evidence; and (iv) whether there is a reliable body of knowledge or experience to underpin the expert's evidence. This is a question for the judge to decide prior to allowing the evidence to be admitted.

[7] This is a Scottish case but as Glover (2017, p. 623) points out, 'Pending a Supreme Court decision on the law in England and Wales, this decision is likely to be highly persuasive'.

The witness must demonstrate sufficient knowledge and experience to render their evidence potentially of value.[8]

That would appear to apply to the relevant professional bodies governing Williams and Soap.

[8] You could point out that the court also stated *that expert evidence could still be excluded if the court considered it would not assist the court for whatever reason.*

Hearsay and Expert Evidence

Another point to note is that an expert is entitled to rely on the work of others in reaching his conclusion. We are told that Williams is relying on US publications for his research. In civil proceedings hearsay statements are admissible under the **Civil Evidence Act 1995** since, with certain provisos, such statements are admissible as 'any representation of fact or opinion however made'.

Oral Testimony

As regards whether Williams or Soap can be called to give evidence (for cases not on the fast track), this is governed by **r. 35.4**. This provides that no party shall call an expert without the court's permission. When permission is sought from the court, the party must identify the field in which he wishes to rely on the expert evidence and, where practicable, the expert in that field on whose evidence he wishes to rely.[9]

[9] In civil cases there are strict rules about advance notice of expert evidence (see **Civil Evidence Act 1972, s. 2(3)**). Under the **CPR** a party who fails to disclose an expert's report may not use the report at trial or call the expert as a witness without the court's permission (**r. 35.11**).

Both Sarah and the Henfield Health Authority should be warned that they should be certain they want to use the experts' reports before disclosing them to the other side. Under the **CPR** any party to whom such a report is disclosed can put it in evidence, legal professional privilege being lost at that point (see **Chapter 10**). CPR, **r. 35.7(1)** states that 'where two or more parties wish to submit expert evidence on a particular issue, the court may direct that the evidence on that issue is to be given by one expert only'. It may well be the case that the parties wish to call evidence on these issues and if they cannot agree on the expert the court may select an expert from a list submitted by the parties or give directions on how the expert should be selected. Once selected, each party can instruct the expert, although they must send copies of the instructions to the other side.

One problem Williams may face is that he may be in breach of a court order in his delay in responding to the request for a statement of agreements or disagreements with the experts of the other side. In a similar situation in *Stevens v Gullis* [2000] 1 All ER 527 the judge held the expert had debarred himself from giving evidence.[10]

[10] This decision highlights the duty experts owe to the court.

Finally, both parties can expect the judgment to reflect the reasons why the views of the expert have been accepted. In *English v Emery Reimbold and Strick Ltd* [2002] 3 All ER 385 the court stated that the judge should provide an explanation as to why he has accepted the evidence of one expert and rejected that of the other.[11]

[11] However, the appeal was lost although there were shortcomings in the judgment. An unsuccessful party should not seek to overturn a judgment for inadequacy of reasons unless, despite the advantage of considering the judgment with knowledge of the evidence and submissions at trial, that party was unable to understand why the judge had reached an adverse decision.

Conclusion

Before the evidence of John Williams and Joan Soap can be adduced, permission will have to be obtained from the court and the way the evidence will be presented will be by way of a written report. If the parties wish to call experts to give oral testimony, then permission of the court has to be obtained and would depend on the circumstances of the case as to whether the court will allow such testimony to be given. Each can also appoint their own expert but the two experts will then have to meet to agree the reports to the court. There may be grounds of appeal if the judge prefers lay opinion to uncontradicted expert opinion on a matter on which expert opinion is appropriate (see *Re B (A Minor)* [2000] 1 WLR 790).

LOOKING FOR EXTRA MARKS?

- It would be appropriate to point out that the **CPR** recommend that the parties appoint a single joint expert in situations such as the question presents.
- In answers to problem questions such as this you should avoid using the case law mechanistically since each case will turn on its own specific facts.

QUESTION | 2

Jurors do not need psychiatrists to tell them how ordinary folk who are not suffering from any mental illness are likely to react to the stresses and strains of life.

(*R v Turner* [1975] QB 834 per Lawton LJ)

Critically evaluate the current approach of the courts to the admissibility of expert psychiatric evidence in criminal trials.

CAUTION!

- This appears to be a relatively straightforward question but you should avoid the temptation to give a narrative account of the law and instead display your analytical knowledge of some of the controversies in this area, such as whether criminal trials should move towards court-appointed experts as in civil cases and whether the law in the area needs codifying.
- Display your knowledge that recent cases about flawed expert evidence have shone the spotlight on this area of law, particularly on the question of whether the distinction between fact and opinion is a meaningful one.
- Note that the question is asking you to respond on the matter of psychiatric evidence specifically and you should not superficially cover expert evidence more generally.

DIAGRAM ANSWER PLAN

Introduction: current procedure for admissibility, conceptual framework for admissibility highlighted in *Turner*.

Examples of admissible psychiatric expert evidence; procedural issues.

Examples of inadmissible expert psychiatric evidence: intention and credibility.

Examples of admissible psychiatric evidence: confessions and personality disorder.

The status of expert knowledge, new areas of expertise, and the importance of preserving social trust in verdicts.

Conclusion: critiques of the current position and the difficulty of reform.

SUGGESTED ANSWER

Introduction

The overall picture in relation to the use of expert evidence in criminal trials has changed since the landmark case of *Turner* quoted in the question. Expert opinion evidence generally is of growing importance but as the quotation suggests there are still significant reservations about the admissibility of evidence from psychiatrists or psychologists concerning the mental or emotional state of witnesses, particularly the defendant. The general rule is that expert evidence is only to be admitted on matters where a judge or jury cannot form their own conclusions.[1] In *Turner* the defendant's mental vulnerability to provocation was a matter for the jury to decide and they could do this, according to the court, without 'help' from an expert. The issues this decision raises are: when and why is evidence from psychiatrists admissible because it is helpful to the jury, when and why is it not admissible. Furthermore, is the approach of the court conducive to a fair trial. Each of these issues will be covered in turn but first the procedure for admissibility will be outlined.

Procedure for Admissibility

The question of the admissibility of expert evidence on mental state has to be seen in the context of the more general problem of when expertise opinion is admissible. Admissibility is a matter of law for the judge to decide. There is as yet no statutory framework in criminal trials but guidance is given in the **Criminal Procedure Rules 2015**.[2] **Part 19** draws on the 'active case management' principles previously introduced in civil cases. The Government rejected the imposition of a statutory code recommended by the Report of the Law Commission, *Expert Evidence in Criminal Proceedings* (2011). The test for admissibility would be 'reliability' and judges would be provided with a list of generic factors to apply. Roberts and Zuckerman (2010, p. 483) comment that 'English law is notably liberal in its approach to the admissibility of expert evidence' and Keane and McKeown (2016, p. 593)

---

[1] In *Turner* itself the defendant, on trial for killing his girlfriend, claimed he had been provoked by her saying he was not the father of her expected child. He wanted to adduce evidence from a psychiatrist to say he was not a violent person by nature but he had a personality such that he could have been provoked and that he was likely to be telling the truth. The evidence was held to be irrelevant because his mental health was not in issue.

[2] The question of cost was a factor in the Government's rejection of a statutory Code. Under the Law Commission's proposal the judge would have acted as gate-keeeper. Keane and McKeown (2016, p. 593) point out that this raises complex questions such as whether the scientific techniques are accepted by the academic community. They cite the US case *Daubert v Merrell Dow Pharmaceuticals*, 509 US 579 (1993).

refer to a 'relaxed approach'. An example is *R v Lutrell* **[2004] EWCA Crim 1344**, a case concerned with the admissibility of evidence from a lip-reading expert, which expressed the general rule. As scientific and technological knowledge advances, formerly fringe areas become mainstream, see for example the recognition of earprinting as a field of expertise (*R v Dallagher* **[2003] 1 Cr App R 145**). Areas of mental health and psychiatric traits have arguably, however, been treated more conservatively in part because of concern that it will impinge on the main plank of criminal justice—the concepts of free will and individual responsibility exemplified in '*mens rea*'.

Admissible Psychiatric Expert Evidence

For expert evidence to be admissible the evidence has to be relevant, the witness, from study or experience, had an authority that others not so qualified did not have, and the witness must be so qualified to express the opinion. There are a number of cases concerning psychiatric evidence specifically where these conditions are fulfilled. These involve instances of mental disturbance or personality disorder as the quotation above suggests. In some instances the medical conditions clearly indicate expert evidence is need: for example, in *R v Toner* **[1991]**. Other cases are not so clear-cut but the court has exceptionally accepted that they merit expert witness testimony. For example, in *Toohey v MPC* **[1965] AC 595** the alleged victim of an assault had been found by police in a hysterical state. Medical evidence on his mental state was admissible, an example of where, in the words quoted from *Turner,* the jury would be helped in deciding whether to believe his account. There was an objective reason for the difficulty the witness appeared to have in telling the truth. Similarly in *DPP v A&B Chewing Gum Ltd* **[1968] 1 QB 159**, an expert in child psychiatry was called to show that the cards would have a tendency to deprave or corrupt children. *Lowery v R* **[1974] AC 85** is a more controversial case. Two men were accused of murdering a girl. Each blamed the other. Lowery's co-defendant called a psychiatrist to give evidence that Lowery's personality made it more likely that he had committed the offence. The Privy Council held the evidence had been rightly admitted in this Australian case. The court in *Turner* explained, however, that this was a limited authority. It was decided on its own special facts.[3]

These cases present somewhat extreme circumstances prompting admissibility of expertise.

Inadmissible Expert Psychiatric Evidence: *Mens Rea* and Credibility

More complex are cases involving the credibility of a witness, the reason being that the basis of the criminal justice system is the question

---

[3] Pattenden (1986) doubts the decision is as limited as the court in *Turner* suggests and welcomes it as an instance where expert evidence was admissible where the defendant was not 'abnormal'.

of guilt. Whether to believe the defendant's not guilty plea is a moral not a technical issue. Thus it is for the jury to pronounce on credibility in the ordinary run of cases. In *R v Chard* (1971) 56 Cr App R 268, evidence from an expert on the alleged inability of the accused to form the necessary *mens rea* of the offence was disallowed by the Court of Appeal. The court emphasised that where there was no issue of mental instability or illness, it is inappropriate to allow evidence from a medical witness as to the state of the accused's mind.

Thus the restriction on the admissibility of expert evidence on matters for which the jury requires no assistance includes also a restriction on expert evidence on the credibility of a witness or the accused save in exceptional circumstances. In *R v Rimmer* [1983] Crim LR 250, the trial judge refused to allow the evidence of an expert on the basis that this related only to the credibility of the accused. However, the case of *R v Weir, R v Somanathan* [2006] 1 WLR 1885, illustrates the difficulty of applying the principle that expert evidence should not be allowed on the credibility of a witness.[4] The Court of Appeal held that the evidence was rightly admitted. Arguably, however, the evidence was directed at the credibility of the sexual allegations given the context in which they were made.

Inadmissible Psychiatric Evidence: New Areas of Knowledge

Lawton LJ's observation in *Turner* indicates how the courts call on experts for evidence on 'scientific information which is likely to be outside the experience and knowledge of a judge or jury'. However, it does not indicate how such areas can be identified. In practice the courts have had to consider the difficult question of at what point modish discoveries in mental conditions become a new science. Unlike mainstream medical science, psychiatric medical evidence does not achieve widespread acceptance. In *R v Gilfoyle (No. 2)* [2001] 2 Cr App R 57 the court held that evidence of a 'psychological autopsy' for the purpose of determining whether an alleged murder victim had in fact committed suicide was not admissible. Such autopsies did not have real scientific basis. Roberts and Zuckerman comment (2010, p. 501) that 'The unsatisfactory state of the law is exemplified by *Gilfoyle*.'[5] They argue that the decision was based on an 'unsystematic and unpredictable fashion in which the court goes about its task'. In *H (JR) (Childhood Amnesia)* [2006] 1 Cr App R 10 the Court of Appeal held that a psychiatrist's evidence on recovered memory syndrome would only be rarely admitted.

Confessions and Expert Evidence

In one particular respect the quotation from *Turner* needs some revision. In a case involving fraud by misrepresentation, *R v*

[4] Kennedy LJ stated (at para. 49) that counsel did not ask the witness to express a view on the truth of the claims '. . . but the jury was entitled to know from an expert whether or not within the Hindu community an allegation of this kind was unusual'.

[5] They write, referring to the six grounds the Court of Appeal gave for rejecting the defence evidence, 'It is not that these factors are irrelevant to an assessment of admissibility, or even that they could not for the most part be brought under the umbrella of the helpfulness test. The problem lies in the unsystematic and unpredictable fashion in which the court goes about its task.'

Jackson-Mason [2014] EWCA Crim 1993, the defendant pleaded that she was not dishonest because she believed she was helping the men who approached her to carry out the misrepresentation. She had a learning disability, an IQ of 77 (the disability range being 70–80), and was vulnerability to exploitation. The court upheld the judge's decision that the jury did not need expert evidence on her state of mind. It observed (at para. 11) that 'This was because the courts have long held that, save in respect of confession evidence, evidence of an IQ being greater than 69 is inadmissible'. There is a growing body of case law on the need for expert witnesses where a defendant who has a significantly abnormal personality disorder which might make a pre-trial confession unreliable and there is evidence that the condition predated the confession. In the notorious miscarriage of justice case *R v Ward* [1993] 1 WLR 619, expert evidence should have been admitted to explain the defendant's suggestible personality which led her to confess to crimes she could not have committed.[6] In *R v Blackburn* [2005] EWCA Crim 1349 the court held that evidence of a forensic psychologist was admissible as relevant to the reliability of a vulnerable teenager who did not have a mental disorder.[7] However, in *R v Weightman* (1990) 92 Cr App R 291 the court cited the observation from *Turner* above and stated (at 29), 'In our judgment they would not have been helped by having a psychiatrist talking about "emotional superficiality" and "impaired capacity to develop and sustain deep or enduring relationships".'

Assessment of the Place of Psychiatric Evidence

One argument for caution over the admissibility of expert evidence, including psychiatric evidence, is that the jury and the lawyers may be too deferential to it.[8] In *R v Tilly* [1981] 1 WLR 1309 the Court of Appeal overturned a guilty verdict where the expert evidence was unchallenged and clearly suggested the verdict was unsustainable. Edmond (2002, p. 58) points out that 'Scientific evidence is an important component of most high profile miscarriage of justice cases.' He also suggests (p. 59) that a 'common concern is that excessive reliance is placed on scientific evidence: that its potential fallibility is not recognised'. This is all the more significant in view of the 'meagre resources' available to the defence to challenge such prosecution evidence.

Some commentators argue that psychiatric evidence should more readily be admitted. Pattenden (1986) points out that where the witness is 'abnormal', as in cases of diminished responsibility, psychiatric evidence is uncontroversially admitted.[9] She suggests that psychiatric evidence could be given about a 'normal individual' including on questions of veracity of a witness or the reliability of

[6] You must of course study the judgments to appreciate the legal reasoning. You may find the chart on p. 182 *Evidence Concentrate* (2017) a helpful preliminary guide.

[7] See also *R v Everett* [1988] Crim LR 826.

[8] Arguably one of the causes of recent miscarriages of justice such as *R v Clark (No. 2)* [2003] EWCA Crim 102.

[9] Her article was written over three decades ago but it is still pertinent suggesting as it does the slowness of change in this area.

out-of-court statements by the accused. She claims that psychiatrists or psychologists make systematic observations, attempt to discount their own preconceptions, and try to see beyond popular mythology and common-sense conclusions. Roberts and Zuckerman (2010, p. 468), on the other hand, stress the need to preserve the moral role of the jury in maintaining 'the durability of social trust in the legitimacy of criminal verdicts'. They also, however, think the current position untenable, particularly in the light of the decision in *Gilfoyle*. Moreover as Roberts (2009, p. 558) points out in relation to the Law Commission proposals, admissibility is not the only question. There are other weaknesses in the procedure for evaluating and receiving expert evidence. Similarly Edmond (2012) sees the problem of one of the need for a deep-going cultural change in the legal profession and the criminal justice system, citing the need to address the reluctance to engage with 'exogenous (i.e. non legal knowledge)'. This arguably includes a greater understanding of the discipline of psychiatry. Other arguments have been advanced for a system of court-appointed experts (perhaps as well as party-appointed experts) to be established in criminal cases. Court-appointed experts were introduced in civil cases by the Woolf reforms in 1997/1998 but in criminal cases they may be more problematic. [10] The criminal trial paradigm is still an adversarial one, with the search for a conclusion based on the conflict between two sides, and society is arguably not ready for trial by experts. In addition, it is a fallacy to think that there is necessarily only one version of scientific evidence. The question is most often that of probabilities, not certainties. As Howard (1991, p. 101) points out, 'It is slightly mysterious that it should be thought that experts are venal mountebanks when engaged by the parties but transformed into paragons of objectivity when employed by the court.'

Conclusion

What is undeniable is that there is increasing public attention and some unease about the treatment of expert evidence in criminal cases. In March 2005 the House of Commons Science and Technology Committee published a report entitled *Forensic Science on Trial*. The Committee conclusions noted (para. 189) the complacency of the legal profession in regard to the lack of safeguards to prevent miscarriages of justice. Such complacency arguably attaches to a reluctance in the legal professions to engage with scientific developments including those in psychiatry.

The law on opinion evidence over 40 years after *Turner* is thus still evolving. Education in science and statistics for juries and legal personnel is one way forward although as the court in *Adams* **[1996] 2 Cr App R 467** stated, trials are about common sense, not mathematical or scientific reasoning. [11] Roberts recommends 'the

[10] The Report led to changes in the Civil Procedure Rules.

[11] Thus the court in *R v Adams* [1962] 2 Cr App R 467 held that Bayes' theorem was not appropriate to use in trials.

adoption of pre-trial procedures which provide for direct involvement of experts in the gate-keeping process'. *R v Brennan* **[2014] EWCA 2387** is a further change, providing that juries may not decline to accept uncontradicted expert evidence without good reason.

The often controversial outcomes of attempts to introduce reforms over recent years, however, suggest that simply moving away from the restrictive proposition set out in *Turner* is not the solution. In conclusion, it is arguable that the limitation of the approach suggested in the quotation from *Turner* is that admissibility is regarded as the central issue. At the heart of this complex question of expertise is therefore not simply fairness to the parties but what Edmond (2002) calls 'the social legitimacy' of legal institutions.

LOOKING FOR EXTRA MARKS?

- You would gain credit for a perceptive appreciation of the reasoning in *Turner* and the theoretical question of what society expected of lay jurors.
- It is advisable to exhibit your knowledge of procedure in this area and in particular engage with the criticism that the Law Commission Report has, as Edmond and Roberts (2011, p. 862) point out, 'insufficiently engaged with principle, particularly the principles motivating the accusatorial criminal jury trials'.

TAKING THINGS FURTHER

- Edmond, G., 'Constructing Miscarriages of Justice: Misunderstanding Scientific Evidence in High Profile Criminal Appeals' (2002) 22 OJLS 53.

  Suggests that one way of addressing the problem of an overly idealised view of the capacities of scientific evidence could be an examination of the different conceptual approaches to scientific evidence used to acquit and comparing it with that used to convict.

- Edmond, G., 'Is Reliability Sufficient? The Law Commission and Expert Evidence in International and Interdisciplinary Perspective' Part 1 (2012) E & P 30.

  See reference in text to answer.

- Edmond, G. and Roberts, A., 'The Law Commission's Report on Expert Evidence in Criminal Proceedings' [2011] Crim LR 844.

  Gives a critique of the Report and is critical of its lack of theoretical analysis of the principles of the adversarial trial.

- House of Commons Science and Technology Committee, 7th Report, *Forensic Science on Trial* (HL96-1) (London: TSO, 2005), http://www.publications.parliament.uk/pa/cm200001/cmselect/cmsctech/291/29102.htm.

- Howard N.M., 'The Neutral Expert: A Plausible Threat to Justice' [1991] Crim LR 98.

  Comments on lack of safeguards to prevent miscarriages of justice from happening.

- Law Commission Report No. 325, *Expert Evidence in Criminal Proceedings in England and Wales* (London: TSO, 2011), http://www.gov.uk/government/uploads/system/uploads/attachment_data/file/229043/0829.pdf.

- Pattenden, R., 'Conflicting Approaches to Psychiatric Evidence' [1986] Crim LR 92.

  Presents a criticism of the reluctance of the English courts to admit psychiatric evidence for witnesses other than those held to be 'abnormal'.

- Roberts, A., 'Drawing on Expertise: Legal Decision-Making and the Reception of Expert Evidence' [2008] Crim LR 443.

  Argues that the prevailing liberal approach to admitting expert evidence has resulted in miscarriages of justice and that the role played by judges and lawyers in such cases has not been sufficiently critically examined.

- Roberts, A., 'Rejecting General Acceptance, Confounding the Gatekeeper: The Law Commission and Expert Evidence' [2009] Crim LR 551.

  See reference in text to answer.

- Roberts, P. and Zuckerman, A., *Criminal Evidence* (Oxford: OUP, 2010), ch. 11.

  A theoretical account identifying the role of social trust in securing the legitimacy of expert evidence.

- Ward, T., 'Usurping the Role of the Jury? Expert Evidence and Witness Credibility in English Criminal Trials' (2009) 13 E & P 83.

  Suggests that, particularly in rape and sexual abuse cases, there are good reasons for admitting some forms of expert evidence of credibility.

- Ward, T., 'Expert Evidence and the Law Commission's Reform Proposals; Implementation Without Legislation?' [2013] Crim LR 561.

  Defends the decision not to introduce legislation and defends the common law principles identified as a broad test of prima facie admissibility coupled with discretionary power to exclude evidence whose potential prejudicial effect outweighs its probative value.

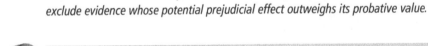

Online Resources

www.oup.com/uk/qanda/

Go online for extra essay and problem questions, a glossary of key terms, online versions of all the answer plans and audio commentary on how selected ones were put together, and a range of podcasts which include advice on exam and coursework technique and advice for other assessment methods.

9 Examination and cross-examination

KEY DEBATES

Debate: in rape trials is the prior sexual experience of the complainant with the defendant relevant to the instant charge?

Under s. 41 of the Youth Justice and Criminal Evidence Act 1941 (YJCEA) leave of the court is required before questioning the complainant on prior sexual experience with other partners including the defendant. Some commentators condemned the decision in *R v A (No. 2)* [2001] UKHL 25, allowing judicial discretion in determining the relevance of questioning a complainant about previous sexual behaviour with the defendant. They argue that this entrenches a male perspective that a woman who has engaged in consensual sexual activity with a particular man is more likely to be consenting to sex with the same man, the subject of the instant charge.

Debate: is it good practice to prepare witnesses for the experience of cross-examination before the trial?

Witness prior familiarisation with the demands of the adversarial system has been given judicial approval in *R v Morodou* [2005] 1 WLR 3442 but in practice it rarely happens. Arguably, this means that many witnesses are not assisted to testify effectively. A distinction must be drawn between such familiarisation by means of mock questioning and the coaching of witnesses on the evidence in the forthcoming trial. The former is acceptable but the latter is objectionable.

QUESTION 1

Daniel, a police constable, in response to a call on his radio, went to investigate an alleged burglary at Henfield Road. As he drove up to the scene of the crime, he saw Henry dressed in a T-shirt and running shorts and carrying a holdall on his back, running in the opposite direction. Daniel chased after him but soon lost him. Daniel made a note of what he had seen in his notebook, but did not do so until nearly six months later, just before the trial. Just after the incident, following an appeal for witnesses, Henry went voluntarily to the police station and was interviewed. He said that the reason that he was in the area at the material time was because he had been out jogging, as he was training for the London Marathon and that the holdall contained bricks to weigh him down. Henry is subsequently arrested and charged with the burglary.

Advise on the following evidential matters:
(Each part of the question is worth equal marks.)

(a) Can Daniel refresh his memory from his notebook outside court before giving evidence? If Daniel then gives evidence for the prosecution without referring to the notebook can the defence cross-examine him as to the contents of the notebook?

(b) Can Daniel refresh his memory from his notebook in court? And if so, can it be put in evidence?

(c) What use can the defence make of Henry's voluntary statement at the police station?

 CAUTION!

▨ Make sure that you have revised both the common law and statutory provisions under **s. 120 of the Criminal Justice Act (CJA) 2003** on refreshing memory.

▨ In assessing evidential worth you need to be aware of how evidence of consistency differs from evidence of the truth stated.

DIAGRAM ANSWER PLAN

Identify the issues	■ The legal issues are: (a) law relating to refreshing memory out of court and whether witness can be cross-examined on source; (b) law relating to refreshing memory in court; (c) admissibility and evidential worth of previous consistent statements.
Relevant law	■ (a) The relevant statutory section is **CJA 2003, s. 120(3)** and related case law; (b) **s. 139** covers this area and **s. 120(3)** also applies; (c) see common law cases since **CJA** has not affected the law on the admissibility of previous consistent statements but note that **s. 114** inclusionary discretion for hearsay statements may apply.
Apply the law	■ (a) This concerns the use by Daniel of a memory-refreshing document out of court and needs consideration whether it is necessary for the document to be contemporaneous; (b) the judge will have to agree that Daniel can consult the document in court, apply **CJA 2003, s. 139**; (c) **Henry's statement is admissible.**
Conclude	■ Assess the outcome for each witness.

SUGGESTED ANSWER

(a) Refreshing Memory Outside Court

It is common for witnesses, such as Daniel as a prosecution witness, to look at written statements which they have made, in order to refresh their memory, before testifying on the witness stand. This practice was recognised by the Court of Appeal in *R v Richardson* **[1971] 2 QB 484.**[1]

In *Richardson*, four prosecution witnesses were given their statements prior to their testimony. The statements were not sufficiently contemporaneous for them to be used to refresh their memory in court. The accused argued on appeal that as the statements were not contemporaneous for the purpose of the rule on refreshing memory in court, their evidence should not have been admitted. The Court of Appeal rejected this argument and approved the dicta in *Lau Pak Ngam v R* **[1966] Crim LR 443**. In that case, the Supreme Court of Hong Kong stated that if witnesses were deprived of the

[1] You could point out that such a rule would probably be unenforceable.

opportunity of checking their recollection beforehand by reference to statements or notes made near to the time of the events in question, testimony in the witness box would be no more than a test of memory, rather than of truthfulness.[2] Further, refusal of access to the statements would create difficulties for honest witnesses, but would not hamper dishonest ones. Subsequently, the court held in *R v Da Silva* **[1990] 1 All ER 29**, that the judge has a discretion to allow a witness to withdraw from the witness stand in order to refresh his memory from a statement made near or at the time of the events in question. The judge has this discretion even where the statement is not contemporaneous with the events.[3] Before he exercises his discretion, the judge must be satisfied that Daniel recalls the events in question because of lapse of time, that he had made a statement near the time of the event representing his recollection of them, that he had not read the statement before testifying, and that he wishes to read the statement before he continues to give evidence. In *R v South Ribble Magistrates' Court, ex p Cochrane* **[1996] 2 Cr App R 544**, the Divisional Court made it clear that *R v Da Silva* did not lay down a rule of law that all four conditions must be satisfied. So he is likely to be able to consult even if it is unclear whether Daniel made the note contemporaneously with the events in question.

Cross-examination on contents

The next issue is whether the defence can cross-examine Daniel as to the contents of the notebook if he consults it before trial.[4] The Court of Appeal in *R v Westwell* **[1976] 2 All ER 812** decided that if the prosecution counsel is aware that his witness has refreshed his or her memory outside the court, it was 'desirable but not essential' that the defence should be informed of this fact. Once the defence is aware that Daniel has refreshed his memory from his notebook outside the court, they are entitled to inspect the notebook, and cross-examine Daniel on the relevant matters contained in it: see *Owen v Edwards* **(1983) 77 Cr App R 191**. However, the court made it clear that if the defence counsel cross-examines a witness on material in the notebook or statement, which has not been used by the witness to refresh his memory, they run the risk of the notebook or statement being put in evidence. **Section 120(3) of the Criminal Justice Act (CJA) 2003** provides that if a witness's memory-refreshing statement becomes admissible as a result of cross-examination then it is admissible evidence of any matter stated of which oral evidence by the witness would be admissible.[5] See also *R v Chinn* **[2012] EWCA Crim 501** where the Court of Appeal addressed the construction of this section.

[2] Note that this area is not closely regulated by law. Arguably there is a case for reform.

[3] In relation to the witness refreshing his/her memory in the witness box under the **CJA 2003**, there is no need for the document to have been made contemporaneously with the event.

[4] It is important you organise your answer to cover the two issues separately.

[5] There are a number of reasons why it might be relevant evidence which are set out in **s. 120(2)(e)**.

(b) Refreshing Memory in Court

Daniel may be entitled to refresh his memory by referring to his notebook in court provided the pre-conditions are satisfied, see **s. 139 of the CJA 2003**. The new test allows a witness to consult a document if it was made when his recollection is likely to have been 'significantly better' when he made or verified it. In other words, the court will look at the quality of the evidence in the notebook rather than the time it was made. In *R v McAfee (John James)* **[2006] EWCA Crim 2914** the Court of Appeal examined the question of what is meant by the witness's recollection being 'significantly better' when they make their note.[6] The court noted that contemporaneity was not required and that the trial judge was best placed to pronounce on whether a witness's memory when he made the statement was likely to have been significantly better than when testifying. In this case the court approved the trial judge's decision to allow the memory-refreshing police document made four-and-a-half months after the incident. The court took the view that the judge must have a residual discretion to refuse a **s. 139** application even if the statutory conditions are met. However, there were no good reasons for refusal in this case.[7] It is likely therefore that Daniel will be able to refresh his memory from his note.

The notebook should be handed to the defence counsel or the court so that it may be inspected and the witness cross-examined on its contents. The defence counsel can request that the jury be shown the notebook if it is necessary for the determination of an issue: *R v Bass* **[1953] 1 QB 680**.

Under the common law rule, which survives the **CJA 2003**, the notebook could not be evidence in the case. But it should be available for inspection by the defence. *R v Sekhon* **(1987) 85 Cr App R 19** sets out guidelines whereby memory-refreshing documents may be shown to the jury to help them follow the cross-examination. If the cross-examiner only refers to parts of the document which the witness used in refreshing his memory then the party calling the witness cannot require that the document becomes evidence. If, however, the cross-examination uses other parts the witness has not relied upon then the party calling the witness may insist that the document becomes evidence (*Senat v Senat* **[1965] P 172**). Daniel should be advised that **s. 120(3) of the CJA 2003** would then apply and the document would be evidence not only of consistency, as under the common law, but of the truth of its contents. However, under **s. 122 of the CJA 2003** the document must not accompany

[6] The defence may argue, for example, that a note made shortly before the trial and many months after the incident would not satisfy this provision.

[7] The court took the view that the prosecution were entitled to present their best case to the jury and that this was the object of many of the provisions in the 2003 Act.

the jury when they retire to consider their verdict unless all parties to the proceedings agree or the judge gives his permission. The risk is the jury will attach disproportionate weight to what is a hearsay statement. In *R v Hulme* [2007] 1 Cr App R 26 the Court of Appeal held that the judge had been wrong to allow a witness statement to be taken into the jury room.

(c) Previous Consistent Statements

The general rule is that a witness may not give evidence, during examination-in-chief, of a previous consistent statement. Although there are a number of exceptions to the general rule, the only one which may apply here is where the accused has made a statement on being accused of the crime. This is in principle admissible in evidence of the facts stated therein.[8] Where the accused denies the charge, the statement, whilst it may be admissible in some circumstances, for instance to show the accused's reaction when taxed with incriminating facts, is admissible only to show consistency of the accused's testimony and goes only to credit. It is not evidence of the facts stated therein: *R v Storey* (1968) 52 Cr App R 334 and *R v Pearce* (1979) 69 Cr App R 365. The CJA 2003 has not affected this specific exception to the rule against narrative.[9]

One issue is whether Henry's statement is taken to be exculpatory, inculpatory, or mixed. It is assumed here that the defence is arguing that the statement is an exculpatory one, although arguable it may be taken to be mixed since it puts him at the scene. In either case it may be admissible. Henry should be warned that not all previous consistent exculpatory or mixed statements will be admitted. In *R v Tooke* (1989) 90 Cr App R 417 a written statement was not admitted since it did not add to a previous oral statement. Henry appears to have made the statement promptly.

Conclusion to (a), (b), and (c)

(a) Depending on the extent of the cross-examination, the notebook will not be put in evidence.

(b) It is likely that Daniel can consult the document in court.

(c) The statement is not evidence of the facts stated in it.[10] Henry's statement may alternatively be admissible as evidence of the truth of its contents under **s. 114(1)(d) of the CJA 2003** if the 'interests of justice' test is satisfied.

[8] You are demonstrating here that you understand the difference between inculpatory and exculpatory statements.

[9] The statutory exceptions are listed in s. 120 of the CJA 2003.

[10] This is the application of the rule against hearsay.

LOOKING FOR EXTRA MARKS

- You will gain extra marks if you demonstrate you are aware that the original common law rule was that a witness could only refresh his memory from an original document but modern practice is that a copy is acceptable.

- In relation to memory-refreshing out of court, counsel has a professional duty to advise the other side what has occurred.

QUESTION | 2

Frank is prosecuted for dangerous driving after he knocked down a pedestrian, Jennice. Jennice alleges that as she was crossing Middlefield Road, Frank hit her with his car, causing a fracture of her left leg. She states that Frank was driving his car at an excessive speed and without due care and attention. Frank's defence is that Jennice lurched out onto the road suddenly and appeared to be drunk. He was unable to avoid hitting her. He admits that the accident took place and the injuries suffered by Jennice.

Advise Frank on the following evidential matters:

(Each part of the question is worth equal marks.)

(a) Dr Lee gives evidence for the prosecution that when he examined Jennice in the casualty department where she was brought after the accident, there were no signs of recent intoxication. Can he be cross-examined on the fact that the next day he had told Lisa, a nurse at the hospital, that Jennice appeared to be drunk when she was brought into the hospital? Can evidence in rebuttal be called if Dr Lee denies the conversation?

(b) Herbert, an eyewitness to the accident, has given evidence that he saw Frank driving erratically immediately prior to the accident. Can he be cross-examined that he was convicted of perjury seven years ago, that he had attempted suicide a few months ago, and that he is very short-sighted?

(c) Before the trial, Paul, the manager of Toasters, a wine bar, has given a written statement to Frank's solicitor. In the statement, Paul said that he served Jennice three to four Singapore Slings, a cocktail, an hour before the accident. When testifying for the defence, he states that Jennice came into the wine bar to use the ladies room and did not have anything to drink. What use can be made of his written statement?

CAUTION!

- Make sure that you differentiate the questions of admissibility and evidential value.

- Distinguish the statutory provisions on the cross-examination of non-defendant witnesses on bad character from those for defendants.

DIAGRAM ANSWER PLAN

Identify the issues	■ The legal issues are: (a) admissibility and evidential worth of a previous statement inconsistent with current testimony; (b) admissibility of bad character and physical disability of non-defendant witnesses; (c) procedure when a party's witness does not come up to proof.
Relevant law	■ (a) Criminal Procedure Act 1865, ss. 4 and 5 and CJA 2003, s. 119; (b) application of ss. 98 and 101 on character of non-defendant witness and **Criminal Procedure Act 1865, s. 6**; (c) **Criminal Procedure Act 1865, s. 3** and CJA 2003, s. 119.
Apply the law	■ (a) Lee's conversation with Lisa is inconsistent with his testimony so the prosecution will want to adduce it—see **Criminal Procedure Act 1865, s. 4** on oral or written prior inconsistent statements; (b) the defence will want to discredit Herbert as a witness so consider the application of **CJA 2003, ss. 98 and 100**, rule of finality on collateral questions; (c) Paul's testimony may lead to claim that he is a 'hostile witness'—**Criminal Procedure Act 1865, s. 3**.
Conclude	■ Summary of advice for Lee, Herbert, and Jennice. Advise Frank on the evidential matters.

SUGGESTED ANSWER

(a) Previous Inconsistent Statement

Dr Lee's earlier conversation with Lisa is inconsistent with his present testimony.[1] **Section 4 of the Criminal Procedure Act 1865** states that if a witness is asked during cross-examination about a prior statement (whether oral or written) made by him which is inconsistent with his present testimony, and does not admit that he had made such a previous inconsistent statement, the cross-examining party may adduce evidence of that inconsistent statement. Before the inconsistent statement can be adduced, the procedure in **s. 4** has to be complied with; namely, the circumstances in which the previous inconsistent statement was made must be put to the witness and he must then be asked whether he had made such a statement.

Thus if Dr Lee denies making such a statement, evidence of the prior inconsistent statement can be adduced. This may take the form of calling Lisa as a rebuttal witness. If, on the other hand, Dr Lee admits making the statement, then the normal practice would be to ask him whether he still wishes to stand by his previous testimony. In most instances, when faced with such a situation, it is unlikely that the witness will stand by his previous testimony.

On the facts of this case, the previous inconsistent statement will help the defence's case that Jennice lurched suddenly onto the road, possibly because she was intoxicated.

Section 119(1) of the Criminal Justice Act (CJA) 2003 provides that a prior inconsistent statement which is admissible into evidence, is admissible as evidence of the facts stated therein and is not merely evidence of the consistency or inconsistency of the witness.[2]

[2] There is no need in a problem question to give an account of the earlier common law position.

(b) Bad Character and Disability of Non-Defendant

Herbert will be a witness for the prosecution. Frank should be advised that under **s. 6 of the Criminal Procedure Act 1865**, a witness may be questioned as to whether he or she has been convicted of any offence, and if he or she denies it or does not admit that fact, or refuses to answer the question, evidence can be adduced to prove such a conviction. The court does retain a discretion not to allow the cross-examination of a witness regarding his or her previous spent conviction. The judge in considering whether to exercise his or her discretion should weigh the degree of relevance of the spent conviction against the prejudice it may cause against the witness. An unfair degree of prejudice may lead to an unfair trial.[3]

[3] It is unlikely that the offence will be spent since a conviction usually involves lengthy imprisonment.

Thus, whether Herbert can be questioned about his conviction for perjury would depend in part on whether it is a spent conviction under the **Rehabilitation of Offenders Act 1974** and whether, if it was a spent conviction, the court would be prepared to allow the cross-examination about it on the basis that justice could not otherwise be done. That is a question for the court to decide. However, bearing in mind that the conviction is for perjury, even if it is spent, it is likely that the court may allow the cross-examination of Herbert regarding it.[4]

[4] Obviously a conviction for perjury would undermine a witness's credibility.

It should also be noted that it is a matter of judicial discretion how far the cross-examination of a witness may go about his or her previous conviction under **s. 6 of the Criminal Procedure Act 1865**.[5] The fact of the conviction can be proved by a certificate from the court of the conviction under **s. 74(1) of the Police and Criminal Evidence Act 1984 (PACE)**. In relation to Herbert's eyesight, arguably this is relevant to the accuracy of his testimony. A witness can be further questioned about such medical evidence, see **Toohey v MPC [1965] AC 595**.[6]

[5] Note that this is an exception to the rule of finality on collateral questions.

[6] Another exception to the rule of finality on collateral questions.

However, Frank should be aware that cross-examination of witnesses in criminal proceedings is also now limited by **ss. 98** and **100 of the CJA 2003. Section 100(1)** provides that in criminal proceedings the bad character (as defined in **s. 98**) of a person other than the defendant is admissible if and only if it is important explanatory evidence, or it has substantial probative value in relation to a matter which is a matter in issue in the proceedings and is of substantial importance in the context of the case as a whole, or all parties to the proceedings agree to the evidence being admitted. A perjury conviction clearly falls within the **s. 98** definition as 'the commission of an offence or other reprehensible behaviour'. It is arguably relevant evidence in questioning Herbert's credibility. However, attempting suicide arguably does not fall within **s. 98** as 'other reprehensible behaviour' and is prima facie admissible under the common law although its relevance would first have to be established (see ***R v Hall-Chung*** **[2007] EWCA Crim 3429).**[7]

Thus, an application to have Herbert's convictions admitted would have to be made to the court. Here it is arguable that the perjury conviction has 'substantial probative value' and is admissible under **s. 100(1)(b) in** that it is of 'substantial importance in the context of the case as a whole'.[8]

(c) Hostile Witness

In this situation, Frank should be advised that his witness, Paul, is not coming up to proof. The general rule is that a party may not impeach his own witness. This means that Frank cannot call evidence from another source to show that Paul is lying, forgetful, or mistaken. He can, of course, call other witnesses who may be able to testify as to what Jennice drank at the wine bar, if there were any.[9]

In order for exceptions to apply, it is necessary to determine whether Paul is merely an unfavourable witness or a hostile one. An unfavourable witness is one who is not coming up to proof whether because they are mistaken, foolish, or forgetful. Such a witness cannot be attacked as to his credit or challenged as to his previous inconsistent statement. At common law, however, a previous inconsistent statement can be put to a hostile witness and leading questions to test his memory and perception may be asked. A witness is regarded as hostile when he is not desirous of telling the truth at the instance of the party calling him.

Since his previous statement to the solicitor is clear and unambiguous, Paul may be treated as a hostile witness. The procedure then is counsel can make an application to the judge to treat the witness as hostile. The judge can decide whether the witness is hostile by looking at the prior statement and the witness's demeanour and attitude.

[7] It is important in answering all problem questions to refer to relevance. More information is needed about whether the attempted suicide suggests Herbert's perception of reality was flawed.

[8] Bear in mind in applying **s. 100 of the CJA 2003** that one intent of the statute was to give more protection to witnesses to encourage them to testify.

[9] You could distinguish here hostile witnesses and those who do not adduce evidence through fear (*R v Honeyghon and Sayles* [1999] Crim LR 221).

If the judge decides that Paul is a hostile witness, then he may be asked leading questions and may be cross-examined by the defence as to his previous inconsistent statement (see *R v Thompson* (1976) **64 Cr App R 96**) under **s. 3 of the Criminal Procedure Act 1865**. Before the defence can prove that Paul made a previous inconsistent statement, he must be reminded of the circumstances of the previous statement sufficient to designate the particular occasion and must be asked whether or not he has made such a statement.

If Paul refuses to admit making such a statement, **s. 3** of the 1865 Act allows the party calling the witness to prove that such a statement was made by the witness. The Act sets out the procedure for cross-examining a hostile (described here as 'adverse') witness on 'a statement inconsistent with his present testimony'. This will apply whether Paul gives testimony that differs from the earlier statement or says nothing at all (*R v Thompson* (1976) **64 Cr App R 96**). Paul may then be cross-examined on the earlier statement. **Section 4** deals with proof of 'contradictory statements of adverse witnesses' and **s. 5** with cross-examination on a previous statement in writing.

The prosecution should be reminded that cross-examination is only allowed on previous inconsistent statements on matters relevant to facts in issue—not to those on credibility (*R v C & B* [2003] **EWCA Crim 29**).

In *Joyce v Joyce* [2005] **EWCA Crim 1785** the Court of Appeal considered the impact of **s. 119 of the CJA 2003**, which allows previous inconsistent statements to be admissible as evidence of the truth of any matter stated even if the maker of the statement does not accept that it was true. This is a change from the previous law, which only allowed such statements to be evidence of lack of credibility. The defence may also rely on *R v Gibbons* [2008] **EWCA Crim 1574**. The Court of Appeal held that under **s. 11 of the CJA 2003** the jury could decide whether the contents of a prior statement of a hostile witness were true even where the witness did not accept making it. Finally, as *Gibbons* makes clear, even if Paul is not declared a hostile witness **s. 119** would allow the statement to be adduced as evidence of its truth if he admits making it, see **ss. 125** and **126 CJA 2003**.[10]

[10] Note that exclusion under **s. 78** PACE only applies to prosecution evidence.

Conclusion to (a), (b), and (c)

(a) The statement by Dr Lee to Lisa would be admissible as evidence suggesting her intoxication.

(b) Herbert's convictions are likely to be admissible.

(c) The defence is advised that the prior statement may be admissible to assist its case.

LOOKING FOR EXTRA MARKS?

▨ For (b) you would gain credit for giving more details and comment on the high test for admissibility under **s. 100**.

▨ For (c) it would be appropriate to expand on the drastic process of declaring a witness hostile, for example it would be advisable to ask the witness first to 'refresh his memory'.

QUESTION | 3

John is charged with the attempted rape of Patricia. He denies the offence and claims that they had met in the park and he chatted to her about her dog. He claims that she invented the attempted rape.

(a) Advise on the likely admissibility of evidence from Patricia's flatmate Julia that Patricia had come home on one occasion sobbing and when asked what was the matter said she had been 'assaulted a week ago'.

(b) When first arrested, John tells police that he stopped Patricia simply to chat about her dog when she was out walking. He says he had an identical breed of dog. He repeats this claim in oral testimony at the trial. The prosecution accuse him of having made this explanation up. Advise the defence.

(c) The defence wish also to call evidence that Patricia had made previous allegations of sexual assault which turned out to be fabricated. Are they likely to succeed?

CAUTION!

This question will test your knowledge of the case law on a number of quite complex procedural points:

▨ in part (a), it will be necessary to discuss the general rule with respect to the admissibility of prior consistent statements and the exception to that rule in cases involving sexual offences;

▨ in (b) the question is whether evidence can be given of John's immediate reaction and the prosecution allegation that he is lying and for this you require knowledge of the common law rule;

▨ you should not attempt this question unless you are also familiar with the growing body of case law under **s. 41 of the YJCEA 1999** and the specific issue in part (c) whether lying about a rape allegation is 'sexual behaviour' and thus questioning of the complainant is prima facie excluded.

DIAGRAM ANSWER PLAN

Identify the issues	■ The legal issues are: (a) admissibility of an out-of-court statement of sexual assault by a complainant; (b) admissibility of an out-of-court statement to rebut an allegation of fabrication; (c) permissible cross-examination of complainants in sexual cases of alleged previous false complaints.
Relevant law	■ (a) CJA 2003, s. 120; (b) common law on admissibility and s. 120(2) on evidential worth, inclusionary discretion, s. 114; (c) whether YJCEA, s. 41 is engaged, CJA 2003, s. 100.
Apply the law	▦ (a) Patricia's statement likely to be admitted; (b) John can rebut allegation of recent fabrication; (c) defence must produce evidential basis for the claim of false allegations which may not be 'sexual behaviour' under s. 41.
Conclude	▦ Assess the likely outcomes.

SUGGESTED ANSWER

(a) Previous Consistent Statement

The general common law rule was that a witness may not be asked in examination-in-chief whether he or she had made a prior statement, either oral or written, consistent with his or her testimony.[1] There are, however, exceptions to this. It may be possible for evidence to be given of Patricia's statement to her flatmate under a statutory exception.

[1] Under the common law such statements were admissible in rape allegations but there were more stringent requirements which have been overtaken by statute.

Section 120 CJA 2003

Section 120(4)(b) admits a statement which consists of a complaint about conduct made by a witness (whether to a person in authority or not) who claims to be a person against whom an offence has been committed. The statement must consist of a complaint made by the witness about conduct which would, if proved, constitute the offence or part of the offence. It should not be made as a result of a threat or a promise, and before the statement is adduced the witness must give oral evidence in connection with its subject matter.[2] Whilst giving evidence the witness must indicate that to the best of his belief

[2] Note that the statute does not preclude responses to leading questions.

he made the statement, and it states the truth. There are two significant departures from the common law; **s. 120(8)** provides that it is irrelevant that the complaint was elicited by a leading question and the requirement that the complaint was made as soon as reasonably practicable was abolished in 2009.

The prosecution may rely on *R v Xhabri* **[2005] EWCA Crim 3135**. In this case the complainant alleged she had been raped and forced to work as a prostitute. She had made a number of telephone calls to her parents and others about her plight and the question was whether the evidence of the receivers of the calls could be received. At trial the judge allowed them in under **s. 120(5)** (previous identification), **s. 120(6)** (a fresh statement when the witness could not be expected to recall), and **s. 120(7)** (recent complaints).

The court held that **s. 120(7)** was rightly applied but not **s. 120(5)** and **(6)**.[3]

Article 6

There was no conflict in the case with **Art. 6**. The hearsay provisions under the statute applied to both defence and prosecution and so the principle of the equality of arms was upheld. **Article 6(3)(d)** did not give a defendant an absolute right to examine every witness whose testimony was adduced against him. The touchstone was whether fairness of the trial required that in the present case almost all the hearsay evidence derived directly or indirectly from the complainant. She was available for cross-examination and so this satisfied the requirements of **Art. 6(3)(d)**.

The fact that in the question the alleged rape occurred a week before this statement and that the statement was in response to a question is not a bar to admissibility. Patricia's statement to Julia if admitted will be evidence of the truth of its contents, as an exception to the rule against hearsay.

(b) Allegation of Recent Fabrication

The first question to address is whether the prosecution is simply arguing that John should not be believed or whether it is alleging he has made up this explanation. If it is the latter then the rule against the admissibility of previous consistent statements applies.[4] In *R v Oyesiku* **(1971) 56 Cr App R 240** it was held that a previous statement may be admissible to disprove the accusation of 'recent fabrication'. The statement was not evidence of the truth of its contents but of the credibility of the witness (*R v Y* **[1995] Crim LR 155**). This area of law, however, has been changed by **s. 120(2) of the CJA 2003**. Admissibility is not affected. That is a matter for the judge.

[4] The issue will be left to the defence to produce evidence in rebuttal and the jury will decide who to believe.

Evidential worth

In *R v Athwal* [2009] EWCA Crim 789 the Court of Appeal considered the relationship between common law principles and the CJA 2003. In that case, defence counsel made an allegation against a prosecution witness and the trial judge applied *Oyesiku* but did not consider **s. 114(1)(d)** and **s. 120(1)(2) of the CJA 2003**. Under the latter provision 'if a previous statement by the witness is admitted as evidence to rebut a suggestion that his oral evidence has been fabricated, that statement is admissible as evidence of any matter stated of which oral evidence by the witness would be admissible'. Thus the statement may be admitted under the inclusionary discretion under **s. 114**.

The Court of Appeal in *Athwal* emphasised that it was not necessary to consider how 'recently' the account had been fabricated, as was the issue under the common law.[5]

(c) False Allegations

The defence claims that the complainant Patricia is making a false allegation and that she has made it before. In relation to the prior complaints, **s. 41(2)** may not apply since making a false allegation is not about 'sexual behaviour'. **Section 41(2)** provides that if at trial a person is charged with a sexual offence no evidence can be adduced nor questions asked in cross-examination about any sexual behaviour of the victim without leave of the court. The Court of Appeal set out guidelines for questioning on false allegations in *R v C & B* [2003] **EWCA Crim 29.** The defence should establish that the previous allegations were made and were false and that there is an evidentiary basis for the claim.[6] Thus John should be warned that there must be an evidential basis for his claim. The courts took a restrictive approach in *R v E* [2004] EWCA Crim 1313 in holding there was no evidential basis for cross-examination on previously false allegations.

Sexual behaviour

If proof of falsity requires questions on sexual behaviour, then **s. 41(2)** would possibly apply. In *R v S* [2003] **EWCA Crim 485** a defence allegation that the claimant had lied about her previous sexual behaviour by claiming to be a virgin at the time of the alleged rape which was the subject of the charge was held to be an allegation of sexual behaviour.[7] In *R v Davarifar* [2009] **EWCA Crim 2294** the Court of Appeal held that questions about previous false statements made by the complainant were not about 'sexual behaviour'. In *R v Garaxo (Shino)* [2005] EWCA Crim 1170 the Court of Appeal held that the trial judge should have allowed cross-examination on

[5] The court in this case emphasised that there must be care not to simply allow what were described as 'unjustified excursions into self-corroboration'.

[6] Simply put, the allegation is about lies not about sexual behaviour.

[7] Glover (2017, p. 576) writes, 'It is not always possible to segregate the evidential issues into neat categories.'

two previous allegations of sexual assault made by the complainant. Although the judge held there was insufficient evidence that these were untrue the Court of Appeal noted that, depending on the answers given by the complainant, a jury could have concluded the allegations had been false.

A related question if **s. 41(2)** is engaged is that **s. 41(4)** may apply if the claim of prior false allegation is 'impugning the credibility of the complainant'. In such a case the judge should not give leave for the questioning. John should be aware that the courts have exhibited a pro-defendant stance. The court held in *R v T, R v H* **[2001] EWCA Crim 1877** that the questioning on false allegations should not have been excluded even if it went primarily to credibility.[8]

[8]Notably the basis of the decision was that the evidence was relevant.

Section 100 CJA 2003

If the defence wish to cross-examine on previous false allegations they may have to satisfy the conditions of **s. 100 of the CJA 2003**. The non-defendant witness can only be questioned on bad character on the grounds set out in the statute which set a high test for admissibility and which also requires leave of the court. However, Patricia should note that **s. 112(3)(b) of the CJA 2003** provides that **s. 100** does not affect the exclusion of evidence under **s. 41** on grounds other than the fact that it is evidence of a person's bad character.[9]

[9]In other words, **s. 41** is expressly preserved.

Section 41(2) makes it clear that the court will not grant leave unless it is satisfied that the evidence is of the kind specified in **s. 41(3)** which applies where the issue is other than consent, as is the case here. In short, in order to have the false allegations admitted John will have to satisfy the court that he is not trying to bring in questions about sexual behaviour. More information is required to establish whether the allegations of falsehoods on the part of Patricia would also reveal sexual behaviour in which case the judge can only grant leave if a refusal might have the effect of rendering a conviction unsafe, see **s. 41(2)(b)**.[10]

[10]This exacts a high test in that the refusal of leave has in effect to lead to a possible miscarriage of justice.

Conclusion to (a), (b), and (c)

(a) Patricia's complaint to her flatmate would be admissible.

(b) John is advised to rely on **s. 120(2)** admitting his previous statement as evidence of the truth of its contents.

(c) Whether **s. 41(2)** applies depends on the circumstances of the previous complaints which the defence claim have been made by Patricia. John should realise that the judge will exercise discretion.

LOOKING FOR EXTRA MARKS

- In (a) you could give more explanation about the historic reason for the rule on prior consistent statements. See *Corke v Corke and Cook* **[1958] P 93**; *R v Roberts* **[1942] 1 All ER 187**.

- In (c) you could cite *R v Knight* **[2013] EWCA Civ 2486** where the defence in making allegations of false allegation by the complainant which also contained evidence of sexual behaviour had to seek leave under **s. 100(4) of the CJA 2003** and **s. 41 of the YJCEA**.

QUESTION | 4

How far do the current evidential rules in relation to rape victims ensure fairness?

CAUTION!

- Ensure that you develop your answer in the form of an argument not a narrative of the law.

- Note that the question refers to 'evidential rules' in general so you should cover cross-examination under **s. 41** in some depth, but also make reference to Special Measures Directions, removal of corroboration requirements, and admissibility of prior complaints.

- Be sure you explain that 'fairness' should embrace the defendant, the complainant, and the public.

DIAGRAM ANSWER PLAN

Explain the background to the change in the law in 1999 and outline the main provisions of s. 41 and other relevant changes in this area.

▼

Review the difficulties in this area, i.e. the 'myths' of female behaviour.

▼

Discuss arguments to suggest unfairness to defendants.

▼

Discuss arguments to suggest unfairness to complainants.

▼

Discuss arguments to suggest law is even-handed.

▼

Conclusion: note public interest in convicting the guilty and observing fair trial rights, arguable that statutory amendments are needed.

Background to Changes in Law

In rape trials that turn on consent, as Birch (2003, p. 370) comments, often 'a jury has little more to go on than one person's word against another'. She cites the phenomenon of the 'twin myths' that sexual experience is erroneously assumed to be related to a propensity to consent and to lack of credibility. The reluctance of complainants to come forward, in part because of such stereotyping, and the difficulty of proof are the context for unacceptably low conviction rates for this offence. Faced with unfairness, irrationality, and danger to individual security, there have been several reforms in the law of evidence. However, controversy remains in that some argue the changes have been overly protective of complainants to the detriment of defendants while others say that the statutory reforms and the case law indicate that the changes do not go far enough to safeguard victims. [1]

The historical evolution of the law largely turns on three areas. One is the exercise of judicial discretion to admit evidence of prior sexual behaviour of the complainant and Parliament's attempts to control that discretion. Secondly, the law has attempted to give particular protection to complainants in these cases in relation to the way they give evidence, and here the provision of anonymity and the availability of protection such as screens and video links have been provided. [2] Thirdly, other procedural changes have been introduced, such as the abolition of corroboration provisions and broader conditions for admissibility of prior complaints. The fairness of the law should be assessed in the light of other less specific changes, for example the presumption under the **Criminal Justice Act (CJA) 2003** for the admissibility of the defendant's bad character.

In relation to cross-examination there was undoubtedly general agreement that the **Sexual Offences (Amendment) Act 1976** was ripe for reform. The Heilbron Committee recommended changes which resulted in **s. 2** of the 1976 Act. Under this the court could draw a distinction between questions or evidence concerning the victim's sexual relationship with the accused and with other men. In the case of the latter, leave of the court had to be obtained before the victim could be asked such questions and this was, in some views, too readily granted. [3]

Current Provisions

The current complex new provisions on cross-examination are contained in **ss. 41–43 of the Youth Justice and Criminal Evidence Act 1999 (YJCEA)**. **Section 2** of the 1976 Act was replaced by **s. 41**

[1] Section 41 of the YJCEA is so complex that if you spend time summarising it you will have no time for argument. It is best to refer to the provisions in the course of your argument.

[2] The relevant sections are ss. 32–39 of the YJCEA.

[3] The shortcomings in **s. 2** of the 1976 Act, were illustrated in *R v Viola* [1982] 3 All ER 73.

of the YJCEA. Unlike the earlier law, this applies to any sexual offence as defined in **s. 62** of the 1999 Act. The purpose of the legislation was to provide more protection for complainants, to encourage reporting of allegations, and make convictions more likely. The Government stated that it had taken account in setting the limits of a 'rape-shield' of the decision in the Canadian case, *R v Seaboyer* (1991) 83 DLR 193.[4]

[4] This held that fair trial rights were violated by a blanket ban on cross-examination on prior sexual history.

Arguments to Suggest Unfairness to Defendants

Those, such as Birch, who regard **s. 41** as less fair to defendants, cite a number of reasons. **Section 41(2)(b)** makes it clear that the court will not grant leave for cross-examination, unless it is satisfied that the evidence is of the very high test specified in **s. 41(3)** or **(5)**, and a refusal of leave might render unsafe a conclusion of the jury on any relevant issues in the case.[5] Secondly, the Act arguably is not fair to the defendant in that it does not draw a distinction between questions relating to the victim's sexual relationship with the accused and other men. This weakness was addressed in the landmark ruling of the House of Lords *R v A (No. 2)* [2002] 1 AC 45. The legal issue was the fairness of the provision in **s. 41** which imposed the same exclusionary provisions on a complainant's sexual experiences with the accused as it did with other men. The House concluded that it was a matter for the trial judge in each case to actually determine whether or not the evidence was sufficiently probative to merit admission. It declared that since ordinary canons of statutory interpretation of **s. 41** did not allow admission of such evidence, the section should be interpreted in the light of **s. 3 of the Human Rights Act 1998** to allow compliance with the provisions of **Art. 6**. In a unanimous judgment, a number of the speeches indicated that excluding such evidence might jeopardise the fairness of the trial. It is indeed the case that relevance depends on context and that legislating too narrowly on it may be unwise.[6] The House of Lords addressed the problem by ingeniously stretching the interpretation of **s. 41(3)(c)**, the similar facts section, to allow questioning on the previous sexual encounter with the defendant. They applied **s. 3 of the Human Rights Act 1998**, which as Lord Steyn put it (para. 45) 'requires the court to subordinate the niceties of the language of **s. 41(3)(c)** and in particular, the touchstone of coincidence, to broader considerations of relevance judged by logical and common sense criteria of time and circumstances.'[7] Lord Steyn stated (at para. 46): 'The effect of the decision today is that under **section 41(3)(c)** of the 1999 Act, construed where necessary by applying the interpretative obligation under **section 3 of the Human Rights Act 1998**, and due regard always being paid to the importance of seeking to protect the complainant from indignity and from humiliating questions, the test of admissibility is whether the evidence (and

[5] You will find Figure 8.2 on p. 17 of *Evidence Concentrate* (OUP, 2017) a useful overview prior to studying the statutory sections.

[6] The point is that relevance depends on context and legislating too narrowly on it may be unwise.

[7] The House's approach has additionally been criticised as unprincipled by a number of commentators who suggest that the reasoning is tortuous and that a declaration of incompatibility would have been preferable. However, this point about judicial strategy is not pertinent to your argument here since you are arguing that the Act is deficient and the judgment upholds this.

questioning in relation to it) is nevertheless so relevant to the issue of consent that to exclude it would endanger the fairness of the trial under article 6 of the convention. If this test is satisfied the evidence should not be excluded.'

Thus arguably the House of Lords has by this interpretation gone some way to correct the balance of fairness in favour of the defendant in **s. 41**. In **R v White (2004)** the Court of Appeal held that **s. 3 of the Human Rights Act** was to be employed cautiously in relation to **s. 41**. Choo (2018, p. 373) points out, however, that this injunction 'sits uneasily with the much-discussed decision in **R v Evans (Chedwyn)**'. Choo argues that the evidence of prior sexual behaviour which the Court of Appeal held admissible under **s. 41(3)(c)(i)** 'should have been held to be inadmissible'. Thus, in practice **s. 41** has not consistently demonstrated a pro-prosecution bias.

A third criticism of the Act as being too pro-prosecution is that it has to be seen in the context of other measures which have possibly harmed the rights of defendants, such as the more ready admissibility of bad character evidence under **s. 101 of the CJA 2003** contrasted with the greater protection of the non-defendant, including complainants in **s. 101**. On this, Birch points out that the jury is kept in the dark where it might be better to educate them about the irrationality of the myths referred to above.[8]

Arguments to Suggest Unfairness to Complainants

Contrasting arguments are put by those who argue on the other hand that the current provisions in **s. 41 of the YJCEA** undermine complainants. First, it is argued that the concept of relevance is not value-free and in a male-dominated judiciary might reflect a male perspective hostile to that of women's experience. McGlynn (p. 225) criticises the interpretations of relevance.[9] She denies the suggestion that **s. 41** undermines defendants' rights but appears to limit the scope of these rights. She suggests that the sexual history evidence at issue in **R v A** was either irrelevant or of little probative value and outweighed by significant risk of prejudice so that its admission is rightly circumscribed.[10] Redmayne also deplores the use of similar fact concepts and the 'coincidence' test as it was applied in **R v A**. He noted (2003, p. 100) that 'once the requirement that the coincidence be relativised to the complainant's non-consent is loosened the section lurches back to unrestricted admissibility'.

Arguments to Suggest Law is Balanced

There are thus powerful arguments to suggest unfairness. On the other hand, there are examples also of an even-handed approach by the courts. To give one example, there has been some concern that

[8] Birch asks why defendants should be treated worse than complainants and suggests that juries should be educated out of their preconceptions.

[9] Her alternative feminist judgment vividly illuminates these points.

[10] *R v Seaboyer* [1991] 2 SCR 577 is illuminating on this.

the allegation of making a false complaint in the past might be pre-cluded as 'sexual behaviour' under **s. 41(2)** but this was held not to be the case in *R v Davarifar* **[2009] EWCA Crim 2294** thus assist-ing the defence. Similarly in *R v T, R v H* **[2002] 1 WLR 632** allega-tions of making a false complaint did not impugn the credibility of the complainant under **s. 41(4)**. The courts have been cautious about applying *R v A*. In *R v S* **[2010]**, concerning a rape allegation against an estranged husband, the court stated, 'There is no logical connec-tion between the last act of consensual intercourse between husband and wife and the event of the alleged rape'. On the other hand in *R v Andrade* **[2015] EWCA Crim 1722** the defendant, who argued consent, was wrongly refused permission for the complainant to be questioned on her sexual history.

There are also available less contentious ways the law of evidence manifests for protecting complainants, such as Special Measures Directions, since they are automatically assumed to be in 'fear and distress' (**YJCEA, s. 17(4)**) and entitled to measures such as screens in court. However, this again may be unfair to the defendant since it might impinge on the jury's perception of the case and also ham-per meaningful cross-examination. The measures contrast with those available to vulnerable defendants.[11] The complainant in sexual cases is treated differently from other victims. In some ways he or she is more protected, as this account has shown; in others he or she is trusted, for example by the removal of corroboration warnings in 1994. Overall, however, it has been suggested that the problem of the low conviction rate is caused not so much by evidential provisions which are unfair to victims but by societal attitudes.

[11] You may not have covered this in your course but if you have it is good to show you appreciate how the various aspects of the law of evidence connect.

Conclusion

Kelly, Temkin, and Griffiths (2006), in the Home Office Report on the operation of this law, give some figures on applications under **s. 41(2)**. Defence applications were made in one-quarter of the trials studied and two-thirds were granted. More applications were made where a pre-existing relationship between the complainant and the defendant was claimed and these applications were granted more often.

Dennis (2006, p. 869) comments, 'Defence lawyers do not generally come well out of this report; they are accused at various points of evad-ing the legislation by not making necessary applications, or flouting the judges' rulings, or of using devious ploys to attack the complainant's credibility in contravention of **s. 41(4)**. Such judgments will inevitably be contested.' Dennis acknowledges, however, that 'there is clearly still scope for improvement, even if one does not support the authors' rec-ommendations for further tightening of the section.' Both reform of the statute and more education are needed to meet the unfairness cited here.

LOOKING FOR EXTRA MARKS?

▦ This is an area which is very often on the news. It is a good idea to collect some up-to-date statistics on conviction rates and reports on possible miscarriages of justice and proposals for reform of the law.

▦ You could gain marks by pointing out that in the controversial case of *R v Mukadi* **[2003] EWCA Crim 3765** the weakness of the 'coincidence' test was displayed. The Court of Appeal held that evidence that the complainant had, some hours before the alleged rape, climbed into the car of an older male driver and exchanged telephone numbers with him should have been admitted.

TAKING THINGS FURTHER

▦ Birch, D., 'Untangling Sexual History Evidence: A Rejoinder to Professor Temkin' [2003] Crim LR 37.
*Presents the differing arguments on **s. 41**.*

▦ Dennis, I., 'Sexual History Evidence: Evaluating Section 41' [2006] Crim LR 869.
A comprehensive review of the debate on the legislation.

▦ Durston, G., 'Previous (In)Consistent Statements' [2005] Crim LR 206.
A helpful explanation of statutory changes.

▦ Hunter, R., McGlynn, C., and Rackley, E. (eds), *Feminist Judgments: From Theory to Practice* (Oxford: Hart Publishing, 2010), ch. 12, 'Commentary on *R v A (No 2)*'.
This applies feminist theory to the controversial House of Lords decision.

▦ Kelly, L., Temkin, J., and Griffiths, S., 'Section 41: An Evaluation of New Legislation Limiting Sexual History Evidence in Rape Trials', Home Office Online Report 20/06 (London: Home Office, 2006).
See reference in text to answer.

▦ McGlynn C., '*R v A (No. 2)* Judgment' in R. Hunter, C. McGlynn, and E. Rackley (eds), *Feminist Judgments: From Theory to Practice* (Oxford: Hart Publishing, 2010), p. 211.
See reference in text to answer.

▦ Redmayne, M., 'Myths, Relationships and Conferences. The New Problems of Sexual History' (2003) 7 E & P 75.
See reference in text to answer.

Online Resources

www.oup.com/uk/qanda/

Go online for extra essay and problem questions, a glossary of key terms, online versions of all the answer plans and audio commentary on how selected ones were put together, and a range of podcasts which include advice on exam and coursework technique and advice for other assessment methods.

10 Privilege and public policy

ARE YOU READY?

In order to perform well in these questions you should have revised the following:

- the privilege against self-incrimination in civil trials and in administrative investigations, and the impact of the **European Convention on Human Rights**
- the absolute status of legal professional privilege, including the denial of defence requests for disclosure
- an outline of the role of public interest immunity in securing non-disclosure of documents and in the protection of informers in civil and criminal trials
- the role of special counsel in public interest immunity claims and *ex parte* hearings

KEY DEBATES

Debate: equality of arms, Public Interest Immunity (PII), and Closed Material Procedures (CMPs).

Parliament decided that the doctrine of public interest immunity was inadequate to safeguard national security and has legislated for CMPs to be used in tribunals and the common law civil courts. CMPs allow a court to consider evidence submitted by one party which is disclosed neither to the other party nor their counsel. It is available as evidence to one party only, usually a government body. By contrast, if PII applies neither party can use the material as evidence. Critics of the procedure argue that this poses a threat to the principle of equality of arms.

Debate: does legal professional privilege apply to evidence gathering?

Legal professional privilege applies to the content of communications between lawyers and clients. It cannot be used in evidence unless the privilege is lost under one of the acceptable grounds.

Controversially, however, statute allows the police or security services to conduct covert surveillance of lawyers' communication with clients in custody in cases of serious crime such as murder and terrorism. Some commentators argue that sanctioning such pre-trial investigatory procedures undermines legal professional privilege because the lawyer and her client cannot be sure that their communications are confidential.

Debate: the limited nature of the privileges recognised in English law.

English common law recognises two privileges, namely the privilege against self-incrimination and legal professional privilege. The scope of the former is restricted in certain circumstances by statute such as **ss. 34–38 of the Criminal Justice and Public Order Act 1994.** Unlike the position in some other jurisdictions, English law has not extended privilege to other relationships such as those between medical advisers and patients or between ministers of religion and those who confide in them.

QUESTION | 1

Emily is suing Heathcliff Translation Services (HTS) for failure to deliver the translation of her novel. Rochester, a translator under contract with HTS, is refusing to respond to pre-trial requests for information from Emily because he fears his involvement in submitting invoices for work that he had not done may expose him and his wife Rosa to fraud charges. At the same time, HTS is subject to a separate investigation by the (imaginary) Translators Regulatory Body (TRB), an organisation set up under statute. The TRB argue that HTS do not comply with their minimum standards. The TRB has statutory powers for their inspectors to examine documents and records. Carlyle, the owner of HTS, at first refuses to allow an inspection, claiming his privilege against self-incrimination, but he then allows the search to go ahead. Inspectors examine Carlyle's computers and find evidence of both child pornography and poor business practices. Carlyle corresponds by email with the lawyers in HTS asking advice on whether he can prevent the material being handed to the police. James, who works in the lawyers' department, and who is a friend of Emily, printed out and forwarded to her copies of this email exchange. Emily wants to use extracts from the emails as part of her suit against HTS.

Advise the parties.

CAUTION!

- A good answer requires you to display understanding of claims for privilege in relation to pre-existing documents; that is, existing independently of the party's will.

- Do not lose marks by overlooking what might misleadingly appear to be a detail in a question, here the reference to copies and legal professional privilege.

- Refer to the possibility of remedies such as injunctive relief.

- Consider the importance of **Art. 6 of the European Convention on Human Rights** in this area.

DIAGRAM ANSWER PLAN

Identify the issues	▨ The legal issues are: claims of privilege against self-incrimination by Rochester and Carlyle; whether legal professional privilege applies to Emily's request for disclosure.
Relevant law	▨ Privilege against self-incrimination in civil proceedings and in administrative investigations; compliance with **Art. 6**; application of legal professional privilege to copies of documents and possible equitable remedy.
Apply the law	▨ Consider whether the application of privilege against self-incrimination would deprive Emily of a remedy; whether the 'documents' in Carlyle's claim are 'independent' evidence; and the application of legal professional privilege to copies.
Conclude	▨ Assess the outcomes for Rochester, Carlyle, and Emily.

SUGGESTED ANSWER

Privilege Against Self-Incrimination

These are civil proceedings and Rochester and Carlyle are seeking to exercise the privilege against self-incrimination. Presumably Emily will challenge Rochester's claim for privilege because it may deprive her of material to pursue the suit against HTS. Rochester should be aware that the privilege is based on common law and the scope of the privilege was set out by the Court of Appeal in *Blunt v Park Lane Hotel* [1942] **2 KB 253**. It is acknowledged in **s. 14(1) of the Civil Evidence Act 1968. Section 14(1)(b)** refers to the right to refuse to answer any question or produce any document or thing if to do so would tend to expose the husband or wife of that person to proceedings for a criminal offence. So Rosa is also in principle covered by the principle.

The privilege against self-incrimination, according to Glover (2017, p. 684) has two aspects;[1] namely, the right not to be compelled to give evidence and the right not to make incriminating statements when confronted with an alleged offence. Lord Mustill in *R v Director of Serious Fraud Office, ex p Smith* [1993] AC 1, 30, a House of Lords judgment, identifies a general immunity which is '... possessed by all persons and bodies, from being compelled on pain of punishment to answer questions the answers to which may incriminate them'.[2]

[1] Arguably both of these aspects are at issue here.

[2] The judgment contains an illuminating typology of the six aspects of the privilege.

The justification for the existence of the privilege, according to Lord Templeman in *AT&T Istel Ltd v Tully* **[1993] AC 45**, is first that it discourages the ill-treatment of a suspect and, secondly, that it discourages the production of dubious confessions.

Rochester should be informed that the privilege would not extend to any possible charges in another jurisdiction so more information is needed to see if his work has a global reach and whether this applies in his case. The authority for this is **s. 14(1) of the Civil Evidence Act 1968**.

The privilege extends to pre-trial proceedings and it is for Rochester to persuade the judge that he needs its protection. He will need to provide evidence that his answers might expose him and Rosa to criminal proceedings. He may rely on the case of *Rank Film Distribution Ltd v Video Information Centre* **[1982] AC 380**. There the House of Lords upheld the claim for privilege because there was a real danger of a criminal charge of conspiracy to defraud against the defendant.

The Privilege and Opportunity of a Remedy for Claimant

One consideration which will be relevant to Rochester is how far the application of the privilege may restrict the recovery of money or property by Emily. The House of Lords in *AT&T Istel Ltd v Tully* **[1993] AC 45** established that there is no reason to allow a defendant in civil proceedings to rely on it, thus depriving a claimant of his rights, where the defendant's own protection can be secured in other ways. Lord Templeman (at 53) stated that the privilege should not be 'blatantly exploited' to deprive the plaintiffs of their civil rights if it was not necessary to protect the defendant.[3] Referring to the defendant, Lord Templeman said that he would be entitled to rely on the privilege against self-incrimination only insofar as the testimony would provide evidence against him in a criminal trial. The plaintiff was making a claim for damages and repayment of money obtained by fraud. At the same time, a police investigation was set up. The plaintiffs were granted orders requiring the defendants to disclose all dealings concerning the money. The order contained a condition that it would not be used in the prosecution of a criminal offence. The order was later varied and the plaintiff appealed against the variation. The House of Lords varied the order after the Crown Prosecution Service gave an informal assurance that it would not seek to use the divulged material. Thus, if in the instant case the judge was assured that the answers would not be relied on in criminal proceedings, there might be no obstacle to the requirement that Rochester answer the questions.

If the Crown Prosecution Service gave no such undertaking, Rochester's failure to answer questions involves then a clash between

[3] Obviously under examination conditions it is difficult to remember quotations but short phrases may be possible.

two principles, namely the duty to testify and the privilege against self-incrimination. A final point is that it should be noted that some statutes such as the **Theft Act 1968** expressly remove the privilege in certain situations.[4] However, there is no indication from the facts in this question of the existence of a statute which has abolished the privilege in the prevailing circumstances.

The issue then arises as to whether Emily will succeed in getting an order to compel Rochester to answer, violation of which would be contempt of court. Whether Rochester was ordered to respond or not would therefore depend on the likelihood of his facing a criminal trial.

Reservations About the Privilege

Rochester (and Carlyle) should be aware, in relation to the likely response of the courts, that the privilege has been subject to judicial criticism. In **Tully** Lord Templeman stated (at 53): 'I regard the privilege against self-incrimination exercisable in civil proceedings as an archaic and unjustifiable survival from the past when the court directs the production of relevant documents and requires the defendant to specify his dealings with the plaintiff's property or money.'

Privilege and Documents

Carlyle also claims the privilege against self-incrimination.[5] He wishes to resist the handing over of material obtained in the course of what was initially an administrative or regulatory inquiry but subsequently a possible criminal one. Carlyle did not claim the privilege for the initial search. It is unlikely that he would have succeeded even if he had, although more information is needed about the investigative powers of TRB to see if there was a statutory basis for the search. If there was not, Carlyle in any criminal proceedings could possibly claim the material was obtained unlawfully and ask for a stay of prosecution or exclusion of evidence under **s. 78 of the Police and Criminal Evidence Act 1984 (PACE)**. The immediate issue is whether the computer material can be handed to the prosecuting authorities. In **Saunders v UK (1997) 23 EHRR 313** the Strasbourg Court drew a distinction between statements made under compulsion, to which the privilege applied, and evidence having an existence independent of the will of the suspect, such as pre-existing documents.[6]

Subsequent case law suggests that Carlyle may be on particularly weak ground in resisting disclosure of the material found as a result of the search. In **C Plc v P (Attorney General intervening) [2007] EWCA Civ 493** the Court of Appeal drew a distinction between response to questions and 'independent' evidence. In this case a search order issued to discover materials relating to copyright infringement unexpectedly revealed child pornography. The pornography could

[4] Dennis (2013, p. 158) has a succinct account of this issue. See also *Beghal v DPP* [2015] UKSC 49 on implied statutory abrogation of the privilege.

[5] There is no need to repeat the general outline of the law you have given above.

[6] You could acknowledge that it is not always easy to make the distinction: see Dennis (2013, p. 163).

therefore be handed to the police and Carlyle may be the subject of a police investigation.

Legal Professional Privilege and Injunctive Relief

The final issue in the problem involves the note of the discussion between Carlyle and the company lawyer. Carlyle is seeking immunity for communications with the lawyer for the purpose of giving or receiving advice.

Legal professional privilege attaches to certain communications between lawyer and client and although it is a common law privilege, its scope is summarised by **s. 10 PACE**. There is an 'iniquity exception' that the privilege does not arise where the relationship between the lawyer and client is based on the commission of crime or other fraud or dishonesty. In *R v Central Criminal Court, ex p Francis & Francis* **[1989] AC 346** the House of Lords held that the privilege is lost even where the criminal intent is that of a third party.[7] The facts of the problem do not suggest the privilege is lost on grounds of crime or fraud since Carlyle is asking for advice rather than seeking to commit an offence.

The fact that the lawyer is employed by the company does not exclude his communications from the scope of the privilege but Carlyle should be warned that copies of the communications are not privileged. Here the copies are of a document which originated as emails but it is submitted that the same principle applies as to paper originals. In *Calcraft v Guest* **[1898] 1 QB 759** the court held that legal professional privilege only attached to the originals of the document and copies were acceptable in evidence.[8] However, Carlyle may have a remedy in that he should be advised that until the documents are before the court he could be granted an injunction to restrain their use. Since it appears they were obtained in breach of confidence then *Lord Ashburton v Pape* **[1913] 2 Ch 469** may apply.[9] However, Carlyle may not need to apply for an injunction. **Rule 31.20 of the Civil Procedure Rules 1998** allows such documents to be used only with permission of the court. Hence, when Emily seeks to use the documents, Carlyle may be able to apply to the court to prevent their disclosure.[10]

Conclusion

If the likelihood of Rochester facing criminal charges is remote then he may succeed in his assertion of the privilege against self-incrimination. Recent case law suggests that Carlyle will not succeed in his assertion. However, if he acts promptly, Carlyle is likely to succeed in his claim for legal professional privilege.

[7] A recent example of fraud is *JSC BTA Bank v Ablayzov* [2014] EWHC 2778 (Comm) which concerned dishonesty in relation to disclosure of assets.

[8] Note that the position in relation to private privilege is different from that of public interest immunity where if PII applies then copies of the documents or their use by the witness recalling details are not admissible.

[9] See *Goddard v Nationwide Building Society* [1987] QB 670 where the Court of Appeal attempted to reconcile these two cases.

[10] For a useful review of the law in this area see *Al-Fayed v Commissioner of Police of the Metropolis (No. 1)* [2002] EWCA Civ 780 at para. 16.

LOOKING FOR EXTRA MARKS?

- Gain extra marks by extending your analysis of *C Plc*. The child pornography constituted evidence independent of the accused since it was discovered as a result of a lawful search warrant.
- You could expand your assessment of the impact of **Art. 6** in relation to the privilege against self-incrimination by pointing out that there may be a breach in the view of the Strasbourg Court if there is compulsion to cooperate with the state, see for example *Shannon v UK* **(2006) 42 EHRR 31**.

QUESTION | **2**

(a) Brenda is charged with unlawful possession of pornographic photographs discovered after a legally conducted police raid on her flat. Her defence is that they were sent through the post to her unsolicited and she, although disgusted and puzzled, had put them on one side and had forgotten to destroy them. She noted that they purported to be from an organisation called the Partners Exchange. She recalls that Archie, a member of her sports club, who had made several unwelcome sexual advances to her, had mentioned that he belonged to the Partners Exchange, which he said arranged 'interesting introductions'. Having spurned his advances, she thought no more of the matter but now she suspects that Archie, who was known to the police as a drug user, may have sent the mail and then informed on her. Brenda denies the charge and demands as part of her defence that the identity of Archie is disclosed at the trial.

Advise Brenda.

(Worth 70 per cent of the total marks for the question.)

(b) Geraldine is facing prosecution for carrying out unauthorised cosmetic surgery at her home. The prosecution had film from a CCTV camera of women with bandaged faces leaving her house. Unfortunately the film had been accidentally erased after it had been viewed by police officers. They do not wish to reveal that the camera was placed secretly on Sanjay's shop opposite Geraldine's house. Police also do not want to disclose that police officer Joan, dressed in a milk deliverer's uniform, kept the house under surveillance from a fake milk float in the street. Geraldine denies the charge and wishes to obtain disclosure of details of the observations of her house.

Advise Geraldine.

(Worth 30 per cent of the total marks for the question.)

CAUTION!

- Only attempt this question if you are familiar with the case law on informants in criminal cases. You must stress that there is a principle of non-disclosure and it is for the accused to show there is good reason arising from the facts of the defence to reverse the presumption.

- Make sure the length and detail of your answers to the two parts in terms of range of analysis and length reflect the allocation of marks.

DIAGRAM ANSWER PLAN

Identify the issues	■ The legal issues are: (a) the disclosure of the identity of an informer; (b) the disclosure of the whereabouts of police observation points, camera film evidence.
Relevant law	■ (a) and (b) Common law public interest immunity rules, statutory procedural provisions under the **Criminal Procedure and Investigations Act (Disclosure) Rules 1997** and the **Criminal Procedure Rules 2015: Art. 6** rights.
Apply the law	■ (a) Brenda suspects Archie framed her not just that he informed and so it is arguable that disclosure of his identity is necessary to ensure Art. 6 fair trial rights; (b) Geraldine's defence is misidentification so may also have grounds of disclosure.
Conclude	■ (a) and (b) Assess how judge is likely to decide on disclosure.

SUGGESTED ANSWER

(a) Naming of Police Informers

A long-established rule applying to criminal proceedings prevents witnesses being asked, or answering, questions about the names of police informers or the nature of the information given. The reason is that public interest requires it to prosecute criminal activity successfully. The rule applies as long as information about the informer is not necessary to establish guilt: see ***Marks v Beyfus*** **(1890) 25 QBD 494.** The rationale of the rule was explained by Lord Reid in ***Conway v Rimmer*** **[1968] AC 910, 953**: pointing out the social problem of the 'war with criminals'.[1]

[1] Since many criminals were highly intelligent it was essential to deny them useful information.

Disclosure rules

However, *R v Ward* [1993] **1 WLR 619**, on the other hand, placed the prosecution under an obligation to disclose to the defence all the material on which the prosecution is based. This area is now covered by the **Criminal Procedure and Investigations Act 1996. Section 21(2)** preserves the common law rule as to whether disclosure is in the public interest. It is for the courts to decide what should not be disclosed.[2] Brenda should be informed that the prosecution must assert a claim to public interest immunity (PII) if evidence of the identity of informers is to be excluded. Under the **Criminal Procedure and Investigations Act 1996** primary disclosure must be made under **s. 3(1)(a)** of any prosecution material which has not previously been disclosed to the accused and which in the prosecutor's opinion might undermine the case for the prosecution against the accused. Secondary disclosure under **s. 7(2)(a)** is to be made, following delivery of a defence statement, of previously undisclosed material which might be reasonably expected to assist the accused's defence. The **Criminal Justice Act (CJA) 2003** amended **s. 3(1)(a)** so as to require primary disclosure of any previously undisclosed material 'which might reasonably be considered capable of undermining the case for the prosecution against the accused or of assisting the case for the accused'. Applications by the prosecution to withhold material must be made in writing and served on the defendant but only to the extent that this would not disclose what the prosecution maintains should not be disclosed. The rules are now enshrined in the **Criminal Procedure Rules (2015).**[3]

[2] The authority for the rule that the court makes the final decision on PII claims is *Conway v Rimmer* (1968).

[3] Check that you are applying the latest version of the Rules, see http://www.justice.gov.uk/courts/procedure-rules/criminal.

Article 6

Brenda may find some support in the principle of the right to a fair trial enshrined in **Art. 6(1) of the European Convention on Human Rights (ECHR).** The Strasbourg Court had discussed the issue in a number of cases, including *Rowe and Davis v UK* (2000) **30 EHRR 1**, *Jasper v UK* (2000) **30 EHRR 441**, and *Fitt v UK* (2000) **30 EHRR 480**. In *Fitt v UK* (para. 45) the Court stressed that 'only such measures restricting the rights of the defence which are strictly necessary are permissible under **art. 6(1).**' It was accepted that the entitlement to disclosure of relevant evidence is not an absolute right.[4] The House of Lords reviewed the principles involved in *R v H, R v C* [2004] **UKHL 3**. Brenda may be assisted by this ruling where the House set out the procedure to be followed when the prosecution refuses to disclose evidence on the grounds of public interest. The applicants were convicted of conspiracy to supply heroin. They demanded disclosure of details of police undercover surveillance which had led to the charges. The judge had ruled in favour of the appointment of a

[4] The court pointed out that 'In some cases it may be necessary to withhold certain evidence from the defence so as to preserve the fundamental rights of another individual or to safeguard an important public interest.'

special advocate. The procedure first introduced under the **Special Immigration Appeals Commission Act 1997** may apply. This allows for the appointment of an independent special counsel, who will be shown the disputed evidence.[5] Special advocates are charged with representing the applicants' interests but since they may not disclose the secret material disclosed to them they do not have the normal professional responsibility to their clients.

The House dismissed the appeal and held that this was not a case where a PII hearing should be held. The decision to appoint a special advocate was premature. The judgment gives a detailed review of the role of special advocates in PII hearings in criminal cases considering (para. 22) that 'Such an appointment will always be exceptional, never automatic; a course of last and never first resort.'

Brenda's counsel will refer to the detailed test set out in the judgment for PII claims in similar cases involving police informers. It stressed that any derogation from the principle of full disclosure had always to be the minimum necessary to protect the public interest in question and must never threaten the overall fairness of the trial.

Ex parte hearings

The prosecution is placed under an obligation to reveal first any evidence that might determine the prosecution case and, later, information which assists the defence case. The procedure differs according to the sensitivity of the material. The judge may hear an application for disclosure either *inter partes*, or in extremely sensitive cases *ex parte*. Where the revelation of the existence of an informer would otherwise require the abandonment of the prosecution, application can be made *ex parte* by the Crown without notice to the defence.[6]

[6] Note how if PII is applied the information on the informant cannot be used in evidence by either side thus preserving equality of arms, unlike the position in relation to Closed Material Procedures.

Since Brenda only suspects and does not have confirmation of the existence of the informer, the prosecution may rely on this procedure under the authority of *R v Davis* **[1993] 1 WLR 613**. The court will normally exclude evidence of an informer's identity, but where the judge is of the opinion that disclosure is necessary to establish the accused's innocence, it is a rule of law that the judge must allow the question to be asked and require an answer: *Marks v Beyfus* **(1890) 25 QBD 494**. It is for the accused to show that there is good reason to expect that disclosure is necessary to establish his innocence. This should normally be done before the trial in proceedings to set aside a witness summons or subpoena for the appropriate Crown witness: *R v Hennessy* **(1978) 68 Cr App R 419**. Brenda may rely on *R v Agar* **(1989) 90 Cr App R 318**, where it was held on appeal that disclosure of the name of an informer in a drugs case was necessary where the defendant claimed to have been set up by the informer and the police acting together. In reaching its decision whether to allow disclosure, the court can take into account the informer's willingness to be named, but this is not conclusive: *Savage v Chief Constable of Hampshire* **[1997] 1 WLR 1061**. In *R v Slowcombe* **[1991] Crim LR 198**, where the identity of the informer would have contributed little or nothing to the issue before the jury, disclosure was refused.

Here, Brenda is claiming that Archie framed her and not just that he informed. If she is able to put up some evidence that Archie did trap her, the jury may well conclude that her story may be true, so her counsel should be permitted to ask the police whether Archie was the informant. The association with the Partners Exchange may well be relevant evidence and lead to an inference of Archie's involvement. If Archie was not the informer, the police would not be required to name the informer, however, and the jury would be asked to believe Brenda's case without that knowledge.

(b) PII and Observation Posts on Private Property

Geraldine will be advised to argue that her right to a fair trial is arguably threatened if disclosure is not made of the details of the observations of her house so she can challenge the interpretation of the evidence.

Geraldine should be advised that the courts have established that PII may apply to police observation posts since residents who might include business proprietors may wish to remain anonymous for their security or financial interest and the supply of posts might dry up if addresses were revealed. However, in *R v Rankine* **[1986] 2 WLR 1075** the Court of Appeal held that if the accused can convince the court of a relevant evidential reason why he should know the identity of the post then it should be revealed. If Geraldine is claiming mistaken interpretation of the condition of the women allegedly leaving her premises then the court might decide this should be tested by revealing the address of the CCTV on Sanjay's shop. In *R v Johnson* **[1988] 1 WLR 1377** the Court of Appeal set out the information which should be given in a voir dire in order to assist the court in deciding whether to uphold the PII claim. Brenda should be assured that the final decision on disclosure rest on the judge. However, in *R (on the application of WV) v Crown Prosecution Service* **[2011] EWHC 2480 (Admin)** the court affirmed the importance of protecting informers.[7] The sergeant in charge of the surveillance should give evidence that he had spoken to the residents before the operation began and ascertained their views on disclosure of their identity.[8] Also a senior officer should give evidence that, just before the trial, he had spoken to the occupants to confirm their wishes. If the judge rules that disclosure of the placing of the CCTV should not be made, he must explain the reasons to the jury and the effect of his ruling.

[7] Hungerford-Welch commenting on this case (2012, p. 460) pointed out that if the defence need to know the identity of the informant in order to have a fair trial but this would endanger the informant or his family, then the prosecution should be dropped.

[8] Note also the case of *Blake v DPP* (1993) 97 Cr App R 169, which held that it was not necessary to show that an actual threat had been made to the occupier of the premises.

Police surveillance

Geraldine might have more success in determining the identity of the milk float, relying on *R v Brown* **(1987) 87 Cr App R 52.** In that case the court held that if the occupants are police then they do not need protection.[9] On the other hand, the prosecution may argue that there is a public interest in protecting police methods which here include disguise as a milk deliverer.

[9]Here the Court of Appeal refused to extend the rule of non-disclosure to cover the identification of unmarked police cars which were on surveillance duty.

There is no issue of PII as regards the outcome of the CCTV camera since the film constitutes real evidence. The prosecution may rely on *Taylor v Chief Constable of Cheshire* **[1986] 1 WLR 1479** where it was held that evidence from police officers who had reviewed a film before it was erased was admissible.[10] However, the defence may argue that it is not admissible evidence if its location is not revealed.

[10]This case illustrates the point that the rule that 'primary' (i.e. not 'secondary') evidence must be produced of the contents of a document, if relied upon by a party as direct evidence, only applies to written material.

Conclusion to (a) and (b)

In (a) Brenda should be assured that the final decision on disclosure is with the judge and on the facts given it is unlikely that she will be awarded this. In *R (on the application of WV) v Crown Prosecution Service* **[2011] EWHC 2480 (Admin)** the importance that is attached to protecting the identity of informers was affirmed. The informant should have had his identity protected and the Crown Prosecution Service had been wrong to seek to break this confidentiality.

In (b) Geraldine is unlikely to succeed in having details of Sanjay's shop revealed but may have more success in arguing that it is necessary to cross-examine Joan on what she claims is an eyewitness account so her identity and location should be made available.

LOOKING FOR EXTRA MARKS?

- In (a) you could advise that Brenda's counsel should also consider *R v McDonald* **[2004] EWCA Crim 2614** in which the Court of Appeal set out guidelines for appeals from the Crown Court on PII hearings.

- In (b) you would gain extra credit by a more detailed examination of the test in *R v H*. Brenda should be aware that the judge should review the progress of the trial as it proceeds and consider if it was still fair. Full disclosure could be ordered at that later stage even if that meant the prosecution was stayed.

- For (a) and (b) you could develop the socio-legal context of your answer by referring to the history of reform of PII in criminal cases and the significance of the collapse of the Matrix Churchill trial and the subsequent Scott Inquiry.

(a) Mr X is suing the Rural Retreat Nursing Home for negligently causing the death of his wife. He alleges that Gloria, a nursing auxiliary, administered a drug overdose. He wishes to adduce in evidence a letter and a report drawn up by the Home's directors for the Home's insurers. This was compiled after the death of Mrs X in preparation for a health and safety inquiry in which other staff were to give evidence that there was lax management in the Home and that bottles were often mislabelled. A copy of the report was sent by the Nursing Home to their lawyers. Jane, Mr X's neighbour who works as a clerk for the Home's lawyers, took a photocopy of the report and sent it anonymously to Mr X. Mr X also asks for discovery of correspondence between Rural Retreat and their accountants because he suspects that the Nursing Home was in financial difficulty and had made a number of its experienced staff redundant. He plans to argue that this was a factor in the poor nursing care.

Advise on admissibility of the report to the insurers and of the correspondence between the Home and the accountants.

(Worth 70 per cent of the total marks for the question.)

(b) Olaf (O), Patrick (P), and Sarah (S) were charged with conspiracy to rob. They all consulted solicitors separately and all planned initially to plead not guilty. O claims that S told him that she told her solicitor, Y, that he, O, had nothing to do with the conspiracy. S now denies having said this to O. S had subsequently entered into an agreement with the prosecution to plead guilty and give evidence against O and P who both plead not guilty. At the start of the trial S gives evidence-in-chief for the prosecution. In preparing to cross-examine S, Mary (M), O's defence counsel, wants discovery of the interview files between S and Y. M also plans to use as evidence an email which S had addressed to Y after giving evidence in which she said that she could not be sure that she had given correctly the dates of meetings she had said had taken place between O and S as part of the alleged conspiracy. Dispute over the timings of these alleged meetings is part of O's defence case. S had sent the email by mistake to O instead of to Y. S is refusing to grant permission to see the interview transcript and is questioning the admissibility of the misdirected email.

Advise O's defence on how the judge is likely to rule.

(Worth 30 per cent of the total marks for the question.)

CAUTION!

▪ You need to be sure to cover the admissibility of two items of evidence, namely the lawyer's report for the insurers and the correspondence with the accountants. The specific questions here on legal professional privilege are: how far does it stretch to correspondence with third parties? What is the status of copies? If the privilege is lost, can use of the document be restrained by an injunction on grounds of confidentiality? How do the **Civil Procedure Rules (CPR) 1998** affect this?

This second part of the question requires you to have knowledge of the law governing legal professional privilege in criminal proceedings and in particular the principle that it still holds even in the face of a possible miscarriage of justice. Note that there are two contested documents here, the record of the initial interview between S and her solicitor and the misaddressed email. Here note that the facts are not dissimilar to those in *R v Tomkins* **(1977) 67 Cr App R 181** so providing an example of how those students who have read the full case report are at a significant advantage in assessments.

 Note the different marks awarded to each part and allocate your time and the detail of your answer accordingly.

DIAGRAM ANSWER PLAN

Identify the issues	The legal issues are: (a) legal professional litigation and advice privilege involving correspondence with third parties; whether there is privilege for correspondence with accountants; (b) whether privilege has been waived by mistake in a criminal case.
Relevant law	Legal professional privilege and third parties, privilege and accountants; 'the dominant purpose' of the creation of the document. (b) **Section 10 PACE** and legal professional privilege in criminal cases.
Apply the law	The report is a communication with a third party but doubtful if litigation is the 'dominant purpose'; copies of the correspondence with lawyers is arguably covered by legal professional privilege, privilege does not extend to communications with accountants; (b) interview transcript unlikely to be admitted even if would help prove innocence, but privilege might have been waived inadvertently in the case of misdirected email.
Conclude	(a) Likely outcome for Mr X; (b) likely outcome for O.

SUGGESTED ANSWER

(a) The Report to the Insurers

 [1] It is good practice to stress that a party has to pass the evidential burden and cannot just go on a fishing expedition for material.

The report to the insurers contains cogent evidence of the state of affairs in the Home at the time of Mrs X's death and would clearly be relevant to Mr X's suit.[1]

Third party or litigation privilege covers communication between the party and a third party, or communications between the party's lawyers and a third party. The report requested by Mr X is a communication between the Home and a third party. Legal advice privilege applies to communications between the party and their lawyers. The Home is unlikely to succeed in claiming advice privilege by sending the report to the lawyers directly. This would not confer on the report legal professional privilege which it did not already possess, see *R v Peterborough JJ, ex p Hicks* **[1977] 1 WLR 1371**, a case decided in the Divisional Court.[2]

[2]As the court stated, if this were not so every litigant could protect embarrassing documents merely by sending them to their legal representatives.

It may be argued that the Home is entitled to claim litigation privilege for the Home's report to its insurers. The House of Lords in *Waugh v BRB* **[1980] AC 521** held that this would be so, provided the report was compiled with a view to pending or contemplated litigation with the dominant purpose of obtaining legal advice. In that case the defendants were sued under the **Fatal Accidents Act 1976**. The plaintiff's husband had died in a railway collision. The widow asked for discovery of an internal report by the defendants submitted to the railway inspectorate and the ministry. However, the report was also intended to give details to the Railway Board's solicitor so he could give advice. There was no privilege because the intended or contemplated litigation was not on the facts 'at least the dominant purpose' of creating the document. The question here is whether the 'dominant purpose' of the report was the prospect of the health and safety inquiry or whether it was the prospect of a civil suit from Mr X. On the facts it appears that it might be the former in which case Mr X might have disclosure.

[3]The ruling has been criticized by academics. Choo (2018, p. 277) suggests it is 'debatable' whether the distinction between litigation and advice privilege is convincing. He maintains that it is 'at least arguable' that the House should have decided that *R v Derby Magistrate's Court, ex p B* [1996] AC 487 was wrongly decided. See also Zuckerman (1996).

The Home may claim, however, that the health and safety inquiry was litigation. More information is needed about the nature of this inquiry but the courts have taken a narrow view of what is litigation. In *Re L (A Minor) (Police Investigation: Privilege)* **[1997] AC 16** the House of Lords decided that legal professional litigation privilege applies only in adversarial proceedings.[3] The House held that while legal professional privilege in the form of communication between lawyer and client was absolute, it did not apply to confidential communications with third parties in relation to non-adversarial care proceedings brought under the **Children Act 1989**. Note that the House of Lords also held that *Derby Magistrates' Court, ex p B* **[1996] AC 487** was distinguished since its ruling on the absolute nature of legal professional privilege was confined to legal advice privilege. Thus if the Home claims litigation privilege they may not succeed.[4]

[4]In *Re L* the welfare of a child was at stake. One issue in *Re L* was the use of the document in possible criminal proceedings against a mother, a drug addict, who had communicated confidentially with an expert.

If Mr X does not in fact succeed in these claims then he may argue that any privilege extends only to the original document. The contents of a privileged document can be proved by secondary evidence, including the production of copies, following the Court of Appeal deci-sion in *Calcraft v Guest* [1898] 1 QB 759. This rule was explained in *Lord Ashburton v Pape* [1913] 2 Ch 469 by Cozens-Hardy MR, as arising from the fact that the court, in an action where it is sought to prove the contents of a privileged document from secondary sources, is not trying the circumstances under which the document was pro-duced. But that rule, as he pointed out, had no bearing on a case where the whole subject matter of the action is the right to retain the copy of a document which is privileged. *Ashburton* established the availability of equitable relief to restrain the use of copies of docu-ments which were subject to a duty of confidence and possession of which had been wrongfully obtained. Despite some attempt to recon-cile these principles, uncertainty arises as to the result in such cases. This has now been simplified by the **Civil Procedure Rules (CPR) 1998**.

Rule 31.20 of the CPR 1998 provides that where a party inad-vertently allows a privileged document to be inspected, the party who has inspected the document may use it or its contents only with the permission of the court. The consequence of this is that a party seek-ing to restrain the use of a privileged document, whether a primary or secondary copy, does not have to apply for an injunction to restrain its use. Under this rule the court can of its own motion, or on the applica-tion of a party to the case, order the return of the document which is privileged without separate proceedings being commenced. It should be noted that this rule does not affect the question as to how the court decides whether a document is privileged.

The difficulty is that the court must decide whether the document has been 'inadvertently' inspected. There remains the question as to whether this applies to cases where the document has been obtained by fraud or trick. At common law, the court took the view that how the document was obtained was not relevant and the issue was whether the party claiming its return was entitled to have it: *Goddard v Nationwide Building Society* [1987] QB 670.

The Court of Appeal in *Derby & Co. Ltd v Weldon (No. 8)* [1990] 3 All ER 362 emphasised that no balancing exercise is required when a party seeks to vindicate privilege in documents mistakenly disclosed.[5] It should be noted that under r. 31.20 of the CPR, if a party inadvertently permits a privileged document to be inspected, it may only be used with the permission of the court by the party who has inspected it. However, here disclosure seems to be deliberate not inadvertent.

It is clearly the case here that Jane, the clerk, is subject to the duty of confidence as against her employer. She has broken her obligation of secrecy in passing the document to Mr X, even if the documents

[5] Dennis (2013, p. 424) highlights the growing problem 'of mistakes in pre-trial disclosure in commercial litigation'.

had been obtained without any reprehensible conduct. The Home could ask for the return of any privileged documents when Mr X seeks leave of the court to use the document under **r. 31.20.** Mr X should be warned that the courts have taken a rather strict approach since the **CPR** were introduced.[6]

Finally Mr X is advised that privilege only applies to legal profession-als. He could rely on *R (Prudential plc) v Special Commissioners of Income Tax* **[2013] UKSC 1** to ask for disclosure of the communica-tion of Rural Retreat with accountants.

(b) The Disputed Evidence

The disputed evidence is arguably relevant and therefore disclosure is likely to be requested. The transcript of the interview with the solicitor goes to an issue in the trial, namely how far S's evidence truthfully gives an account of O's involvement. O's defence barrister will want to cross-examine S on the alleged verbal statement to O which S now denies having made. The record of the interview could be used as a previous inconsistent statement.[7]

There is no information that S has waived the privilege. The courts take an absolutist stance in relation to non-disclosure of material subject to legal professional privilege as illustrated by the case of *R v Grant* **[2006] QB 60**. In that case the Court of Appeal quashed a conviction because the police, in recording G's conversations with his solicitor, had violated the privilege. It was not material that G's defence had not been prejudiced as a result of the disclosure. It is unlikely that O will be able to claim that the privilege has been waived by the agreement with the prosecution: see *R v Daniels* **[2011] 1 Cr App R 18** decided in the Court of Appeal.[8] Neither will it benefit O to claim that the record of the interview is required to prevent a possible miscarriage of justice. In *Derby Magistrates' Court, ex p B* **[1996] AC 487, 507,** Lord Taylor of Gosforth CJ explained that the rationale for legal professional privilege was that a man must be able to consult his lawyers in confidence, since otherwise he might hold back half the truth.[9]

In that case the stepfather in a murder trial was expected to give evidence against the defendant and the evidence covered by legal professional privilege could, if admitted, have been used either as a previous inconsistent statement or as admissible hearsay under **s. 114(1)(d) of the Criminal Justice Act 2003**. The advice to O is that the evidence is unlikely to be admitted.

This evidence is clearly relevant in that it could raise reasonable doubt about the veracity of S's evidence for the prosecution. The email falls into the same category of evidence, namely protected by legal professional privilege, as identified earlier. There is one difference

[6] See *USP Strategies v London General Holdings* [2004] EWHC 373 (Ch).

[7] You could add references here to ss. 4 and 5 of the Criminal Procedure Act 1865 and s. 119 of the CJA 2003.

[8] The Court of Appeal held that waiver could not be implied in a situation whereby the appellant had entered into an agreement to give evidence against alleged accomplices. Note that the court acknowledged, however, that there was a question mark over the reliability of prosecution evidence obtained in such circumstances.

[9] The judgment made a ringing endorsement of the absolutist position that legal professional privilege is a fundamental condition on which the administration of justice as a whole rests.

here, however, that the answer to the question, has the privilege been waived, is yes. Legal professional privilege will be lost when evidence falls into the hands of the other side innocently or by mistake on the part of the party claiming privilege. O can rely on the case of *R v Tompkins* **(1977) 67 Cr App R 181** where the privilege was lost.[10] The prosecution was able to use in cross-examination the contents of a note which a legal assistant had found on the floor of the courtroom. The defendant had written a note to his barrister which arguably contradicted his testimony.

[10]Munday (2017, p. 133) comments that such a case 'would look vulnerable from a human rights point of view'.

Conclusion

(a) Mr X is likely to be successful in obtaining disclosure of the report to the insurers and the communication with accountants if the material is held to be relevant. (b) O may be able to rely on recent case law to adduce the contested evidence.

LOOKING FOR EXTRA MARKS?

- In (a) you could add that Mr X's counsel may be under ethical restraints under the Code of Conduct for the Bar, which may prevent him using communications that have come into Mr X's hands by such unorthodox means.

- In (b) you could gain extra marks by explaining that legal professional privilege is defined in **s. 10(1)(a) of the Police and Criminal Evidence Act 1984 (PACE)** as 'communications between a professional legal adviser and his client or any person representing his client made in connection with the giving of legal advice to the client'.

TAKING THINGS FURTHER

- Hungerford-Welch, P., *'Case Comment, R (on the application of WV) v CPS'* [2011] Crim LR 456.
  See reference in answer to Question 2 in the text.

- Jackson, J., 'Justice, Security and the Right to a Fair Trial: Is the Use of Secret Evidence Ever Fair?' [2013] Public Law 720.
  A review of the effect of 'closed material procedures' on defendants' rights to know the case against them.

- Leigh, I., 'Reforming Public Interest Immunity' [1995] 2 Web JCLI 89.
  Gives a detailed account of the collapse of the Matrix Churchill trial and the reforms proposed to PII claims in criminal cases in the Scott Inquiry.

- Loughrey, J., 'Legal Advice Privilege and the Corporate Client' (2005) 9 (5) International Journal of Evidence and Proof 183.
  Considers which corporate communications are covered by legal advice privilege.

▨ Redmayne, M., 'Rethinking the Privilege against Self-Incrimination' (2007) 2 OJLS 209.
Argues that no distinction should be drawn between requirement to speak and requirement to produce documents.

▨ Spencer, M., 'Coping with *Conway v Rimmer* [1968] AC 910: How Civil Servants Control Access to Justice' (2010) 37 JLS 387.
A socio-legal account of the role of the executive in litigation management when public interest immunity is claimed.

▨ Zuckerman, A., 'Legal Professional Privilege: The Cost of Absolutism' (1996) 112 LQR 535.
A critical examination of the effect of the absolutist approach to legal professional privilege and suggests that communications between client and lawyer might be disclosed in litigation.

Online Resources

www.oup.com/uk/qanda/

Go online for extra essay and problem questions, a glossary of key terms, online versions of all the answer plans and audio commentary on how selected ones were put together, and a range of podcasts which include advice on exam and coursework technique and advice for other assessment methods.

Mixed topic questions

11

QUESTION | 1

Jones and Watkins are both accused of the murder of Simpson. Both blame the other for the offence. Jones has three previous convictions for disorderly behaviour, while Watkins has five previous convictions for robbery, in two of which he had been part of a gang which had used knives and pickaxes and had threatened their victims. Freda, aged 19 years, was a witness to the killing of Simpson and she gave a statement to the police but also claimed that Jones afterwards threatened to harm her if she told what she had seen. Jones denies this. Watkins's counsel wishes to adduce evidence that Jones had pleaded not guilty to all the previous charges of disorderly behaviour of which he had been convicted. Watkins had previously worked as a security guard in a college. The prosecution wish to call evidence of an internal college disciplinary hearing over an allegation of assault on a student. As a result, Watkins had been dismissed. At the investigation stage Jones had refused to answer police questions but his solicitor read out a prepared statement. Freda has a conviction for shoplifting. She states she is too afraid to give evidence at trial. Jones had pleaded not guilty to the previous charges on which he was convicted.

Advise on evidence.

CAUTION!

- Be aware that the question covers several areas: the character provisions of the **Criminal Justice Act (CJA) 2003**, the provisions on silence in the **Criminal Justice and Public Order Act 1994 (CJPOA)**, and the special provisions relating to witnesses who claim they are afraid to give evidence (Special Measures Directions (SMDs)).

- Note the particular issue of an allegation of propensity for untruthfulness arising from Jones's not guilty pleas.

- Bear in mind also the hearsay provisions for witnesses in fear and possibility of witnesses being allowed to give anonymous evidence.

- Be careful to distinguish the bad character rules relating to defendants from those for non-defendants.

DIAGRAM ANSWER PLAN

Identify the issues	▪ The legal issues are: is the bad character of the defendants and witness admissible; if so, what is their evidential worth; what protection is available to a witness in fear; can an inference of guilt be drawn from a defendant's submission of a written statement instead of verbal responses to police?
Relevant law	▪ CJA 2003, ss. 98–103; CJA 2003, s. 116(2); SMD and YJCEA 1999; CJPOA 1994, s. 34.
Apply the law	▪ CJA 2003, s. 101(1)(d), (e), and (g) may apply to J and W; ss. 100 and 116(2) applies to Freda; s. 34 may apply to J.
Conclude	▪ Assess likely outcome for J, W, and F.

Bad Character of Defendants

The two co-defendants, Jones and Watkins, and the witness, Freda, have previous convictions and/or instances of reprehensible behaviour. Before examining whether these are likely to be admissible at trial, it is necessary to examine whether **s. 98 of the Criminal Justice Act (CJA) 2003** applies.[1] The definition of bad character is likely to cover all the behaviours cited, namely the previous convictions and Watkins's disciplinary charge. However, with regard to the alleged threat made by Jones to Freda, para. 357 of the Explanatory Note makes it clear that this evidence is likely to be regarded as evidence relating to the facts of the offence and so will be admissible outside the **s. 98** provisions.[2] If there was a material basis for them they would be admitted under **s. 98(a)** as evidence 'which has to do with the alleged facts of the offence with which the defendant is charged'.

Character of Non-Defendant

- The prosecution will consider Freda's shoplifting offence is admissible. **Section 100 of the CJA 2003** specifies that evidence of the bad character of a person other than a defendant is not to be given without the permission of the court (**s. 100(4)**) and this can only be given if it meets one of three conditions. They are that it is important explanatory evidence, it is of substantial probative value to a matter in issue, and that issue is one of substantial importance in the case or the prosecution and defence agree that the evidence should be admitted.

- Here we are told that there is a dispute between Jones and Freda as to what happened. It is arguable therefore that if Jones's counsel applies to have the evidence admitted under the second head above, the court may give permission. Jones should then be aware, however, that it may be arguable that he has now 'attacked the character of another person' and that the prosecution may seek to have his previous convictions admitted under **s. 101(1)(g)** (see later).

Special Measures Directions (SMDs)

Freda is frightened to give evidence. This may bring into play **s. 19 of the Youth Justice and Criminal Evidence Act 1999 (YJCEA)** which covers Special Measures for the giving of evidence by fearful witnesses. The question then arises as to whether Freda falls into one of the categories of witnesses, not including the defendant, who are eligible for 'special measures'.[3] She is a witness to a violent offence so will be covered by **Sch. 1A** and **s. 17 of the YJCEA**. This extends the category of automatically eligible witnesses to those who

---

[1] You need to judge how much explanation of the scope of the bad character definition to include. Point out that the disciplinary hearing is covered by 'reprehensible behaviour'.

[2] It reads, 'Evidence that the defendant had tried to intimidate prosecution witnesses would also be admissible outside this scheme [s. 98] as evidence of misconduct in connection with, as appropriate, the investigation or the prosecution of the offence, as would allegations by the defendant that evidence had been planted.'

[3] Her age does not qualify her for s. 16(1)(a) since she must be under 18. We are not told she has mental, or physical, impairment so s. 16(2) will not apply. She is not a complainant in a sexual offence so s. 17(4) does not apply.

were witnesses to killing/GBH/ABH or other assaults using a firearm or knife. The court will consider the relevant criteria applying to witnesses where the quality of their evidence is likely to be diminished by reason of fear or distress. The judge may consider the use of such measures as live links or video screens.

Hearsay and Anonymity

An alternative approach is for Freda's pre-trial statement to be admitted under the hearsay provisions of the **CJA 2003**. **Section 116(2)** sets out a procedure which may apply where 'through fear the relevant person does not give (or does not continue to give) oral evidence in the proceedings, either at all or in connection with the subject matter of the statement, and the court gives leave for the statement to be given in evidence'. Fear is to be 'widely construed'. The admissibility of Freda's evidence in this way will depend upon the exercise of the court's discretion, which will include a consideration of fairness in view of the impossibility of cross-examining Freda. The court may exercise its discretion not to allow this hearsay evidence since Freda will not be cross-examined, thus arguably undermining the defence. Evidence of Freda's lack of credibility may be given even if she does not appear. Freda should be warned that a hearsay statement cannot be given anonymously: see *R v Mayers* **[2008] EWCA Crim 2989**. It does not appear on the facts that this is one of the extreme cases where the prosecution will be able to succeed under **ss. 89–97 of the Coroners and Justice Act 2009** in obtaining an anonymity order.[4]

[4]See *R v Donovan* [2012] EWCA Crim 2749.

Co-Defendants and Criminal Record

Jones and/or the prosecution may try to have Watkins's previous convictions admitted as evidence. The prosecution may argue that they are admissible under **s. 101(1)(d)** as relevant to an important matter in issue between the defendant and prosecution. *R v Hanson* **[2005] 1 WLR 3169** sets out the test for admissibility. The court must consider whether the history of convictions establishes a propensity to commit offences of the kind charged and whether that propensity makes it more likely that the defendant committed the offence charged. In this case the previous convictions arguably show a propensity to violence if not to murder. In *R v Mitchell* **(2017)** the Supreme Court held that the jury may assess the prior incidents 'in the round' since 'obvious similarities in various incidents may constitute mutual corroboration of those incidents'. Even if the judge decides the offences are eligible to be considered under this head she must apply her exclusionary discretion under **s. 101(3)** if it appears to the court that the admission of the evidence would have such an adverse effect on the fairness of the proceedings that the court ought not to admit it.[5] If the evidence is admissible under this head then Jones may make use of it also to try and establish his innocence.

[5]She must also consider **s. 103(3)**, which refers to 'the length of time since the conviction or for any other reason, that it would be unjust for it to apply in this case'.

However, even if the court ruled the convictions and the disciplinary charge inadmissible for the prosecution under this section it would still be open to the co-defendant Jones to put in an application to have the character of Watkins put in evidence. The relevant section is **s. 101(1)(e)**. Under this, evidence must have substantial probative value in relation to an important matter in issue between the defendant and the co-defendant. In *R v Platt* (2016) the Court of Appeal, rejecting reliance on the common law precedents including *R v Randall* (2003), held that 'substantial' 'should be given its ordinary unelaborated meaning'. In that case the accused's propensity did not have substantial probative value such as to be admitted under **s. 101(1)(e)**. Since each blames the other for the offence, it is likely that Jones will argue that Watkins's previous convictions and the reason for his dismissal demonstrate a propensity to violence which he, Jones, does not have, albeit he has a criminal record.

With regard to the evidential value of the bad character evidence, in *R v Randall* [2003] UKHL 69 the House of Lords made it clear that where two defendants were jointly charged with a crime and each blamed the other for its commission, one accused could rely on the more significant criminal propensity of the other in order to prove his innocence. In that case, the co-defendants were charged with murder and each claimed the other had killed the victim. The evidence of the antecedents of the co-defendant was relevant not only to lack of credibility but also to the issue of which of them was more likely to have committed the offence.[6] The exclusionary discretion in relation to **s. 101(3)** does not apply to **s. 101(1)(e)**.

Jones's convictions arguably do not show a propensity to violence and so may not be admissible under **s. 101(1)(d)**. Jones may decide to put his convictions in evidence on the basis that they do not demonstrate a propensity to such violence. This would be covered by **s. 101(1)(b)**. Alternatively, the evidence may be admissible by the prosecution under **s. 101(1)(g)** if Jones has successfully adduced Freda's convictions. In this case the court has discretion not to admit the evidence under **s. 101(3)**. The explanatory note on **s. 101(1)(g)** states that such evidence 'will primarily go to the credit of the defendant'.

Depending on how the evidence of Jones's criminal record is treated in the trial it is possible that even if it is not admitted under **s. 101(1)(e)** that Watkins's counsel, relying on *R v Highton* [2005] EWCA 1985, may be able to cross-examine Jones on it.[7]

It may be that Watkins can argue that the fact that Jones pleaded not guilty in the previous trials is of substantive probative value to the matter in issue between the two defendants. The issue is who is telling the truth. **Section 104** further explains 'matter in issue between the defendant and a co-defendant'. It states that 'Evidence

[6] That case was decided upon under the **Criminal Evidence Act 1898**, but it was relied upon in *R v Dennis Robinson* [2005] EWCA Crim 3233 under the CJA 2003. There the Court of Appeal held that the judge had been entitled to direct the jury to consider all the evidence, including evidence adduced by one of the co-defendants as to the bad character of her co-accused.

[7] The case is authority for the proposition that once evidence of bad character became admissible through one of the 'gateways' in the CJA 2003 the use to which it could be put depended upon the matters to which it was relevant rather than upon the gateway through which it was admitted. The key consideration is relevance.

which is relevant to the question whether the defendant has a propensity to be untruthful is admissible on that basis under **section 101(1)(e)** only if the nature or conduct of his defence is to undermine the co-defendant's defence.' That seems to be the case here.

In *R v Hanson* the Court of Appeal stated that a propensity to be untruthful was evidenced, inter alia, 'by a plea of not guilty and the defendant gave an account on arrest, in interview, or in evidence, which the jury must have disbelieved'.[8]

[8]It stated that 'propensity to untruthfulness', was 'not the same as propensity to dishonesty'.

Thus, further information is needed to assess whether the earlier not guilty pleas indicate that degree of untruthfulness on the part of Jones. Watkins will be aided by the decision in *R v Lawson* **[2007] 1 WLR 1191** where the Court of Appeal held that a judge was correct to allow the prosecution to adduce bad character evidence in order to establish a defendant's propensity as to truthfulness where there were inconsistencies between the defences of the two co-accused and the evidence was of substantive probative value. Here the bad character evidence was a previous conviction for unlawful wounding.[9]

[9]Munday (2015, p. 40) comments that 'The judicial role is not to hamper and embarrass defendants in the conduct of their defence.'

Silence at Interview

Finally, with regard to Jones's failure to respond to police questions at interview and his submission of a statement, Jones (if he testifies and gives evidence he might reasonably have stated earlier) may rely on *R v Knight* **[2003] EWCA Crim 1977**, where the Court of Appeal discussed what was meant by the defendant's failure to mention at interview facts later relied on for his defence under **s. 34 of the Criminal Justice and Public Order Act 1994.** Accordingly, a statement given to the police at the time of the defendant's failure to answer oral questions, put later in evidence and read out by the judge in the summing-up, meant that inferences under **s. 34** could not be drawn.[10]

[10]The court held that 'failure' was not meant to be that of refusing to answer questions at interview.

➕ LOOKING FOR EXTRA MARKS?

▪ You could expand on the examination of propensity for untruthfulness. It was noted in *R v Campbell* **[2007] EWCA Crim 1472** that a propensity for untruthfulness will not normally be of assistance in assessing guilt. If they apply common sense the jury will conclude that a defendant who has committed a criminal offence may well be prepared to lie about it even if he has not shown a propensity for lying, whereas a defendant who has not committed the offence charged will be likely to tell the truth, even if he has shown a propensity for telling 'lies'. However, note that in *R v N* **[2014] EWCA Crim 419** the Court of Appeal departed from the restrictive approach in *Campbell*.

▪ You could make the important procedural point that both Jones and Watkins should be aware that the **CJA 2003** applies in relation to the admissibility of their bad character whether they give evidence or not.

Alerted by a burglar alarm, police from a nearby station arrived at a house in Meadow Way at 9.00 p.m. on Thursday night. They found a window smashed by a stone. While two officers searched the house and interviewed Jack's wife, a third searched the street in a police car for suspects. Meanwhile the owner of the house, Jack, went out on foot looking for the suspect. He found Wayne running several streets away and grabbed him. 'You rat,' Jack shouted, 'you've tried to burgle my house.' Wayne said nothing but tried to shake Jack off. The police car arrived and Wayne was arrested and cautioned by the police. At the police station he was cautioned and questioned in a series of interviews. Before the first interview Wayne requested access to a solicitor, but this was denied by Inspector Brown on the grounds that they suspected Wayne had an accomplice who could be alerted by calling a solicitor. At the first interview, beginning at 7.00 a.m. on Friday morning, Wayne refused to cooperate with the questioning. At the second interview Wayne was again denied a solicitor. He then offered to 'tell what he knows', if the police promise to put in a good word for him to the judge. The inspector nodded his assent. Wayne then said that he had been out drinking with his friends and when making his way home he had vomited into Jack's garden in Meadow Way. He ran off because he was ashamed at what he had done. He gives no explanation why he had two large stones in his pocket. This second interview began at 12 noon on Friday and ended at midnight. He was given no food. Wayne was later charged with attempted burglary and entered a plea of not guilty. At trial the prosecution put it to him that he had failed to mention at interview that Jack had had an affair with his wife. They allege that Wayne had a reason to attack Jack's property. Wayne accepted that he had known about the affair.

Advise on evidence.

(!) CAUTION!

- Among the issues you must consider are possible 'implied' inculpatory statements such as fleeing from the scene and silence in the face of questioning by a person in authority and by an ordinary citizen.

- In addition, you will have to deal with the possibility of breach of **s. 58 of the Police and Criminal Evidence Act 1984 (PACE)** and the Codes of Practice. The Codes are very comprehensive and you will obviously not be able to remember all the details, but you must touch on the main points, considering possible breaches in the period of detention and the related question of whether the offence here is an indictable offence.

- The circumstances of the obtaining of Wayne's statement, and whether it is inadmissible under **s. 76** or **78 PACE** should be considered.

- You must identify the various legal issues first and then in turn consider the relevant law in relation to the narrative of events. In these questions it is especially useful to prepare a plan for your answer to ensure your coverage is comprehensive.

DIAGRAM ANSWER PLAN

Identify the issues	▦ The legal issues are: is running away from a crime scene a confession; the evidential value of silence in response to questions from persons of authority and those on 'equal terms'; new information presented to defendant at trial.
Relevant law	▦ Common law on silence as a confession; CJPOA 1994, ss. 34–38; PACE, ss. 76–82 and Code C.
Apply the law	▦ Likely that Wayne has grounds for exclusion of evidence under CJPOA, s. 34 and s. 37 and under PACE, s. 78 on grounds of lack of access to legal advice. ▦ Prosecution is most likely to succeed in adducing 'confession' to Jack.
Conclude	▦ Advise on evidence.

SUGGESTED ANSWER

Wayne's Flight from the Scene

Wayne is seen running from the scene of the crime. Does this have evidential significance? A confession is defined in **s. 82(1) of the Police and Criminal Evidence Act 1984 (PACE)**. It 'includes any statement wholly or partly adverse to the person who made it whether made to a person in authority or not and whether made in words or otherwise.'

It is arguable that this definition is wide enough to include an admission by conduct.[1] It is unlikely that an implied statement by conduct such as running away will be accepted as a confession.

Clearly, however, the fact that Wayne was running away along the street is part of the circumstances of the alleged offence and is therefore relevant as an integral part of the events forming part of the basis of the charge. It would arguably be admissible under **s. 98(a) of the Criminal Justice Act (CJA) 2003** as evidence which 'has to do with the alleged facts of the offence with which the defendant is charged'.[2] Since Wayne himself offers an explanation for running away, **s. 101(1)(b)** may also apply and thus the prosecution will be on weak ground citing it as evidence of guilt.

[1] The Criminal Law Revision Committee in its 11th Report (Cm 4991, 1972) gave as an example of such a confession, a possible admission by conduct, a nod of the head. But that is clearly an express statement by conduct.

[2] Evidence adduced by defendant or given in examination or cross-examination.

Silence at Common Law

Wayne's silence in the face of accusations from Jack is more likely than his fleeing to amount to an admission. The common law rule is that a statement made in the presence of the accused cannot amount to evidence against him, except insofar as he accepts what has been said, as the House of Lords held in *R v Christie* [1914] AC 545. However, if in certain circumstances a reply or rebuttal would reasonably be expected, silence can be taken to be a confession. The test of admissibility of this type of silence is whether the parties are speaking on even terms: see *R v Mitchell* (1892) 17 Cox CC 503 and *Parkes v R* (1977) 64 Cr App R 25. The court will have to decide first whether Jack and Wayne were speaking on even terms, which does seem likely. Thus, any direction by the judge that the silence could amount to a confession is arguably proper. The judge, however, must be careful to apply *R v Chandler* [1976] 1 WLR 585 in directing the jury.[3] Failure to do this may lead to quashing a conviction. This common law principle is preserved in the **Criminal Justice and Public Order Act 1994**, which covers questioning under caution by a police constable.[4]

Failure to Mention a Fact at Interview

In relation to the application of **ss. 36** and **37** of the 1994 Act, Wayne's failure to account for the presence of the stones in his pocket or his presence in the street at the initial interview may be admissible respectively under **ss. 36** and **37**, since the court is permitted to draw inferences under these two sections, whether or not the accused gives an explanation at trial. Before questioning on these matters the investigating officer must give the additional special warning set out in para. 10.10 of Code C. The evidential value of silence in the first interview which is shortly replaced by an explanation of his presence in the second, as is the case here, must be low. However, Wayne has failed at the second interview to explain the presence of the objects (stones in his pocket) under **s. 36** and thus runs the risk of an inference of guilt being drawn.

For **s. 34** but not **s. 36** to apply there must be, inter alia, a 'fact' relied on by Wayne at trial which he could reasonably have been expected to have raised earlier.[5] It seems that the prosecution, by raising the matter of the affair between Jack and Wayne's wife at trial, wished to imply a motive of revenge on the part of Wayne. This would make his possible defence of innocently being in the area less likely to be believed. However, no inference of guilt should be drawn if the fact relied on is true (*R v Webber* [2004] UKHL 1). It appears here that the prosecution is maintaining that the account of the affair is true and Wayne accepts that he knew. There is thus no dispute between the parties at this stage on this issue and if this is so **s. 34** is not likely to apply.

[3] The jury must consider, first, whether the silence does indicate acceptance of what Jack said and, if so, whether guilt could reasonably be inferred from what he had accepted. It was the failure of the judge to leave these two issues to the jury and his suggestion that the defendant's silence could indicate guilt which led the Court of Appeal to quash the conviction in this case.

[4] **Section 34(5)** of the 1994 Act provides that the section does not 'prejudice the admissibility in evidence of the silence or other reaction of the accused in the face of anything said in his presence relating to the conduct in respect of which he is charged . . .'

[5] The purpose of the legislation is to prevent 'ambush defences' or concocted evidence in situations where the prosecution will not have been able to properly mount a challenge.

[6] See also *Murray v UK* (1996) 22 EHRR 29.

However, another consideration which will help the defence is that neither **s. 34** nor **s. 36** should apply here since there has apparently been a serious breach of criminal procedure in the failure to allow access to requested legal advice.[6] It appears that this has been wrongly denied to Wayne since under **s. 58(1) PACE** a suspect interviewed at a police station must be given the opportunity to consult a solicitor and under **s. 34(2A)** and **s. 36(4A)** inferences should not be drawn if the suspect has not been given an opportunity to consult a solicitor. Thus if the prosecution seek to adduce an inference under **s. 36** the defence should apply for exclusion under **s. 78 PACE**.

Confession and 'Mixed Statements'

Wayne's statement at the second interview takes a form which is partly exculpatory and partly inculpatory in that he accepts he was at the scene, i.e. in Meadow Way, but not that he was attempting to burgle. Following the House of Lords decision in *R v Sharp* **[1988] 1 WLR 7**, such mixed statements are admissible as evidence of the facts related. Confessions may be excluded under several provisions of **PACE**. The grounds are oppression under **s. 76(2)(a)**; unreliability under **s. 76(2)(b)**, both of which operate as a rule of law; and unfairness under **s. 78**, which operates as the exercise of discretion. There appear to be no grounds of oppression here, but **s. 76(2)(b) PACE** may be appropriate. Arguably, Wayne may rely on *R v Barry* **(1991) 95 Cr App R 384**, in that he has been induced to make a partly inculpatory statement by a promise of a favour, namely for the police to put in a good word for him at trial.[7] It must be shown that there is a connection between what was said or done and the confession and it is arguable that Wayne was induced to confess by the indication of favourable treatment by the inspector. Thus the nod from the inspector is 'the something said or done' and the 'circumstances existing at the time' are arguably the absence of a solicitor who could witness the collusion of the police (see *R v Mathias* **[1989] Crim LR 64**). There is no need for bad faith on the part of the police for this section to be engaged as *R v Harvey* **[1988] Crim LR 241** demonstrates. However, more seriously for Wayne is the reluctance of the courts to apply **s. 76(2)(b)** in cases where the defendant is not assessed to be 'vulnerable' as in *R v Canale* **[1990] 2 All ER 187**. **Section 76(2)(b) PACE** was not appropriate since the accused had been in the Parachute Regiment and was not therefore in the position of a vulnerable defendant in the face of police questioning.[8]

[7] In that case the promise of bail led to a confession being held potentially unreliable by the Court of Appeal.

[8] It is good to demonstrate how the exclusionary tests for confessions in **PACE** must be applied systematically.

If **s. 76(2)(b) PACE** is not applicable there may be sufficient breaches of other sections of the statute and the Code to warrant exclusion under **s. 78 PACE** by the exercise of the court's discretion. The circumstances in which the statement was obtained reveal a number of possible breaches of the statute and Codes of Practice. First, Wayne has his access to a solicitor denied. The reason for delaying legal advice given by the police, namely fear of alerting another suspect, does appear to comply with **s. 58(8)(b) PACE** but the police must put up cogent evidence to justify such a fear (see *R v Samuel* **[1988] QB 615**). As the offence does constitute an indictable offence, the reason for delay in access to a solicitor appears appropriate, as long as the delay has been authorised by a senior officer. Further, Wayne should have been allowed eight hours' rest in any 24 hours free of questioning, with breaks for refreshment and periodic checks during the questioning.

The courts appear to take the attitude that to justify exclusion under **s. 78 PACE**, the breach or breaches must be 'significant and substantial', as the Court of Appeal held in *R v Keenan* **[1990] 2 QB 54**. A key issue is whether the police acted in bad faith: *R v Alladice* **(1988) 87 Cr App R 380**. In *R v Canale* **[1990] 2 All ER 187** the Court of Appeal held that the officers had shown a cynical disregard of the Code, which they had breached flagrantly. The court held that the confession should have been excluded under **s. 78 PACE**.

In the given scenario, there appear to be breaches of the conditions of detention. In the absence of bad faith, the court will be concerned to look at whether the breaches were operative in leading to potential unreliability under **s. 76(2)(b) PACE** or unfairness to the proceedings under **s. 78**.

Conclusion

Thus Wayne's silence in the face of the accusation from Jack is probably admissible. The cumulative effect of the possibly wrongful denial of legal advice, the apparent inducement, and breach of the statute and Code C are together likely to lead to Wayne's initial silence at interview, his failure to give an explanation under **s. 36**, and his partly inculpatory statement being held inadmissible. [9]

[9] Of course Wayne could be convicted on the confession alone.

LOOKING FOR EXTRA MARKS?

- You would gain credit for referring to human rights law under the **Human Rights Act 1998**. The right to a fair trial under **Art. 6** extends to pre-trial as well as trial proceedings. Evidence obtained at interview may be excluded if it affects the fairness of the proceedings. The Strasbourg Court in *Murray v UK* **(1996) 22 EHRR 29** placed emphasis on the right of access to legal advice in relation to the admissibility of silence as evidence and this led to changes in UK legislation.

- It would be appropriate to give more detail on procedural matters. Thus if the judge accepts breaches of **PACE** and the Codes as an arguable proposition, then the burden of proof is on the prosecution to prove in a voir dire beyond reasonable doubt that the confession was not so obtained. The test is an objective one of whether any confession obtained in such circumstances would be likely to be unreliable.

QUESTION | 3

Fred is charged with sexually assaulting Amanda, a colleague at work. He pleads not guilty. He claims she had engaged in sexual banter with men at work and had invited him to her flat and consented to sexual intercourse. He claims she was showing her gratitude to him for help he had given her at work. He also claims she has a suggestible personality and had been persuaded to invent the assault by work colleagues who knew his past. Fred has a previous conviction for sexual assault on a female co-worker, five years ago. The prosecution are considering calling Amanda's mother to testify that Amanda was very reclusive and she never had a boyfriend. Amanda is also a volunteer youth worker. The prosecution want to call evidence from a psychiatrist that Amanda does not have a 'suggestible' personality. Fred is considering whether to testify.

Advise on evidence.

CAUTION!

- You must first identify the issues which include evidence that can be brought to support a non-defendant witness, expert evidence, and the previous convictions of a defendant.

- Bearing in mind this is a sexual assault case, you should consider the cross-examination of the complainant under **s. 41 of the YJCEA**.

- Fred's decision on whether to testify at trial involves **s. 35 of the CJPOA**.

DIAGRAM ANSWER PLAN

Identify the issues	The legal issues are: admissibility of good character of non-defendant; admissibility of psychiatrist's expert evidence on personality; previous convictions of defendant; defendant's failure to testify.
Relevant law	Rule of collateral finality in relation to non-defendant; common law on expert evidence; CJA 2003, ss. 98–104; YJCEA 1999, s. 41.
Apply the law	Amanda's good character admissible but may trigger cross-examination under YJCEA, s. 41; expert evidence not admissible; Fred's conviction may be propensity evidence; inference of guilt possible from failure to testify.
Conclude	Advise on evidence.

Good Character of Non-Defendant

The prosecution wish to claim that Amanda is of good character. The common law governs the admissibility of good character of a non-defendant witness (see *R v Hamilton* (1998) The Times, 25 June).[1] In general, although a defendant can call evidence of his good character, that is not the case in relation to a witness. However, the prosecution may rely on a developing line of authority in cases involving sexual assault which has to some extent undermined the strict common law position. Thus, in *R v Tobin* [2003] EWCA Crim 190 the defendant, a married man of 36 years, alleged that the complainant, a young girl, had initiated sexual activity in thanks for a lift. The Crown was allowed to call evidence of her good character and the Court of Appeal held that the trial judge had been right to allow the complainant's mother to give evidence that she was a polite and quiet girl.[2] Section 41(5)(a) of the Youth Justice and Criminal Evidence Act 1999 (YJCEA) permits the prosecution to adduce evidence in rebuttal about the sexual behaviour of the complainant. It is possible therefore that the prosecution may be allowed to call Amanda's mother.

Sexual Activity

Any reference to Amanda's lack of boyfriends, however, may be judged to be a 'reference' to sexual activity under s. 41(5)(a) of the YJCEA.[3] If the prosecution lead on Amanda's good character then by s. 41(2) and (5) of the YJCEA the defence may apply to the court for leave to adduce evidence concerning the complainant's sexual behaviour. Thus Fred may raise the allegation of her flirting at work and cross-examine her on that. If the prosecution do not lead on the issue it is likely the court would refuse such cross-examination. It may be advisable for the prosecution therefore to confine the evidence of good character on the part of Amanda to the fact she was a volunteer youth worker and not refer to her lack of encounters with men.

Psychiatrist's Expert Evidence

The evidence from the psychiatrist raises the problem of the admissibility of expert testimony. The law does not admit expert evidence of witness credibility unless there are special circumstances. In *R v Robinson* (1994) 98 Cr App R 370 the Court of Appeal held that evidence from an educational psychologist that the complainant in a rape trial was 'not suggestible' should not have been admitted. The court stated 'the Crown cannot call a witness of fact, and then, without more, call a psychologist or psychiatrist to give reasons why the

---

[1] The witness's credibility is a collateral issue and in this case evidence in rebuttal of an attack on the witness was inadmissible.

[2] Explaining the departure from the general rule, the court stated: '. . . our sense of fair play is not offended but rather affirmed by the admission of the very limited evidence about that complainant's characteristics and conduct which occurred' (paras 16–17).

[3] 'Sexual behaviour' is widely defined in the section as 'any behaviour or other sexual experience'. In *R v S* [2003] EWCA Crim 485 a complainant's lies about her virginity was held to be 'sexual behaviour'.

⁴See further Chapter 10.

jury should regard that witness as reliable.' It does not appear here that Amanda is suffering from a mental illness which would permit expert evidence to be admitted (see *R v Turner* [1975] QB 834).⁴

Previous Convictions

Fred's previous conviction for sexual assault may be admissible under the provisions on bad character in the **Criminal Justice Act (CJA) 2003**. As a conviction it satisfies the test of bad character under **s. 98** and Fred may have triggered its admissibility under two heads and these considerations will apply whether he testifies or not. First, the prosecution may argue that the conviction is admissible under **s. 101(1)(d)** as being relevant to an important matter in issue between prosecution and defence. This section equates to the earlier common law provisions on similar fact, although it is clearly the intention of the 2003 Act that more of such evidence will be admitted (see *R v Hanson* [2005] 2 Cr App R 21). The current test for admissibility is set out in *Hanson*. The court should consider whether the history of the convictions establish a propensity to commit offences of the kind charged and if that propensity makes it more likely that the defendant has committed the offence charged.

Fred's conviction of a sex offence appears to fall into the same category of offence as the current charge, although the current **Categories of Offences Order 2004 (SI 2004/3346)** issued under the **CJA** lists only offences of dishonesty and sexual offences against children. In *Hanson* the Court of Appeal stated that 'In referring to offences of the same description or category, **section 103(2)** is not exhaustive of the type of conviction which might be relied upon to show evidence of propensity to commit offences of the kind charged' (see also *R v Weir* [2006] 1 WLR 1885). The prosecution will rely on case law which does indicate a low threshold for admissibility. In particular, where the offence is a sexual one previous sexual behaviour seems almost routinely to be admitted. In *R v Weir* the Court of Appeal held that evidence of an earlier caution for taking an indecent photograph of a child was rightly admitted in a trial where the defendant was charged with sexually assaulting a 13-year-old girl. It is not fatal to the prosecution's application that Fred has only one previous conviction, especially since this is a charge of a sexual offence. In *Hanson* the Court of Appeal stated that there was no minimum number of events necessary to demonstrate such a propensity. The fewer the number of convictions, the weaker is likely to be the evidence of propensity. It agreed that a single previous conviction for an offence of the same description or category will often not show propensity, however it could be admissible. Admissibility might be appropriate if it shows a tendency to unusual behaviour or where its circumstances demonstrate probative force in relation to the offence charged.⁵

⁵In other words, there is clearly a very low threshold for admissibility.

An alternative route to admissibility is that of **s. 101(1)(g)**. For this the defendant has to have made an attack on another person. If Fred is allowed to cross-examine Amanda on her alleged behaviour at work because the prosecution had introduced the matter of her sexual activity then it may be that **s. 101(1)(g)** is triggered, which would allow another route of admissibility of the previous conviction. However, the exclusionary discretion must be considered.[6] Under **s. 101(3) of the CJA 2003** the court must not admit evidence under **s. 101(1)(d)** or **(g)** if on an application by the defendant to exclude it, it appears to the court that the admission of the evidence would have such an adverse effect on the fairness of the proceedings that the court ought not to admit it. Although evidence admitted under this head goes mainly to credibility, following *R v Highton* [2005] 1 WLR 3472 it may also be evidence of propensity (see also *R v Randall* [2004] 1 WLR 56) as long as it is relevant evidence.[7]

[6] It is important to explain that a specific exclusionary discretion applies to s. 101(1)(d) and (g) of the CJA 2003.

[7] See also *R v D, P and U* [2012] 1 Cr App R 8 where the court stated that the specific gateway is important.

Failure to Testify

If Fred chooses not to give evidence, it should be borne in mind that **s. 35 of the Criminal Justice and Public Order Act 1994** allows the court or the jury to draw such inferences as appear proper from the accused's failure to give evidence without good cause. Thus, there is a risk that the jury may draw adverse inferences from his failure to give evidence in court (see *R v Cowan* [1996] QB 373).[8] Under s. 35(5) a failure to answer questions is presumed to be 'without good cause' unless the accused is entitled under statute not to answer particular questions or enjoys a legal privilege not to answer them or alternatively the court grants discretion not to answer. The judge should follow the Criminal Practice Directions guidelines on Fred's non-appearance to testify. The directions follow those in *Cowan* and are different from those under **ss. 34, 36**, and **37**. In particular, the jury is restricted to considering the prosecution's case in deciding whether it should draw an adverse inference. The points covered should remind the jury of the following: the burden of proof was on the prosecution; the defendant had a right to silence; silence alone could not prove guilt; the jury must first consider whether there was a case to answer and if the answer was 'yes' then ask if the defendant had an answer would he not have gone into the witness box. In *Birchall* [1999] **Crim LR 311** Lord Bingham CJ stated: 'Inescapable logic demands that a jury should not start to consider whether they should draw inferences from a defendant's failure to give oral evidence at his trial until they have concluded that the Crown's case against him is sufficiently compelling to call for an answer.'

[8] You must judge how much of this important test you are able to include in your answer.

In *R v Becouarn* [2005] UKHL 55 the House of Lords held that the then Judicial Studies Board Specimen Direction was sufficiently fair to defendants.[9] The jury could be directed that they could draw an

[9] The *Cowan* direction was approved by the House of Lords in *Becouarn*.

[10]The defendant did not testify because under (now repealed) sections of the **Criminal Evidence Act 1898** he would then have had his criminal record revealed. This situation is less likely to arise now since criminal records may be revealed in certain circumstances even if the defendant does not testify.

adverse inference if they considered the accused to have no answer to the prosecution case, or none that would stand up to cross-examination, even though an additional reason might be that he would have his criminal record revealed if he testified. The House rejected any direction along the lines of *Lucas* [1981] QB 720, pertaining to lies by the defendant that there might be other reasons for the defendant's silence.[10]

LOOKING FOR EXTRA MARKS?

- You could develop your analysis of the departure from the rule of finality to collateral questions and refer to the earlier case of *R v Funderburk* [1990] 1 WLR 587 which demonstrated the difficulty of maintaining a firm distinction between issue and credibility in a case which centred on the complainant's word against that of the defendant.

- You would gain credit for a deeper discussion on the relevance of the 'gateway' in terms of evidential worth. Note that in *R v D, P and U* [2012] 1 Cr App R 8 the court stated that the decision as to the relevant gateway or gateways will normally be of great help in identifying the way or ways in which the evidence can legitimately be used, that is to say the issues to which it is relevant.

QUESTION | 4

Jeremy, Harold, Christine, and Joan are on trial for supplying illegal drugs. They share a flat in which the police find quantities of heroin, £50,000 in used banknotes, and a large quantity of designer clothes. The defendants claim that they had won the money at horse-racing. They claim that the heroin must have been left by a student they had put up for the night, who has now disappeared. At the investigation stage they all have the same solicitor, Good & Co. Before the trial Christine changes solicitor. Jeremy pleads guilty and gives evidence for the prosecution. Christine's counsel has sought leave to produce a statement that Jeremy had made to Good & Co. which is inconsistent with evidence he gives in court and which would help Christine's defence. Harold had made a confession of his responsibility for the drug dealing in a statement to the police, in which he said that Christine was not involved in the offence. Harold's confession is, however, excluded by the trial judge beforehand in a voir dire. The judge employed s. 76(2)(b) on the ground that the confession had been obtained as a result of an inducement made to Harold by the police that they would promise a lighter sentence. Harold has now made another statement to police saying that he had seen Christine selling drugs outside a school. Christine's counsel wishes to adduce his excluded confession. Joan refused to answer a number of questions at a police interview with a solicitor present. She did claim, however, she was not a user of drugs. She plans to claim at trial that she was a recreational user, not a supplier of drugs.

Christine, Joan, and Jeremy are planning to plead not guilty. Harold is considering pleading guilty.

Advise on evidence.

CAUTION!

- Be aware that the question includes a number of areas including legal professional privilege, lies as evidence, and inferences from silence.

- The question requires an appreciation of the complex situation arising when a defendant wishes to adduce a co-defendant's confession or to cross-examine a co-defendant on a confession which has already been ruled inadmissible as part of the prosecution's case.

- You need also familiarity with the concept of relevance and in particular a knowledge of case law on the relevance of 'lifestyle' in drugs cases.

DIAGRAM ANSWER PLAN

Identify the issues	■ The legal issues are: whether 'lifestyle' evidence is admissible in drugs cases; whether legal professional privilege (LPP) can be breached to help a defendant; whether an inadmissible confession can be adduced for a co-defendant; extent of inferences from silence; lies as evidence.
Relevant law	■ Case law on relevance; case law on LPP; PACE, s. 76A; CJPOA, s. 34; *Lucas* direction.
Apply the law	■ Christine is unlikely to succeed in getting either Jeremy's or Harold's statements adduced; Joan runs the risk of a s. 34 inference and a *Lucas* direction on her lie about drug taking.
Conclude	■ Advise on evidence.

SUGGESTED ANSWER

Relevance and 'Lifestyle'

[1] It is a good legal exercise to discuss relevance wherever you find the opportunity since examiners will be looking for skill in inferential reasoning as well as legal knowledge.

All evidence must be relevant, although of course not all relevant evidence is admissible. [1] The first question to address is whether the discovery of the designer clothes is relevant evidence. The test for relevance is a matter of experience and common sense. A number of cases have shown the application of the concept of relevance in connection with drug dealing. In *R v Wright* [1994] Crim LR 55 the Court of Appeal held that the finding of a large quantity of cash was capable of being relevant to the issue of whether the accused was supplying drugs to others. It is clear, however, that the judge must direct that the jury must not treat that evidence as evidence of propensity. In *R v Grant* [1996] 1 Cr App R 73 guidelines for directions to the jury were set out. In order for the finding of the £50,000 to constitute evidence, the jury would have to reject the explanation that it was a result of success at the races and accept that there was no other innocent explanation. If the jury were to conclude that the presence of the money indicated not only past dealing but an ongoing dealing in drugs, then finding the money together with the drugs in question would be a matter which they could take into account in considering whether the necessary intent to supply had been proved. £50,000 is likely to be considered a large enough amount to be relevant but the admissibility of the evidence of designer clothes is less certain. Further information is needed to establish how exclusive they are (Nike, Gap, or Versace?). It has in any case been held that evidence of lavish lifestyle will only rarely be relevant to an issue of intent to supply (*R v Halpin* [1996] Crim LR 112). In *R v Guney* [1998] 2 Cr App R 242, on the other hand, the Court of Appeal said that whether evidence is relevant depends on the particular circumstances of each case.[2] Evidence of cash and lifestyle might even be relevant to possession, but more likely to intent to supply. In that case the Court of Appeal held that the evidence of finding nearly £25,000 in the accused's bedroom near to the drugs was admissible, relevant evidence on the question of possession. The accused had claimed the drugs were planted on him. The court stated, however, that evidence of a lavish lifestyle or possession of large sums of cash was not without more proof of possession.

[2] Munday (2015, p. 19) writes, 'A veritable blizzard of decisions has considered the admissibility of cash and lifestyle evidence in criminal cases in which the defendant is charged with possession of drugs, with or without intent to supply.' He comments that *Guney* is 'an instructive authority on this topic'.

Privilege

There is no general privilege attached to confidential statements made between professional people and their clients. However, the major exception to this is legal professional privilege, which covers certain types of correspondence between a lawyer and his or her client and certain communications between a lawyer and/or client and third parties. The privilege belongs to the client, who can insist on non-disclosure by the lawyer or third party in question. The scope of the privilege is given in s. 10 of the Police and Criminal Evidence Act 1984 (PACE).[3] Jeremy can thus claim legal professional privilege for his statement to Good & Co. He may waive this if he wishes. However, if he fails to do this it will be impossible for Christine to challenge it successfully in the light of a House of Lords ruling. Christine

[3] This gives a useful definition but the principle of exclusion is based on the common law.

might reasonably argue that a refusal to disclose harms her defence and, in the case of *R v Ataou* **[1988] QB 798**, such a claim was heard sympathetically by the Court of Appeal. However, in *R v Derby Magistrates' Court, ex p B* **[1996] AC 487**, the House of Lords over-ruled *Ataou* and the earlier case of *R v Barton* **[1972] 2 All ER 321**. The House held that 'no exception should be allowed to the absolute nature of legal professional privilege once established.' The House also held that the privilege is the same whether it is sought by the prosecution or the defence and the 'refusal of the client to waive his privilege, for whatever reason, or for no reason, cannot be questioned or investigated by the court'. The court considered that 'if a balancing exercise was ever required in the case of legal professional privilege it was performed once and for all in the 16th century'. In that case a witness, B, who had previously been acquitted of a murder, could not be compelled to produce a confession made in the presence of his solicitor in a subsequent trial of his stepfather for the same offence. This decision has been much criticised.[4] The House of Lords limited its scope in *Re L (A minor)* **[1997] AC 16** when it held that the privilege was confined to legal advice privilege and did not apply in care proceedings. It is assumed that Jeremy's statement concerns legal advice privilege. Christine is very unlikely to be allowed to adduce the document.

[4] Choo, for example (2018, p. 225), comments that it 'is open to criticism on the ground that it overlooks the importance of the need to protect the innocent from wrongful conviction'.

Confession

Evidence of Harold's excluded confession is clearly relevant to the trial since it conflicts with his planned evidence in court if he pleads not guilty. He had previously absolved Christine but now he is implicating her. Her counsel is first of all advised to apply for its admission under **s. 76A(1) PACE**.[5] This now states that 'in any proceedings a confession made by an accused person may be given in evidence for another person charged in the same proceedings (a co-accused) in so far as it is relevant to any matter in issue in the proceedings and is not excluded by the court in pursuance of this section'.

[5] This was brought in the wake of the House of Lords decision in *R v Myers* [1997] 3 WLR 552, based on the common law position. Glover points out (2017, p. 429) that 'it is now generally unnecessary to refer *Myers*'.

The court will apply the tests for oppression and reliability, as formulated for evidence tendered by the prosecution but the standard applied to the co-defendant will be the balance of probabilities. In order for the section to be engaged, however, it is necessary for Harold to plead not guilty; that is, be a 'co-accused'.[6] Assuming that he is still a defendant, Christine's counsel will try and convince the judge on a voir dire that on the balance of probabilities it has not been obtained '. . . in consequence of anything said or done which was likely, in the circumstances existing at the time, to render unreliable any confession which might be made by him in consequence thereof'. The trial judge had of course already ruled that was the case

[6] This demonstrates the care with which you read the statutory sections and do not assume that there is only one possible approach.

but the standard for the prosecution to reach was the higher standard of beyond reasonable doubt. As Choo points out (2018, p. 113) the operation of **s. 76A** means that it is possible that a trial judge might have to direct the jury that a statement was evidence for the co-defendant but not for the Crown. Note that the judge cannot exclude the confession if admissible for Christine under **s. 78** since that only applies to prosecution evidence.

If Harold does plead guilty then **s. 76A** is not available to Christine since he is an 'ex-defendant' and no longer an accused person. An alternative route is for her to apply to have Harold's statement admitted under the inclusionary discretion for otherwise inadmissible hearsay: **s. 114(1)(d)**.[7] The prosecution may challenge her request and may rely on the decision in *R v Finch* **[2007] 1 WLR 1645**. In that case F wanted to adduce a statement of his former co-accused, R, which exonerated him of the offence. R pleaded guilty thus his statement was not admissible under **s. 76A PACE**. The application was refused since R could have been compelled to be a witness. The Court of Appeal stated (para. 24) '. . . it is not in short the law that every reluctant witness's evidence automatically can be put before the jury under **s114** of the 2003 Act'. However, the court did not rule out the possibility that **s. 114** could be used for a third party confession.[8]

Silence

The contrast between Joan's statement at trial and her earlier silence at interview raises the possibility of inviting the jury to consider **s. 34** or **s. 36** if the issue at interview was explaining the presence of drugs. More information is needed on the circumstances of the interview, particularly the nature of the legal advice and how much Joan was told of the case against her. In *R v Compton* **[2002] EWCA Crim 2835** the court considered that it was sufficient for the police questioner to say that he was investigating drug trafficking, without being specific about the offence. Joan's explanation appears to go to the central issue; that is, she is denying dealing in drugs. It is established that **s. 34** may apply even if the jury in drawing an adverse inference would effectively determine guilt. Lord Woolf CJ in *Gowland-Wynn* **[2002] 1 Cr App 569** stated that **s. 34** applied when a 'defendant could be expected to comment about something which goes to the heart of his defence'. If other conditions apply then Joan's silence may be admissible.

Joan's Silence and her Lie

The final issue to consider here is that in the interview room Joan said she was not a user of drugs. If the prosecution were to use this it is arguable that a *Lucas* direction is required, since Jane appears to

[7] You see how important it is that you appreciate how close the connection is between hearsay and confessions.

[8] Christine may rely on *R v Y* [2008] 2 All ER 484 where the prosecution was allowed to adduce a confession under **s. 114**.

have told an out-of-court lie. In *R v AO* **[2000] Crim LR 617** the Court of Appeal held that 'where the same response was relied upon both as a lie and a failure to mention a fact relied on by the defence, then both directions should be given'. The judge should therefore give a *Lucas* direction as well as one on failure to mention a fact if the **s. 34** conditions apply. The lie by Joan must be admitted or proved beyond reasonable doubt and the jury told that the mere fact that the defendant lied is not in itself evidence of guilt since defendants may lie for innocent reasons. So only if the jury is sure that Joan did not lie for an innocent reason can the lie support the prosecution case.

LOOKING FOR EXTRA MARKS?

- You could explain that the application of **s. 76A PACE** raises many complex issues of fairness between co-defendants and you may have the opportunity to extend your analysis. One issue that has worried commentators is that under **s. 76A(2)** D2, applying for the admission of D1's excluded confession, may be unsuccessful notwithstanding that the statement 'may be true'.

- You will be credited for explaining in more detail why the courts are reluctant to admit confessions under **s. 114** when they are inadmissible under **PACE**. A major problem is that such confessions are not subject to the protections of **ss. 76** and **78 PACE**. This is an area where both the prosecution and the defence might want to adduce an otherwise inadmissible confession as *R v Y* **[2008] 1 WLR 1683** and *R v Finch* **[2007] 11 WLR 1645** demonstrate.

Online Resources   www.oup.com/uk/qanda/

Go online for extra essay and problem questions, a glossary of key terms, online versions of all the answer plans and audio commentary on how selected ones were put together, and a range of podcasts which include advice on exam and coursework technique and advice for other assessment methods.

12 Skills for success in coursework assessments

Introduction

The general points about study and preparation made in **Chapter 1** will also help you write good answers in coursework. This chapter will expand on the distinguishing features of coursework which are research, authorities, and citation. Your tutors will expect you to have researched in more than usual depth to answer these questions and to give full as well as accurate references for your arguments and analysis.

Coursework may take various forms. The student may be asked to undertake a project or work out the answer to a long problem. Or there may be group work, even the setting up of a web page. Often the course will require a long essay, perhaps on some fairly general topic such as corroboration or hearsay. Seen or open book examinations in a way straddle the two forms of assessment since they enable you to conduct more focused prior research than in a conventional unseen examination.

For many students research presents a daunting task even if they have attended the relevant lectures, listened to the podcasts, or watched the videos. The real challenge for many is to produce any extended piece of writing. Law students need to know that professional legal practitioners must often express themselves fluently in writing, and their teachers are offering them opportunities to learn this key skill.

Writing and Reading

How to begin? Writing and reading are the two sides of written communication and before tackling the coursework assignment, extended systematic reading is essential. A reading list may have been provided along with the assignment and if not the student should certainly ask for one. The list will probably cite a mixture of key cases and academic commentary. It may also refer the student to particular sections of legislation. The student should read them all. As much as anything else this is a way of soaking oneself in the topic, finding out how it fits together with other areas of law, to see how the judges develop law to answer new questions thrown up by real life, to get a feel for the work of academic lawyers, and see how legislation is drafted and interpreted.

There is almost invariably a deadline for the essay or assignment, so it's important to start reading for it as soon as possible. A good essay cannot be thrown together at the last minute, however fluent the student may be. The situation may come as a shock, but the life of almost every legal practitioner is measured out in deadlines, and the course organisers are providing merely a foretaste of what working life will entail.

Sources

Case reports in the law reports are drafted to make the reader's task easier. The student needs to learn how to make full use of them. Confronted with a case citation, the student's first reaction may be to wonder why she has been asked to read this particular case. The catchwords above the headnote may provide some of the answer. These narrow down the reader's focus to highlight in telegraphic form the issues resolved by the judges' decision in the case. English law is a system of precedent in which, for example, the decisions of the Court of Criminal Appeal are binding on the Crown Court or the magistrates. Generally speaking, cases are reported only if they change the existing body of case law in some way.

A succinct summary of the facts of the case will be followed in the report by a paragraph or two setting out the gist of the court's decision, the holding. And in the law reports produced by the Incorporated Council of Law Reporting there will also be a telegraphic account of counsel's arguments before the court, showing which previous cases were cited as authority for the propositions put before the judge(s) by counsel.

The student shouldn't stop reading there. A good writer is almost always a constant reader. Reading the full text of the judgments is the best way for a student to develop a good style and a command of legal language. It often requires concentration and thought but these are exactly the qualities the practitioner needs. And there are unexpected rewards because the judgments are often witty and quotable. Provided it is properly cited, it isn't plagiarism to include a relevant passage of a judgment verbatim in an essay if it makes the point better than anything you could write.

Academic Writing

Much academic writing on the law is commentary on the decisions of the courts. Here the student is being exposed to the controversies and arguments by which the legal system renews itself and develops. A good academic article will clarify some of the subject's obscure features, and provide the student with a good model for his or her own writing. For coursework you should go beyond the standard textbooks (see **Chapter 1**) and read more journal articles and monographs. The latter are specialised studies of one area such as Character Evidence or Hearsay.

Keeping Organised Notes

Students should learn to keep notes of their reading whether by hand using the conventional card index system or by using the sophisticated digital word-processing programs. Recording notes and reflections is easier said than done because even quite a small undergraduate project may involve reading several tens of thousands of words. The student should at least keep a note of the names of the cases and articles read and try and summarise for his or her own benefit the useful points they contain. The skill of thinking critically about what has been read is one that law students need to acquire. You should not simply record but also comment on what you have read, perhaps by comparing different authors' views and deciding what you think.

Analysis

If you have read widely your arguments will be sound. Law students are warned not to simply make personal observations and not simply to adopt a particular academic view. Good students will learn to synthesise arguments from the texts they have consulted in order to address the propositions set in the coursework projects. Law essays are not political manifestos and you must convey a balanced viewpoint with clearly evidenced argument. You may of course in your conclusion adopt a particular stance for which you have given authority. In other words, avoid 'editorialising'. Of course you may address how the law could be reformed but only if you have critically assessed its current state first.

The student has to find a way to generate a coherent piece of writing on the given topic. Undergraduate coursework doesn't usually require the originality of postgraduate work but the student does need to demonstrate an understanding of the issues to show that the leading cases and academic comments have been read and understood. The student is also expected to convey this in appropriate language and in an organised piece of writing.

Writing Style and Referencing

There is no need to strive for a pompous style full of polysyllabic expressions. Avoid pulling fancy words out of the thesaurus. Try and express the concepts and arguments under review in ordinary but appropriate language. Do not use colloquial expressions. If in doubt it is often a good idea to read the offending passage aloud to an understanding friend and gauge their reaction before submission. Don't be afraid to rewrite your material until you are satisfied with it. Writing is a process of constant rewriting and revising. Structure your argument well and present clearly defined paragraphs. Reference using the style recommended, usually OSCOLA.

In the age of information overload students must learn to be discriminating in the use of sources, particularly web-based materials. Question them and assess whether they are authoritative. Beware of using authorities from other jurisdictions, such as the United States or Australia, unless this is specifically asked for. There may be a place, for example, for citing particular pressure groups such as law reform campaigners but you must discriminate soundly based from polemical points. Students should aim to master the art of legal referencing, citing cases in the proper form. Here case lists in the law reports are invaluable, since they have the case details in standard form which the student can copy with confidence. Organising the writing of the essay or project is a lot easier for the student who has read the materials attentively. It should be possible to break the piece of writing down into smaller sections, each dealing with some logical stage or issue in the argument.

Assessment Criteria

In coursework, more so than in examinations, you will usually be given clear assessment criteria so make sure you understand and address them. They will often include terms such as analysis, knowledge, integration, synthesis, use of authorities, structure, and presentation. Sometimes they will include 'reflection' which means you should review the learning you have achieved. Be guided by the criteria in assessing how far you should cover the socio-legal context of the issues.

COURSEWORK QUESTION

Section 38 of the Criminal Justice and Public Order Act 1994 provides that a conviction cannot be based solely on inferences from a suspect's failure to respond to pre-trial police questioning. By contrast the common law allows a conviction to be based solely on a pre-trial confession.

How far are these differing provisions justifiable?

*Your introduction should set out what you take the question to mean. You see that the question centres on the difference between the treatment of confessions on the one hand and silence on the other.

*It asks you to explain how the difference is justified in law and then for you to comment whether the justification is in your view convincing. Bearing in mind this is a law essay you are not asked simply to give a personal evaluation but to back up your points with evidence.

ANSWER GUIDANCE

Introduction

You could use the introduction to explain the differing status between the weight of evidence of guilt from a confession, which is a positive act, and silence which is more ambiguous and subject to misinterpretation. You could cite **s. 38 CJPOA** in relation to silence and explain the common law rule in relation to confessions not needing corroborative evidence.[1] Explain that your answer is (i) going to address in what way and why the law treats these two areas of evidence differently and then (ii) comment on whether the justification given is convincing.

[1] This is a law essay and so you are not asked simply to give a personal evaluation but to back up your points with relevant and supportive evidence.

Body of essay could:

(i) Review possible reasons why the law treats these two areas of evidence differently:

Consider the history of confessions and the privilege against self-incrimination in western culture[2] and explain how the law tries to balance two assumptions: first, that people do not as a rule make statements which are against their own interests and, secondly, that the law should protect the individual from intrusive and oppressive questioning which might lead to unreliable evidence being obtained. To do otherwise would violate individual autonomy and jeopardise the moral integrity of the verdict.

[2] See P. Brooks, *Troubling Confessions* (Chicago: University of Chicago Press, 1999).

● With regard to confessions, **PACE** provides safeguards against the admissibility of confessions which may be obtained in ways which are tainted, i.e. **s. 76** and **s. 78** and also **s. 58** provides for access to legal advice. By contrast there are fewer protections in the **CJPOA** apart from right to a solicitor (see *Murray v UK*) and **s. 38**.[3]

[3] You see that the question does not ask about failure to testify, so references to **s. 35** of the CJPOA are irrelevant.

- The overall approach in English law is to look at the quality of the evidence rather than the quantity: see Dennis (2013) on miscarriages of justice arguing that mechanical application of rules, for example on corroboration, would not overcome the problem of police lack of integrity.

(i) Assess the strength of the justifications:

- Arguments to suggest the current position is satisfactory could give examples where the courts have acted to exclude confessions: e.g. *Samuel*, *Mason*, *Harvey*, *Kirk*. Similarly, the need for corroboration in relation to silence is accompanied by other pro-defence decisions, for example the importance of **Art. 6** in *Murray*, right of access to legal advice in *Cadder*, importance of judicial directions in *Cowan*, decision in *Knight* in relation to written submissions. It could also be argued that English law approaches most items of evidence from the point of view of their weight rather than the number of items of evidence and that technical rules about supportive evidence are difficult to operate.

- Arguments to suggest that the justification of the current law is not convincing could include the psychological studies cited by P. Pattenden, 'Should Confessions be Corroborated?' (1991) 107 LQR 317, which show that defendants may have a compulsion to cooperate with police and make a false confession leading to miscarriages of justice. In addition, the safeguards under **PACE** are weakened by narrow pro-prosecution decisions, for example *Goldenberg*, *Hayter*, *Fulling*. In relation to silence as evidence, the very complication of the law in relation to access to legal advice (see e.g. *Beckles*, *Condron*) makes the safeguard of supportive evidence less powerful. Answers could point out that the possible over-use of confessions and silence as evidence concentrates too much on police interviews and that more proactive forensic evidence gathering should be encouraged to supplement interrogation of the suspect. DNA evidence is one example.

Conclusion

Should give an assessment of the fairness of the law. The argument could be that all confessions should have supportive evidence (compare Scots law) and also that no safeguard can overcome the inherent weakness of silence as evidence, particularly the ambiguity of its meaning, and that, as Dennis argues, **s. 34 of the CJPOA** should be repealed. Alternatively, others may argue that there may be argument from a crime control perspective about the increasing sophistication of criminals and the need for the law to be more robust.

Submission

Make sure you have:

- kept to the word length;
- checked for possible (including inadvertent) plagiarism;
- included a bibliography if required;
- given proper and full citations;
- checked for spelling and grammatical errors.

Make sure you have not:

- used colloquial expressions;
- cited non-scholarly sources such as student revision guides;
- used out-of-date law;
- cited law from other jurisdictions when the criteria do not require this.

Online Resources   www.oup.com/uk/qanda/

Go online for extra essay and problem questions, a glossary of key terms, online versions of all the answer plans and audio commentary on how selected ones were put together, and a range of podcasts which include advice on exam and coursework technique and advice for other assessment methods.

Index

Introductory Note

References such as '178–9' indicate (not necessarily continuous) discussion of a topic across a range of pages. Wherever possible in the case of topics with many references, these have either been divided into sub-topics or only the most significant discussions of the topic are listed. Because the entire work is about 'evidence', the use of this term (and certain others which occur constantly throughout the book) as an entry point has been minimised. Information will be found under the corresponding detailed topics.

Q

R

S